W9-DAS-683

The
Less Developed
Economy

A Critique of Contemporary Theory

KAUSHIK BASU

Basil Blackwell

First published 1984
Basil Blackwell Publisher Limited
108 Cowley Road, Oxford OX4 1JF, England

Basil Blackwell Inc.
432 Park Avenue South, Suite 1505
New York, NY 10016, USA

British Library Cataloguing in Publication Data

Basu, Kaushik
  The less developed economy.
  1. Developing countries – Economic conditions
  I. Title
  330.9172′4   HC59.7

  ISBN 0-631-13111-6

Typeset by Unicus Graphics Ltd, Horsham, West Sussex
Printed in Great Britain by The Pitman Press, Bath

Contents

Preface

Early development economics was a vast subject, covering a whole range of issues, including some quintessential problems of under-development. This was the source of its attraction, but also the cause of its fall from grace. While it raised innumerable important questions, it appeared to have answers for very few, which gave rise to the suspicion that traditional development economics, in the name of asking difficult questions, often ended up asking questions impossible to answer. During the last decade or two, however, the concerns and method of the subject have been changing. Recent development economics, by setting itself more realistic targets and drawing on results in pure economic theory, shows promise of opening up exciting avenues of research. The present book, by formalising some of the early works and by elucidating and developing on recent research, tries to capture this changing face of development economics. The book also brings together work belonging to different ideological strains and shows that beneath the different jargon and contrasting semantic styles are ideas which have much more in common than is generally supposed.

While an attempt has been made to develop new concepts and pursue new directions, the overall approach of this monograph remains – for several reasons, including that of the author's limitations – an economic one. At one stage I did think I would discuss some sociology but restrained myself after hearing some sociologists discuss economics.

The writing of this book was spread over my stay in Belgium, during the academic year 1981/82, and Delhi, thereafter. My interest in development economics goes back to my student days at the London School of Economics. Hla Myint, Max Steuer and especially Amartya Sen played a role in this. After I returned to India this interest continued to grow.

The Delhi School of Economics was a colourful place when I arrived here. Though it had lost some of its best economists by then, it still had a lot to offer. There was Sukhomoy Chakravarty who must be one of the most erudite and knowledgeable economists anywhere. I am tempted to recount an amusing incident involving him. John Hicks was visiting India, and one afternoon while he was having an informal chat with us at the Delhi School of Economics, conversation veered to a relatively unknown paper by him. One of my colleagues queried whether it had been reprinted anywhere. Hicks paused for a few seconds and said hesitantly, 'I *think* not', and on his heels was Chakravarty's response, 'No it *has* not.' In writing this book, I gained from several stimulating conversations with Chakravarty.

It cannot, however, be denied that India has been going through a bad phase as far as research goes. In the name of 'relevance', there is an increasing tendency to cut ourselves off from international academe and research – a convenient and, in the long-run, devastating use of the infant industry argument. Also, there is a dangerous tendency to equate 'relevance' with 'empirical research'. The belittling of abstract theoretical work has meant that Indian researchers are compelled to do their empirical work with theories developed eslewhere and often quite irrelevant to the Indian milieu. The disfavour shown towards theory stems partly from a genuine concern to avoid the excesses of abstraction and the use of mathematics as a façade for trivia, but also in part from the common delusion of believing that what one cannot understand must be unimportant.

In September 1981, I left for Belgium to spend the academic year at the Center for Operations Research and Econometrics, Louvain-la-Neuve, and the Centre d'économie mathématique et d'économétrie, Brussels. My colleagues in Belgium were very agreeable. Most of them, that is. Intellectually and otherwise I benefited much from Jan Gunning, Victor Ginsburgh, Louis Gevers and most of all Jacques Drèze, whose generosity was overwhelming.

Nine months is not a long time if you are trying to write a book, travel and lecture. The work continued for almost a year after my return to Delhi.

My first opportunity to experiment with a more formal and different approach to development economics occurred in 1980, when V. K Chetty invited me to give a 25-lecture series at the Indian Statistical Institute. I have a feeling that mid-way through the series, Professor Chetty began to doubt the wisdom of his decision. But, fortunately, by then it was too late. I also benefited much from our dicussions, and from his many observations.

The list of my indebtedness is long. In addition to the names already mentioned, I would like to thank Alaka Basu, Pinaki Bose, Amit Bhaduri, Mrinal Datta Chaudhuri, J. Krishnamurthy, K. L. Krishna, Ashok Lahiri, René Olivieri, Jean-Phillipe Plateau, Mihir Rakshit, André Sapir, Hans-Bernd Schaffer and Tibor Scitovsky for discussions on this subject and comments on the manuscript. Parts of the book I have presented at seminars in various places. I faced a particularly stimulating audience at the LSE where I gave two lectures in March 1982. Finally, I am grateful to Gigi Ginsburgh and Kulbir Singh for very efficient typing.

The book is arranged so that the chapters get increasingly micro-theoretic and also analytically more demanding. The chapters are divided into three main parts and a brief concluding one. Each part can be read independently. The mathematical prerequisites are minimal since only elementary calculus and algebra have been used. It is more important that the reader should have had a year's training in economic theory. Without this, it is possible to read the book, but not possible to appreciate it fully.

PART I

Introduction and Macro Perspectives

CHAPTER 1

Introduction

1 Introduction

Usually it is the case that what we instinctively feel is true, is so. Many of our woes stem from our presumption that this is always the case. The concerns of less developed economies are, at one level, very obvious: there is poverty, chronic underemployment and exploitation. To these, government after government has responded by trying to raise investment, encouraging labour-intensive techniques of production and legislating against high interest rates and low wages. But the stubborn persistence of most of these problems has increasingly made us aware that economic underdevelopment has more to it than meets the eye.

Development economics dates as far back as economics itself, to Adam Smith (1776), and even earlier, to the works of François Quesnay and other physiocrats. In the early years of the subject, developmental concerns were so pervasive that one could not divide economics into development economics and the rest, without great arbitrariness. The distinction became possible and necessary with the rise of the marginalist school, in particular with the publication of Jevons' (1871) book which caused an emphatic shift of interest. Development economics was left to be practised at the periphery. Indeed it was not to rise into prominence till the middle of the twentieth century.

Writing with a sweep reminiscent of the classical writers, Arthur Lewis analysed the process of development in two long essays (Lewis, 1954, 1958) and together with Nurkse, Rosenstein-Rodan and others put development economics on the map; and it has remained there ever since. Amidst a profusion of language and platitudes, enlivened by the occasional brilliant paper or book, the subject trundled on. But in recent times, once again, there has been a change in its concerns and method. This has been ushered in without any single work marking the crossroads but the change is, never-theless, significant and promising.

This recent development economics is distinguished by being less ambitious and more realistic in its aims. Its concerns are more with the short-run than the long. Attempts to describe the path of development over decades, so popular in the period immediately following Lewis (1954), no longer occupy the centre stage. The focus is now on the problems and structure of underdevelopment and not just on the process of development. Along with this change of focus there has occurred a rather natural change in technique – an increasing use of rigorous analysis and concepts and results from economic theory. This has once again blurred the dividing line between develop-ment economics and economic theory, which had emerged with the rise of the marginalist school.

This monograph briefly formalises some older doctrines and eluci-dates the newer advances, presenting and criticising recent works, trying also to extend frontiers, a little bit here, a little bit there. There is a second objective: to bring together some works which are conventionally kept separate on the ground that they belong to different ideological strains. By analysing these works in the simplest of terms, I try to show that shorn of the differences in jargon of the different schools, the areas of contention turn out to be smaller than generally supposed. Section 4 below is an elaboration on this theme.

In one important way the scope of the present book is limited: while I do refer to some relevant anthropological and sociological writings and conduct some cursory discussions, my approach remains an economic one. There is no attempt to justify this with the claim that there is nothing beyond such an approach. It is, in fact, unfortu-nate that economists in criticising the *works* of sociologists often fail to distinguish between this and the role of *sociological explana-tions* and end up belittling the latter. In the next two sections I try to illustrate the nature and role of sociological factors, before putting them aside in order to concentrate in the rest of the book on the purely economic.[1]

---

[1] While interdisciplinary research has its strong points, it must not be forgotten that, depending on the problem being analysed, the ability of the researcher and a variety of other factors, there is often a case for ignoring the more distant interconnections and conducting an indepth study of some particular aspect of society. I quote a sociologist: 'Clearly, we cannot study all aspects of social life at the same time simply on the ground that there is some interconnexion among them. In practice what the working sociologist does is to select ... a problem, and then to examine those institutional systems that are immediately relevant to his study, leaving out of consideration those which are less directly relevant to his concerns' (Béteille, 1974, p. 9).

2   Economic rationality and norms

It is widely maintained in economics that rational behaviour on the part of individuals can sustain the efficient functioning of an economy. And 'rational behaviour' is typically equated with the maximisation of binary preferences given the assumption that more goods are always preferred to less.

In reality much of human behaviour is shaped by morals, customs and social norms. Most of us would concede this. What is less obvious is that an individual's adherence to certain social norms may be a *necessary* element in many economic models. An attempt is made here to persuade the reader about this claim by constructing an example.

The example centres around a straightforward question: why do we not try to walk off without paying after a taxi-ride? In order to conduct a relatively rigorous discussion let us place the problem at a certain level of abstraction.

Consider an individual who gets out of a taxi at a place where there is no one to bear witness to his paying or not paying the fare. Further, this is a large city and the passenger does not expect to require the services of this cabman in the future. Would the passenger try to walk off without paying? Most of us would agree that, even in this situation, a vast majority of human beings would not choose to default. It is claimed here that to explain this behaviour we have to make allowance for our sense of morality or norms.

I shall try to establish this by negation. Let us therefore assume that it is self-interest which makes a person pay, because if the passenger tried to button up his pockets, the taxi-driver would in all likelihood assail him. This is not an implausible assumption (particularly to a profession that has tried to model marital and even extra-marital relations in terms of maximising behaviour) but as soon as we accept it, we land ourselves in trouble. The crack, however, appears elsewhere. It is now the taxi-driver's rationality which becomes questionable. Why do we expect him to retaliate against a passenger who is trying to defraud him, and to attempt to recover the fare at the risk of an unpleasant scuffle? To me, the most plausible reason seems to be his injured sense of fair play or anger at his customer's violation of social norms (catalysed no doubt by the fact that he is at the receiving end). But to admit this is to grant the role of commonly accepted values – no matter how in-directly – in the prevention of anarchy. This leaves only one way out:

to explain the taxi-driver's response in terms of his selfishness. To do so, one would have to argue that the agony of a scuffle may be less than the reading on the meter. This may well be valid. But now comes the main difficulty. If that is so, why should the taxi-driver not try the same tactic even if the passenger has paid? That is, he could take the fare and then pretend that the passenger never paid and go through the same action as he would if the passenger had attempted to defraud him, and thus end up collecting perhaps twice the correct fare, not to mention the tip. Everybody would agree, taxi-drivers do not behave in this way. Therefore, they must be irrational, because it was supposed, a few lines ago, that this behaviour is the one in conformity with their self-interest. (Some defenders of faith would, however, be pleased to know that in the city of the author's residence, particularly late at night, taxi-drivers do occasionally give evidence of rationality.)

Herein lies the crux of the matter. The object of the above exercise was not to show that human beings are not guided solely by selfishness; but to demonstrate that, given the order that attends the multitude of economic exchanges in society and the absence of anarchy and fraud, this *must* be so. The 'invisible hand' would not be able to coordinate a multitude of selfish acts to bring order – as it is supposed to do – if it was not aided by the adherence of individuals to certain commonly accepted values.[2] It is only when considering markets, like the one for loans, which are characterised by a long time-lag between the acts of the two parties involved in the exchange, do we talk of default (i.e. the possibility of one party backtracking on his part of the contract). What is not usually appreciated is that virtually all economic exchanges involve a time-lag. Like the taxi-driver, the barber brings the bill after the haircut, as does the waiter after the meal. And as the above example shows, it is not possible to explain the absence of widespread default in these situations without making allowances for our sense of values and norms. This also means that to explain the larger incidence of default and fraud in economic transactions in some societies, we do not have to claim an excess or a shortage of rationality on the part of their inhabitants, but may adduce the more reasonable explanation of differing social norms.

Thus while the absence of externalities etc. is necessary for the efficiency of the invisible hand, a more basic assumption is that the

[2] Arrow (1982, p. 271): 'The model of *laissez-faire* world of total self-interest would not survive for ten minutes; its actual working depends on an intricate network of reciprocal obligations, even among competing firms and individuals.'

agents involved in economic exchanges fulfil their obligations. And the ultimate guarantor of this assumption is our system of values and norms.

Once we allow for norms or customary behaviour, we are able to appreciate many features of society without having to construct artificial 'economic' arguments. Consider, for instance, the threat of violence. It is well-known that one way in which a landlord in a backward agricultural region ensures that money owed to him is repaid is by using the threat of violence. This would appear as a paradox to the economist ('Why does he not anyway use such threat and earn money?'): but as soon as we accept the idea of norms and morality such behaviour becomes easy to understand; it is, in fact, analogous to the taxi example. This acceptance also makes us aware of newer dimensions to policymaking.

It will be argued in chapter 12 that one of the reasons behind high rural interest rates is the isolation that exists in rural markets; and the isolation in turn is caused, in part, by the risk of default. To this, the economist's typical policy recommendation would be to argue for a more effective legal machinery. This would make it *rational* for individuals not to default. But the above example shows that rationality or self-interest is not the only motive which prompts human behaviour. It is possible to affect the behaviour of human beings by shaping their system of values. Of course, this cannot be achieved overnight. But education and the media can make inroads steadily. What is important is to recognise that the changing of social norms can alter not only society but even the prices of goods and loans.

Consider a variant of Sen's (1973) delightful application of the non-zero-sum game, the 'Prisoner's Dilemma', to a social problem. Let us assume, as is quite reasonable, (a) that every city dweller prefers his city to be clean rather than dirty, and (b) that one person throwing litter on the streets does not make a clean city dirty. It is easy to see that each individual, acting atomistically, would prefer to throw litter on the street rather than go through the trouble of looking for a litter bin to dispose of it. It being rational for each individual to litter the streets, all citizens – if they were rational – would do so. The city would be a dirty one and (given (a)) everybody would be worse off.

I find this story convincing and therefore believe, facetious though it may sound, that the squalor of, for example, Calcutta is a reflection of the rationality of its inhabitants. This also shows how much we can gain from a little bit of irrationality. Actually there are two ways of solving this problem. One is to impose fines for dirtying the streets; the other is to inculcate in human beings suitable values. The former works by changing what is rational to the individual. The latter works by making people accept a little bit of irrationality. It is true that the latter would take much longer to implement, but it is ethically the more attractive and ought to be the long-run objective.

3   On weighing scales that are known to be biased

Another issue which suggests the presence of non-economic forces in the shaping of economic transactions is consistent cheating. Rural observers and economic anthropologists have written about how some landlords consistently cheat the poorer peasants. What is worse is that the latter are often aware of it but are powerless to resist. Thus Breman (1974, p. 191) describes how in the subdistrict of Gandevigam (in western India) landlords are supposed to pay for the medicines should a *Dubla* (i.e. a farm worker) fall ill; but in practice they either do not pay or they add the payment to the existing debt. What is more, the *Dublas* are aware of this. Similarly others have written about how in some villages the poor are not only forced to buy their merchandise at high prices from the landlord's shop, but the weighing scales are biased against them.

To many social scientists, the fact that the poor peasants *know* that they are being cheated and still cannot resist is taken to be an additional evidence of exploitation. To the neo-classical economist, the fact that the 'cheated' person knew in advance that he would be 'cheated' is what makes the exchange less unfair. He would argue that if a weighing scale is biased and both the buyer and the seller know it, then this is qualitatively no different from a case in which the price is a bit higher but the scales are balanced.

This is a powerful argument, but in putting this forward it is easy to miss out an important question. Why does open cheating take place at all? Why is it that producers do not simply charge a higher price instead of going through this rigmarole of quoting a low price and then using a biased scale? This points to the presence of extra-economic factors which make the rigmarole approach more desirable to the seller even though it is *economically* equivalent to the straightforward one of charging a higher price. What these extra-economic factors are is a subject which lies beyond the realm of our present analysis, but that is no reason for denying their existence.

4 From analysis to prescription

The conflict between different schools of thought are often unnecessarily heightened because of our tendency to read into analyses prescriptions that are not there. Consider first the *so-called* neo-classical claim that in most situations workers are paid their marginal product. If this has to be contested it must be on empirical grounds. But in practice we often object to this claim because we implicitly associate with it the value judgement that 'therefore workers get what they deserve'. There is, however, no reason why we cannot dissociate these positive and normative observations. It is perfectly consistent for a person to find the neo-classical claim acceptable and yet believe in more pay for the workers or even socialism.

As a second example consider a labourer who takes a loan from his landlord and never manages to repay and so gets tied to the landlord for good. Suppose, in addition, that he knows the exact course of events which will follow when he takes the loan. Should he be classified as a bonded labourer? A negative answer here is often regarded as a prescription for non-intervention, as evidence of a belief that the labourer needs no help. This is wrong. It simply means a disinclination to categorise the above labourer separately from other similarly poor ones who prefer not to take a loan and opt instead for lives of greater poverty but fewer obligations to some landlord.

The economist who says that the poor share tenant in a less developed economy has, in opting to be a share tenant, chosen the best of all known alternatives open to him and the one who says that the alternatives open to him were miserable ones are not necessarily individuals in conflict, with different beliefs about reality, with different prescriptions for the world.

These are specific examples of what much of this book, by drawing on works belonging to different schools, has tried to show: that there is greater harmony than is apparent in the diverse strains of thought that have gone into the analysis of economic underdevelopment.

CHAPTER 2

The Vicious Circle of Poverty

1 Poverty and its persistence

Poverty has a tendency to persist. An understanding of why this is so must surely provide some clues to progress. With this in mind, Rosenstein-Rodan, in his well-known paper of 1943, examined the causes of stagnation in the backward areas of Europe. And starting with this, the decade or so that was spent researching into the causes of persistence of poverty provides us with some of the best works in development economics. From the contributions of Rosenstein-Rodan (1943), Singer (1949), Nurkse (1953), Scitovsky (1954) and Fleming (1955), distantly echoing the ideas of Allyn Young (1928), emanated a list of difficult and important concepts – like the vicious circle, balanced growth and the big push – which would be the basis of endless research and debate.

The persistence of underdevelopment despite the many shocks and jolts which every economy receives in the normal course of its existence, raises the suspicion that underdevelopment is a state of equilibrium and that there are forces at work which tend to restore the equilibrium every time there is a small disturbance. It is this suspicion which gives rise to the idea of a vicious circle. A vicious circle of poverty is a 'circular constellation of forces tending to act and react upon one another in such a way as to keep a poor country in a state of poverty' (Nurkse, 1953[1]).

Before enquiring further, it would be useful to become acquainted with a couple of features of a poverty trap, or 'low-level equilibrium trap' to use Nelson's (1956) terminology. First, it is an equilibrium in the sense that, once there, the economy has a tendency to remain there. It is also stable in some limited way because small shocks do

[1] See page 4 of the 1964 Oxford University Press edition.

not disturb it. At the same time the use of the word 'trap' suggests that one *can* get out of it.

It is useful to illustrate these features with an example. I consider a rather naive version of the classical doctrine of subsistence wage (e.g., in Ricardo, 1817[2]). This entails an endogenous theory of population growth, in particular two assumptions: that in economies with low per capita income, (a) whenever per capita income rises above subsistence level, population grows, and (b) whenever it falls below subsistence level, population shrinks. The reasons behind (b) are obvious; those for (a) are usually attributed to declining mortality but it is possible to append to this (particularly with the advent of contraception) arguments about a volitional rise in fertility. The qualification, 'in economies with low per capita income', is important for (a). This is clear from experience and there are also good reasons for it. First, mortality is unlikely to decline endlessly and secondly, with the modernisation of society, there occurs a concomitant change in values which leads to a preference for small families.

Given (a) and (b) the poverty trap is obvious. Consider an original equilibrium with subsistence income. From here, every small disturbance sets up forces which takes the economy back to subsistence. Note, however, that while per capita income remains the same, population and national income may well change between the original equilibrium and a new one. It would therefore not be quite apt to describe the original equilibrium as stable; and so Leibenstein (1957) describes such a situation as 'quasi-stable'. A quasi-stable equilibrium is one where, given a disturbance, some variables tend to return to the original level, even though some others might change. Hence, Leibenstein argues that what we really mean when we speak of a poor country being in a poverty trap is that the economy is in a quasi-stable equilibrium with per capita income being one of the the stable variables.

Note also, that even this limited stability is a local phenomenon because, once per capita income is pushed beyond a certain level, conditions (a) and (b) would cease to hold. Hence the idea of a 'critical minimum effort', that is a thrust sufficiently large to take the economy beyond the whirlpool which keeps pulling it back into poverty. The original situation described in this example can be thought of as a vicious circle of poverty, because it is the low per

---

[2] See pages 52–63 in the 1973 Dent edition. Leibenstein (1957) also discusses a variant of this doctrine.

capita income which sets up forces, namely (a) and (b) which keeps the per capita income low.

Another widely discussed example is the so called 'supply-side vicious circle': capital scarcity implies a low income; a low income, in turn, implies a limited capacity to save; and small savings lead to a limited investment and capital scarcity.

Many other vicious-circle ideas have been explored in the literature (see Nurkse, 1953; Bauer,1971) and in general, once pointed out, these are not difficult to grasp. But there is a particular vicious-circle hypothesis, first pointed out by Rosenstein-Rodan and developed further by Nurkse, which, though quite obvious at first sight, is much more difficult to appreciate in depth. This thesis is also the mainspring of much of the debate on balanced and unbalanced growth.

2   The vicious circle and balanced growth

A shoe factory is considering an expansion of output. This will mean more people would be employed at the shoe factory, more raw material would be bought and more profits would be earned. In short, there will occur an increase in total income; and recalling that profit is a residual income (equal to the value of shoes minus cost), it is clear that the increase in income will be equal to the value of additional shoes. But given that people spend only a small fraction of their income on shoes, the additional supply of shoes would far outstrip the increase in demand. Hence either the price of shoes will fall or (in case price is exogenously fixed) the producer will find that he is unable to sell all the new shoes. It is, therefore, possible that the producer will find the expansion unprofitable.

By this same argument it is quite possible that the producer of each commodity finds an expansion in output not worthwhile because of limitations in the size of the market; i.e. because of a lack in demand.[3] But now consider an increase in the production of all commodities, maintaining the proportionality of demand. The expansion in each commodity, by generating demand for other goods, would provide one another with the required market. Thus the deficiency in demand perceived by each individual producer would now no longer be felt. This is a direct application of John Stuart Mill's more careful formulation of Say's law: 'Every increase

---

[3] One should not confuse between need and demand. In a poor country the need for goods is immense. Demand, on the other hand, is need *expressed* in the market place. If one does not have money one cannot demand anything no matter what the needs are.

of production, if distributed without miscalculation among all kinds of produce in the proportion which private interest would dictate, creates, or rather constitutes, its own demand' (quoted in Nurkse, 1953).

Of course, the fact that a balanced increase in production generates its own demand does not necessarily imply that such an increase is *feasible*. That depends on the availability of the factors of production. If the supply price of the factors are low and do not respond much to changes in demand, then the expansion is *feasible*. I explain all this rigorously in the next section.

The concept of balanced growth has traditionally emerged from the analysis of the poverty trap described above. The balanced-growth doctrine has many variants (usefully surveyed by Dagnino-Pastore, 1963 and Mathur, 1966) but its essence is the assertion that, if we want a poor country to develop, it has to be on the basis of a synchronised expansion in many sectors. The doctrine can be, and has been, interpreted in normative and positive terms. The former amounts to a recommendation to the government that while undertaking new capital investment it should be so *planned* as to be spread across sectors. The latter consists of a statement of feasibility: the only kind of capital formation feasible is a balanced one. I argue in the next section that while Nurkse's vicious circle theory is a powerful analytical idea, the balanced growth doctine (the normative or the positive version) does not follow from it and the conventional emphasis on the doctrine has been misplaced.

Traditionally, the main criticism of this doctrine has come from the so called 'unbalanced growth' school, led by Hirschman (1958). The attack of this school is a combination of positive and ideological criticisms. And its main thrust is supposed to be in the claim that it is in the incentives and strains generated by imbalance that lie the seeds of economic progress. A large investment in one sector generates, through 'linkages', the scope for expansion in other sectors. This school also attacks the pro-planning penchant one discerns in the balanced growth literature. Despite these differences the conflict between Nurkse and the unbalanced growth theories are not as irreconcilable as is traditionally made out to be. I try to show this in the next section.

3 Nurkse in the light of Walras

So much has been written about Rosenstein-Rodan's (1943) and Nurkse's (1953, chapter 1) vicious-circle thesis, and that too with so little formalism,[4] that lots of ambiguities and contradictions have crept into the literature. However, as must be clear from the above dicussion, at the core of their ideas lies a clear and unambiguous claim that *there exist situations where it is not profitable for any single producer in the economy to increase production because of market limitations, though if all producers increased production they would all profit from it*. Nurkse goes on to argue that a trap like this is often the cause of the persistence of underdevelopment in backward economies. This is of course an empirical question; and an attempt to check its validity can be flimsy or fastidious (examples of the former abound in the literature) but has to be based on facts. However, here I wish to attend to a prior theoretical question: Is Nurkse's claim (in italics above) theoretically valid? Given that so many doctrines and debates on underdevelopment, e.g. the 'big push' theory and the balanced and unbalanced growth debate, germinate from Nurkse's claim, this question is a crucial one.

At first sight, Nurkse's claim appears to be something of a paradox to those familiar with Walrasian equilibrium analysis. Scitovsky (1954) was the first person who fully appreciated this difficulty in accommodating both Nurkse and Walras. The problem is this: from a well-known theorem in welfare economics (see, for example, Debreu, 1959, chapter 6) we know that in a Walrasian world, every competitive equilibrium is also a Pareto optimum. This conflicts head on with Nurkse's hypothesis that in many less developed countries (LDCs), while an individual cannot profit from increasing his output, an *overall* increase in production is possible. Scitovsky discusses with lucidity a number of reasons why *in reality* equilibria may be Pareto sub-optimal. But he does not isolate the critical features in *Nurkse's model* which permits his equilibrium to be so different from that of Walras.

In turning to this problem we should first note that in the existing literature there is a certain amount of ambiguity as to whether these vicious circles are to be explained in terms of fixed or flexible price models. Thus, while Rosenstein-Rodan (1943) treats prices as fixed, Scitovsky (1954) treats them as flexible and Nurkse (1953) maintains a considered ambiguity. Considered, because it ought to be possible to formalise in either way. Given the recent developments in the theory of fix-price equilibrium analysis (Drèze, 1975; Malinvaud, 1977), it should be possible to develop the Rosenstein-Rodan–Nurkse thesis in terms of fixed prices and rationings, but I shall

---

[4] An exception is Findlay (1959), who makes an interesting attempt to formalise Nurkse. His model, however, does not capture the full richness of Nurkse because the equilibrium concept that he uses is essentially Walrasian.

adopt the more traditional approach of assuming that prices are flexible, and it is their movement which equates demand and supply. Now note that in Nurkse's world, when an individual considers increasing production, he anticipates a limited market, that is (given the flex-price assumption), he expects the price of the good to fall. In a Walrasian world, each producer treats the price as given, which means that the problem of inadequate demand is not something that an individual producer has to worry about. Whose world is closer to the actual one is an empirical question, but my interest here is an analytical one. The formalisation of Walras is, of course, well known. The same cannot be said about Nurske. So that is what I turn to presently.

The aim is to develop formally Nurkse's concept of an equilibrium. The term equilibrium is used here in a neo-classical sense, to describe a situation where, *given the options open to each agent*, every agent chooses what is best for him and the choices of all agents taken together are consistent. This property is satisfied by such diverse notions as the Arrow–Debreu equilibrium (see Debreu, 1959) and the Drèze equilibrium (Drèze, 1975). Where they differ is in their supposition about what the options open to each agent are. And it is in this that Nurkse differs from the rest.

Let there be two consumer goods, 1 and 2, and one factor of production, labour. There are two producers, one producing good 1 and the other good 2.[5] If X_1 and X_2 units of the two goods are produced at prices p_1 and p_2 respectively, then the total income generated in the economy is $p_1 X_1 + p_2 X_2$.

Let the marginal propensity to consume be the same for everybody and equal to c_1 and c_2 for goods 1 and 2, with $c_1 + c_2 = 1$.[6] Hence the proportion of the total income spent on the ith good is $c_i(p_1 X_1 + p_2 X_2)$. Thus the demand for the ith good is $c_i(p_1 X_1 + p_2 X_2)/p_i$, and the condition, demand equals supply, is written as

$$c_1(p_1 X_1 + p_2 X_2)/p_1 = X_1 \tag{1}$$
$$c_2(p_1 X_1 + p_2 X_2)/p_2 = X_2. \tag{2}$$

Since prices are flexible, given any quantity vector $\mathbf{X} = (X_1, X_2)$, these equations will give us the price vector $\mathbf{p} = (p_1, p_2)$. Note that since $c_2 = (1 - c_1)$, (2) is satisfied whenever (1) is satisfied, as indeed

---

[5] It is possible to think of many producers for each good. The crucial assumption is that producers be aware of the limitations of the market when considering an expansion. It is also implicitly assumed here that each entrepreneur, because of limitations in his capacity, can produce only one commodity.

[6] While I rule out savings, there should be no difficulty in enlarging the model to accommodate it.

one would expect from the Walras law. Thus I concentrate on (1). It is easy to check that if **p** satisfies (1) then any scalar multiple of **p** also satisfies (1). That is, only relative prices are given by (1). For convenience, I shall restrict the price vector such that

$$p_1 + p_2 = 1. \tag{3}$$

From (1) and (3), we get

$$p_1 = p_1(\mathbf{X}) = \frac{c_1 X_2}{c_2 X_1 + c_1 X_2} \tag{4}$$

$$p_2 = p_2(\mathbf{X}) = \frac{c_2 X_1}{c_2 X_1 + c_1 X_2}.$$

Thus, *given* a vector **X**, $p_1(\mathbf{X})$ and $p_2(\mathbf{X})$ are the prices that ensure that **X** is the amount demanded. The vector $[X_1, X_2, p_1(\mathbf{X}), p_2(\mathbf{X})]$ will denote an equilibrium *if* X_1 and X_2 are the chosen supplies of the two producers in this situation. Their choice, of course, depends on the options open to them. And this is where Nurkse's model differs from the standard Walrasian one.

Consider an output vector $\mathbf{X}^* = (X_1^*, X_2^*)$. To check whether $[X_1^*, X_2^*, p_1(\mathbf{X}^*), p_2(\mathbf{X}^*)]$ is a Walrasian equilibrium we assume that the producers treat the prices as fixed at $p_1(\mathbf{X}^*), p_2(\mathbf{X}^*)$ and choose their optimal X_1 and X_2. If these happen to be X_1^* and X_2^*, then we have a Walras competitive equilibrium. Notice that the horizontal demand curve faced by the individual agent in the above Walrasian case, need not be the actual demand curve. It is instead a 'conjecture' in the agents' mind. And, in fact, what is important in defining an equilibrium is the conjectured demand, that is, what the agent *believes* will be the effect on prices of changes in the quantity supplied by him. To appreciate this is to pave the way for other definitions of equilibrium, for example, those of Negishi (1961) and Hahn (1977).[7]

---

[7] The distinction between the actual and the conjectured demand curves was clearly elucidated by Kaldor about 50 years ago. He writes: 'The traditional "market demand curve" for a certain product is *not the same sort of thing* as the demand curve which is relevant in determining the actions of the individual producer. The first denotes a functional relationship between price and the amounts bought from a particular producer. The second concerns the *image* of this functional relationship as it exists in the mind of the entrepreneur' (Kaldor, 1934, p. 40). He goes on to point out rightly that in many situations the actual demand curve may be quite difficult or even impossible to define. Kaldor, however, errs on one point – in his supposition that in perfect competition the dichotomy between the 'imagined' and 'real' demand curves does not arise. From recent advances we know that a downward sloping aggregate demand curve is compatible with horizontal demand for each individual producer only if there is a continuum of producers, which is of course quite unrealistic.

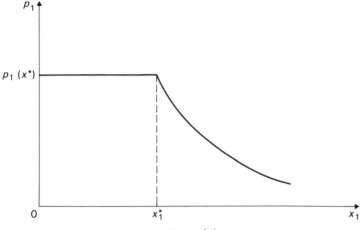

Figure 2.1

Now Nurkse assumed that if a producer starting from X^* produces more of the ith good then p_i falls and the producer *takes this into account* in computing the profitability of producing more. The fall in p_i is just sufficient to clear the market. If, on the other hand, a producer cuts back his production he expects no price response. Thus (producer 1 supposes that) p_1 depends on X_1 in the following way:

$$p_1 = f_1(X_1) = \begin{cases} p_1(\mathbf{X}^*) & \text{if } X_1 \leqslant X_1^* \\ \dfrac{c_1 X_2^*}{c_2 X_1 + c_1 X_2^*} & \text{if } X_1 \geqslant X_1^* \end{cases} \qquad (5)$$

A symmetric equation, $f_2(X_2)$, for good 2.

Equation (5) is illustrated in figure 2.1.[8] If given (5), the ith producer still chooses X_i^*, then $[X_1^*, X_2^*, p_1(\mathbf{X}^*), p_2(\mathbf{X}^*)]$ is a Nurske equilibrium.

The amount forthcoming from the ith producer will depend on the labour-market conditions. Since the purpose of the present exercise is illustrative, I make some very simple assumptions about labour supply. Let L be the total amount of labour available in the

[8] This kinked 'demand curve' is one interpretation of Nurkse. But kinked demand curves in general have a long and independent history and they have received diverse justifications spread over at least 40 years (Sweezy, 1939; Drèze, 1979). There is also the theoretical question as to whether (and, if not, under what conditions) the Nurkse conjectures could be thought of as rational? I make no attempt to pursue this line here.

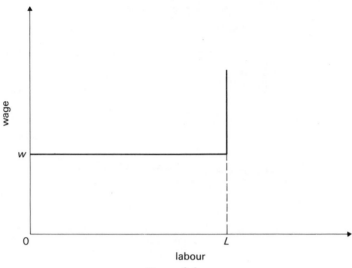

Figure 2.2

economy and suppose that at the subsistence wage, w, the labourers are indifferent between working and not working.[9] Figure 2.2 illustrates the labour supply curve.

Let l_i be the amount of labour needed to produce 1 unit of good i. At $\mathbf{X}^*$, the producer of good 1 will not want to produce any more if his marginal revenue, for *increases* in output (i.e. $X_1 \geqslant X_1^*$), is less than or equal to wl_1. Computing the marginal revenue, using (5), this condition may be written as[10]

$$p_1(\mathbf{X}^*) - \frac{c_2 c_1 X_1^* X_2^*}{(c_2 X_1^* + c_1 X_2^*)^2} \leqslant wl_1.$$

Using (4) and the fact that $(1 - p_2) = p_1$, the above inequality may be rewritten as

$$[p_1(\mathbf{X}^*)]^2 \leqslant wl_1. \tag{6}$$

[9] Strictly speaking, the subsistence wage should be defined in real terms with w deflated by a consumer price index. My assumption that labour supply depends on money wages is purely for reasons of simplicity. Since I do not consider inflation in this chapter and restrict attention only to relative price adjustments, my assumption need not be too disturbing.

[10] The total revenue for firm 1 (given $X_2 = X_2^*$) is given by $X_1 f_1(X_1)$. Since we are considering increases in X_1 starting from X_1^*, clearly $f_1(X_1) = c_1 X_2^*/(c_2 X_1 + c_1 X_2^*)$ (see (5)). Keeping this in mind if we differentiate $X_1 f_1(X_1)$ by X_1 and then insert $X_1 = X_1^*$, we get the marginal revenue at X^*, which is precisely the left-hand expression in the inequality below.

At $\mathbf{X}^*$, the producer of good 1 will not want to produce less if

$$wl_1 \leqslant p_1(\mathbf{X}^*). \tag{7}$$

This is obvious from (5). Therefore if (6) and (7) are satisfied then X_1^* is the optimal output from producer 1's point of view. Symmetric conditions apply to producer 2. The above conditions presuppose, of course, that the demand for labour does not exceed its supply. That is

$$l_1 X_1^* + l_2 X_2^* \leqslant L.$$

All this may be summarised into a brief statement. The vector $[X_1^*, X_2^*, p_1^*, p_2^*]$ is a *Nurkse equilibrium*, if and only if

(i) $p_i^* = p_i(\mathbf{X}^*)$ $i = 1, 2$;

(ii) $[p_i(\mathbf{X}^*)]^2 \leqslant wl_i \leqslant p_i(\mathbf{X}^*)$ $i = 1, 2$;

and

(iii) $l_1 X_1^* + l_2 X_2^* \leqslant L$.

A *Nurkse equilibrium* with (iii) holding as a strict inequality will be referred to as a *poverty trap*.

It should be possible to build a more elaborate model along these lines and analyse formally different aspects of the vicious circle. Even this simple model sheds light on many important issues. First of all, it is easy to check with an example that a Nurkse equilibrium with unemployment can arise. Suppose a certain economy is characterised by:

$$c_1 = c_2 = \tfrac{1}{2};$$

$$l_1 = l_2 = 1;$$

$$w = \tfrac{1}{3};$$

$$L = 5.$$

It is easy to check that $X_1 = X_2 = 1$, $p_1 = p_2 = \tfrac{1}{2}$ is a Nurkse equilibrium. At $X_1 = X_2 = 1$, $p_1(X) = \tfrac{1}{2}$. Hence $[p_1(\mathbf{X})]^2 = \tfrac{1}{4}$. Therefore, wl_1 ($= \tfrac{1}{3}$) is less than $p_1(\mathbf{X})$ and greater than $\{p_1(\mathbf{X})\}^2$. Also, at this point total employment ($= l_1 X_1 + l_2 X_2$) is equal to 2. Hence all properties of a Nurkse equilibrium are satisfied. This is a poverty trap because three-fifths of the labour force is unemployed.

Now if the production of *either* good 1 *or* good 2 is raised, the respective firm will make a loss. If, however, both sectors are expanded in step, that is along the ray (λ, λ), up to the point where $\lambda + \lambda = 5$, then both sectors would make profits.

Using the definition of a Nurkse equilibrium, we can sketch out a region in the (X_1, X_2)-space such that all points in this region indicate output vectors which can be Nurkse equilibria (when supported by suitable prices). Note that conditions (ii) and (iii) can, in this economy, be written as

$$\left[\frac{X_j}{X_i + X_j}\right]^2 \leqslant \frac{1}{3} \leqslant \frac{X_j}{X_i + X_j} \qquad i = 1, 2 \ (i \neq j)$$

and

$$X_1 + X_2 \leqslant 5.$$

The shaded region in figure 2.3 depicts output vectors where the economy could stagnate in the sense of Nurkse.

It is of course definitional that at a Nurkse equilibrium no single producer benefits by increasing output. What is interesting is that if $[X_1^*, X_2^*, p_1^*, p_2^*]$ is a Nurkse equilibrium, then $[\lambda X_1^*, \lambda X_2^*, p_1^*, p_2^*]$ is also a Nurkse equilibrium where λ is a scalar such that $\lambda l_1 X_1^* + \lambda l_2 X_2^* \leqslant L$. This may be proved as follows. Since $[X_1^*, X_2^*, p_1^*, p_2^*]$ is a Nurkse equilibrium, it satisfies conditions (i), (ii) and (iii) above. Now from (4) it is clear that $p_i(\mathbf{X}^*) = p_i(\lambda \mathbf{X}^*)$, for all values of λ

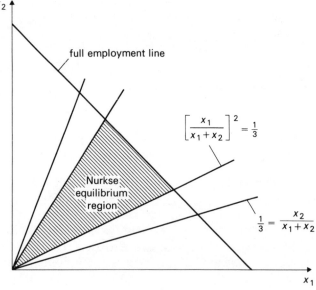

Figure 2.3

(excepting zero). Hence $[\lambda X_1^*, \lambda X_2^*, p_1^*, p_2^*]$ satisfies (i) and (ii), for all values of λ. If in addition λ is restricted such that

$$\lambda l_1 X_1^* + \lambda l_2 X_2^* \leqslant L,$$

then (iii) is also satisfied.

This proposition implies that if $[X_1^*, X_2^*, p_1^*, p_2^*]$ is a poverty trap, i.e. it is a Nurkse equilibrium with

$$l_1 X_1^* + l_2 X_2^* < L,$$

then it is *possible* to move up to the full employment point by increasing the production of all commodities at the same rate. Herein lies the heart of the balanced growth doctrine to which I return in a moment. For the time being just note the emphasis on the word 'possible' above, which suggests that a balance is not *necessary* though it is sufficient for moving up to full employment – a fact which acquires a certain amount of importance in the context of the balanced-growth debate.

It is easy to see that along the balanced growth path the proportionality of the two goods are maintained that is,

$$p_1^* \Delta X_1 / p_2^* \Delta X_2 = c_1 / c_2,$$

where ΔX_i refers to the change in X_i along the balanced growth path. This corresponds to Nurkse's (1953, p. 12) observation: 'An increase in the production of shoes alone does not create its own demand. An increase in production over a wide range of consumables, *so balanced as to correspond with the pattern of consumers' preferences*, does create its own demand' (my italics).

In the vicious circle, no individual producer has the incentive to produce more. This happens, as seen above, if condition (6) is true. This is less likely to be true if c_1 is large. If c_1 is large then a large proportion of the income generated by increasing the output of producer 1 is spent on good 1. That is, the supply from producer 1 generates much of its own demand and so an expansion in the production of good 1 may be profitable. Thus if there is *one* producer with this property then the economy might never get into a poverty trap.

Note that while for simplicity we have only considered one factor of production, labour, the model can be easily adapted so as to comment on capital investment. First, by direct analogy, we get the result that no single firm would make fresh investments while in the poverty trap, even though an investment suitably spread out across all sectors may be worthwhile. Secondly (and this is not analogous to our analysis of labour), with capital, unlike with labour, indivisibilities and increasing returns to scale assume a prominent role. This means that a balanced expansion in capital investment is not only *possible* but it makes room for the use of more sophisticated capital equipment. This is also the crux of Young's (1928) argument.

Now we are better placed to appreciate Fleming's (1955) critique of the Rosenstein-Rodan–Nurkse thesis. Fleming argues that in most situations if the production of good 1 rises, the factor cost, i.e. wages, will rise as well, which will cause a *cut-back* in the production of good 2. Thus, to quote Fleming, 'whereas the balanced-growth doctrine assumes that the relationship between industries is for the most part complementary, the limitation of factor supply ensures that that relationship is for the most part competitive'. While the above model does not speak about wage formation at the full-employment point, Fleming's disagreement with the poverty trap thesis is easy to explain. Fleming argues that more often than not factor supply will be inelastic. And he in fact considers the case of completely inelastic supply. In terms of the above model, suppose that the economy is at (X_1, X_2) such that $l_1 X_1 + l_2 X_2 = L$. Now let there be a technological improvement in the production of good 1. If this augments the use of labour in this sector, then clearly the supply of labour to the other sector must fall. Whether this bids up wages or not, this will cause a drop in the output of good 2. But there is really no conflict between Fleming and Nurkse. Fleming's concern is with a special case of the above model, with the rising part of the labour supply curve in figure 2.2.[11]

Let us now take a look at the big push theory or what Leibenstein (1957) refers to as the Critical Minimum Effort (CME) hypothesis. While this is related to Nurkse's thesis, it is wrong to suppose that it follows logically from Nurkse's model. I clarify at the outset that the CME doctrine has many facets. In particular, Leibenstein claimed that, (a) there exists a certain minimum investment such that a smaller investment is not feasible, and (b) that once this investment is under-taken the economy begins to grow on its own. Here I treat the CME doctrine as equivalent to (a). Of course, the word investment does not make immediate sense in our simple model. So, instead, I consider input use in general.

The belief that a certain minimum input is essential to move away from the poverty trap, arises from the fact that we need to simul-taneously increase output in all sectors. This is not a valid argument because the same input, if it is divisible, can be spread endlessly thin

[11] Fleming's analysis is criticised and extended by Islam (1957).

across all sectors. If, however, there are fixed costs associated with any expansion then this, coupled with Nurkse's vicious circle theory, implies that there is a certain critical minimum effort necessary to move out of the poverty trap. For example, if beginning from $\mathbf{X}^*$ (and assuming that there is adequate labour surplus), sector 1 can employ more labour productively only if it is of the magnitude of ΔN (this is a simple way of capturing the idea of fixed costs), then to increase output, a minimum of

$$\Delta N \left(1 + \frac{p_1^* \, l_2 \, c_2}{p_2^* \, l_1 \, c_1} \right)$$

labour employment has simultaneously to take place.[12]

Finally, let us turn to the most contentious issue: balanced and unbalanced growth. I want to argue here that the doctrine of unbalanced growth does not lie as totally beyond the ambit of Nurkse's model as is usually suggested (see also, Mathur, 1966, and Thirlwall, 1972). First consider the positive aspect. Can unbalanced growth actually occur? Not only has Hirschman (1958) effectively argued in the affirmative, but it appears to me – and I am really speculating here – that if we introduce some elements of dynamics in the model of this section, this possibility can be demonstrated. This may be seen as follows. Consider a situation $\mathbf{X}^*$ where there is a considerable amount of unemployment and condition (6) holds for producer 1 but not for producer 2, i.e.

$$[p_1(\mathbf{X}^*)]^2 \leqslant wl_1 \quad \text{and} \quad [p_2(\mathbf{X}^*)]^2 > wl_2.$$

Then in this situation producer 2 will expand production. Once he has done so, p_1 will rise because of the increase in demand. This may now make it profitable for 1 to expand output, which would raise p_2, thereby making it worthwhile for 2 to go in for another round of expansion. And so on. From this approximate argument it appears that it should be possible to isolate parametric configurations within this model which can alternatively explain unbalanced growth and the poverty trap.

If the latter occurs what should be the government's strategy? This leads us to the normative issue. And here, I feel, the emphasis on balanced growth has been misplaced. What is clear is that, if a country is caught in a low-level equilibrium, some form of governmental

---

[12] It is being assumed that in sector 2 additional labour is divisible. It is easy to check that if employment in sector 1 increases by ΔL_1, for the expansion to be balanced, ΔL_2 must equal $(l_2 c_2 p_1^* \Delta L_1)/l_1 c_1 p_2^*$. Since the minimum feasible ΔL_1 is ΔN, a balanced expansion entails a minimum of $\Delta N[1 + (p_1^* l_2 c_2)/(p_2^* l_1 c_1)]$ new employment.

intervention is necessary, because no producer will individually expand output. It was shown above that a balanced expansion is possible. But this need not be the only way for two reasons.

1 When we say that a balanced growth is possible we mean that a balanced growth confers profits on all producers. But this does not mean that this is the only expansion path that does so. And among all the expansion paths, which generate profits to all producers it is not clear why the balanced one should be considered optimal. For instance, if one believes in maximising aggregate welfare in the traditional sense, then one should recommend an expansion path where the marginal profit rates are the same in different sectors.

2 In case it is the government, i.e. the public sector, which is undertaking the expansion, it is not even necessary that profits are generated to all expanding sectors. Surely a government should allow public-sector firms to make losses (this would typically not require much coaxing) if that results in greater benefit elsewhere. Consider a poverty trap. One option for the government is to undertake additional production in commodity 1. Since the original position was an equilibrium, this activity of the government is bound to result in losses. But this would increase profitability in sector 2 and cause an expansion in output in that sector. This would, in turn, raise the price of good 1 and mean a recovery of some of the losses in this sector in the long run. Thus Nurkse's model is not at all inimical to a strategy where the government concentrates its resources on one sector and expands its production. The strategies of balanced and unbalanced growths do not spring from totally different conceptions of reality.

In the many surveys and modern discussions of poverty traps and balanced growth one person who has consistently been left out is Michał Kalecki. Kalecki's works on development economics are insightful and, shorn of the linguistic and stylistic differences, not very dissimilar to those of Rosenstein-Rodan and Nurkse. In fact, many of his ideas were developed in lectures given in 1953 not too far away (from an unabashedly Asian perspective) from the venue of Nurkse's famous lectures in 1951. Kalecki's venue was Mexico City, Nurkse's Rio de Janeiro.[13]

[13] Educated at Lodz and Gdansk, Kalecki was always on the sidelines of mainstream economics. His works on development economics are even less known because these appeared in scattered and obscure places. Some of the best pieces, however, have now been available for some time in a collected volume – Kalecki (1976).

Kalecki's concern was with two sectors, consumer goods and investment, and his economy (particularly in Kalecki, 1960) *looks* quite similar to the model in this section. Where he coincides with Nurkse he is less meticulous and searching, but in some ways he has a longer reach. Some of these I discuss in the next chapter.

4 Manifestations of unemployment

In LDCs unemployment manifests itself in an amazing diversity of forms. Surplus labour, disguised unemployment, conventional open unemployment are all distinct concepts but they reflect the same underlying problem: an acute inadequacy in the economy's capacity to employ its labour force. Typists in government offices playing cards during working hours, members of large families labouring at snail's pace on tiny plots of land, Arthur Lewis' (1954) 'messengers' employed by 'most businesses in underdeveloped countries', 'whose contribution is almost negligble' are all employed in a conventional sense but are actually expressions of the same phenomenon. One implication of such unusual manifestations of excess supply of labour in India is that its official unemployment statistics are often quite misleading, with unemployment figures which can be 'low enough to put many advanced countries to shame' (Sen, 1975, p. 119).[14]

In the industrialised world excess supply manifests itself mostly in open unemployment with the dole and other social securities taking care of the hapless. In most LDCs no such institutionalised system of support for the unemployed exists; and the myriad forms of under-employment must, in part, be society's response to this – a haphazard attempt to insure against widepsread poverty and also the vicissitudes of markets.

The literature on unemployment is vast.[15] Even in the present book the topic is taken up time and again, in different contexts, in different forms. In fact, Nurkse's theory which we have just examined can explain an interesting kind of unemployment. This unemployment is, however, not involuntary in the Keynesian sense. We shall, in later chapters, encounter several kinds of involuntary unemployment. In reality, I feel, one major cause of its existence lies in the

[14] Sen's remark is in the context of the 1961 census which showed India's unemployment as 1.4 million.

[15] For an overview and a good discussion of the main conceptual issues, one may refer to Myrdal (1968) and Sen (1975).

fact that labour is heterogeneous in quality and yet wage discrimination *within* a firm is typically infeasible. This mean that even if workers are available in the open market at a lower wage than what a firm is paying its workers, the firm may prefer not to lower the wage because by doing so it may lose its more talented workers (who would normally have a higher reservation wage).

Returning to Nurkse's model, recall that at equilibrium, the *social* marginal revenue product of labour may exceed the wage. This means that more labour than the number employed at equilibrium *can* be employed (if the new employment is spread across sectors in a certain way) with all workers being paid a higher wage and, in fact, with everybody in the economy benefiting. This happens because of a divergence between the private and social marginal revenue products of labour confronted by *each* firm. In the poverty trap, each employer finds that the marginal revenue product of employing one more worker is below the wage. So he does not employ more. What escapes his calculation is the additional profit which accrues to the other sectors as a consequence of his employing one more labourer.

It has been argued by many that in a situation like this, efforts to generate more employment in one sector would have a tendency, not only to push prices up once and for all, but to cause inflation. This is a matter that needs careful analysis and this is what I turn to in the next chapter.

CHAPTER 3

Inflation and Structural Disequilibrium

1 Employment policy and the inflation barrier

Given the widespread prevalence of underemployment – using the term with sufficient catholicity to include disguised and open unemployment – in LDCs, what can be done by way of remedy? One approach is through project planning, that is, via appropriate choice of techniques and shadow wages (see Dasgupta, Marglin and Sen, 1972; Little and Mirrlees, 1974). This approach is, however, very specific and it assumes away many of the wider macroeconomic dimensions of employment policy.

The latter loom large in the works of Rao (1952), Kalecki (1976) and some of the Latin American structuralists. Rao considers a standard Keynesian remedy for unemployment – the generation of additional effective demand. And he argues that the consequences of such a policy in an LDC with its *chronic* underemployment will be very different from what allegedly happens in industrialised nations during *episodic* stagnation.[1] In LDCs, because of the inelasticity of capital goods supply, output cannot respond to the additional demand, and the multiplier has its impact on the nominal values by simply pushing up prices. Thus it is the inflation barrier which thwarts full-employment policy.

Kalecki's worry (1954, 1960, 1968) is similar: an attempt to alleviate unemployment in LDCs is likely to result in inflation. But his argument is different. It is not just the capital deficiency that concerns him (though he is well aware of its importance) because he is willing to consider 'pick and shovel' techniques of output expan-

[1] I qualify my remark on Keynes with an 'allegedly' because recent experience and theory (Malinvaud, 1977) makes it clear that, even in developed countries, Keynesian policies work only in a limited *class* of situations.

27

sion. But even this strategy would cause inflation because of another constraint – the wage-goods bottleneck. And it is Kalecki's perception of this bottleneck which is the point of both bifurcation between his and Nurkse's theories and concurrence between him and the structuralists.[2]

In this chapter I first discuss Kalecki's theory of underdevelopment, and then move on to a discussion of inflation in general. Inflation is not a topic in which economics can boast of many successes. The fact that I discuss this topic within a limited context – that pertaining to LCDs – does not in any way change this fact, which is a roundabout way of warning the reader that my comments on inflation should be treated as tentative and experimental.

2   Notes on Michał Kalecki

Kalecki's interest in development economics was not a direct one, but tangential to his general interest in macroeconomics and growth. He spent a lot of effort trying to isolate the fundamental differences between developed and underdeveloped economies. His findings – not dissimilar to those of Rao's (1952) – are best summarised in his own words (Kalecki, 1976, p. 23):

> The crucial problem facing the underdeveloped countries is thus to increase investment considerably, *not for the sake of generating effective demand*, as was the case in an underemployed developed economy, *but for the sake of accelerating the expansion of productive capacity* indispensable for the rapid growth of national income. There will be, however, three important obstacles to stepping up investment. Firstly, it is possible that private investment will not be forthcoming at a desirable rate. Secondly, there may be no physical resources to produce more investment goods. Thirdly, even if the first two difficulties were overcome, there is still the problem of adequate supply of necessities to cover the demand resulting from the increase in employment. (my italics)

Much of Kalecki's work on underdevelopment is focused on this third obstacle and it is in this that the germs of his theory of inflation lie.

Consider a stagnant economy. Capital is in short supply, primary factors like labour are underutilised, per capita income is low and the

---

[2] There is another difference between Rao and Kalecki. In Rao (1952) a rise in effective demand has a multiplier effect on prices. The ripples die out and the net effect is a certain price increase, the magnitude of which depends on the society's marginal propensity to consume. In Kalecki (1954), a rise in demand triggers off an inflation, i.e. a chronic price rise.

techniques of production are primitive. It is in an economy like this that Kalecki considers the possibility and consequences of growth. But a prior question which must arise is why is the economy stagnant in the first place.

While Kalecki[3] has no explicit theory of stagnation, there are many suggestions in his work from which one may assume that his views on this were similar to those of Rosenstein-Rodan and Nurkse. Thus Kalecki also talks about 'balanced development' and about the importance of an output expansion which is consistent with the additional demands generated by it: 'Inflationary pressures may be avoided by planning an increase in the supply of necessities matching the demand for them, which will be generated by the planned increase in national income' (Kalecki, 1976, p. 25). So we could suppose that the economy Kalecki is considering is in a poverty trap of the kind defined in chapter 2. Up to here, Kalecki is in agreement with Nurkse, or rather, there seems to be no harm in assuming agreement (though some difficulties arise later and I take them up then). But at this point two major differences arise. First, Kalecki argues that the expansion of agricultural production in LDCs is not a purely technical matter. Its rigidities are largely *institutional*. In the context of India, he isolates factors like the structure of property rights, 'the operation of many farms under a system of disguised tenancy without security of tenure' and the 'inherent poverty of small peasants enhanced by their dependence on the merchants and moneylenders' (Kalecki, 1976, p. 19). These features of backward agriculture I discuss in later chapters and so the specificities of these need not detain us here. In essence, what Kalecki argues is that while balanced growth, in principle, solves the problem, it is not a feasible strategy without dramatic land reforms and other major instituional changes. A big push is indeed needed, though of a very different kind from the one envisaged by Rosenstein-Rodan.

Even if agricultural output is inelastic (assuming that revolutionary institutional changes are not on the agenda) what about the strategy of concentrating on one or a few sectors? This would result in losses, for reasons discussed in chapter 2, but governmental strategies need not be circumscribed by the criterion of commerical profitability. Now, as noted in chapter 2, an expansion in one sector causes a price rise in the other sectors. The second difference lies in Kalecki's assumption that a price rise like this does not end as a one-shot adjustment but escalates, instead, into a general inflation.

[3] My comments on Kalecki are based primarily on his 1954, 1960 and 1968 papers.

The reason is as follows. If output in the capital goods sector rises, the price of consumer goods rises. Workers in an effort to maintain their real wages, push up nominal wages. Producers respond by raising prices (in an effort to restore the original level of profit) and the spiral continues.

The affinity between Kalecki and the structuralists is obvious. The assumption of fixed real wage and price mark-up is an integral part of structuralism. In Sunkel's (1958) theory it appears as the 'propagation mechanism', waiting to convert price adjustments into inflation.

Before going on to take a closer look at structuralism it is useful to try and formalise Kalecki's argument. There are two sectors: consumer goods 1, and capital goods 2. As in the previous chapter, let X_i, p_i and c_i be the supply and price of good i, and the propensity to consume good i; and assume that $c_1 + c_2 = 1$. Then the condition of equality between the demand and supply of good 1 may be written as

$$X_1 = c_1(p_1X_1 + p_2X_2)/p_1. \tag{1}$$

Since $c_1 + c_2 = 1$, this condition automatically ensures that the demand and supply of good 2 are equal. This was demonstrated in chapter 2 and is easy to check.

Assume that the economy has been static at a certain configuration (X_1, X_2, p_1, p_2) (i.e. using vector notation, $(\mathbf{X}, \mathbf{p})$) which satisfies (1) and also embodies an excess supply of labour, as in the poverty trap. How the economy arrived here, we do not question.

Now assume that the volume of consumer goods (which in a poor country comprise primarily the products of agriculture) are structurally fixed at the level where it happens to be, and it is movements in p_1 which helps clear markets. p_2 is fixed as a mark-up on variable costs:

$$p_2 = ml_2w, \tag{2}$$

where l_2 is the amount of labour (the only variable factor of production) needed for producing 1 unit of good 2, w is the money wage and m is a constant with $(m - 1)$ being the mark-up on cost.

Denoting the real wage by W, the assumption of rigid real wages is given by

$$W = w/p_1. \tag{3}$$

This completes the model. Assume that the original configuration $(\mathbf{X}, \mathbf{p})$ satisfies (2) and (3) also.

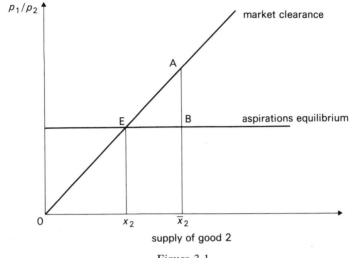

Figure 3.1

Note that (1) may be rewritten as

$$p_1/p_2 = c_1 X_2/(1 - c_1) X_1 \tag{4}$$

and (2) and (3) may be combined and expressed as

$$p_1/p_2 = 1/ml_2 W. \tag{5}$$

(4) and (5) describe Kalecki's model, and will be referred to, respectively, as the market clearance equation and the aspirations equilibrium equation. Recalling that X_1 is fixed, these two equations may be diagrammatically illustrated as in figure 3.1.

Point E in this figure denotes an equilibrium. From (4) and (5) it is obvious that the scaling up of X_1 and X_2 in balance, i.e. to λX_1 and λX_2, creates a new equilibrium with unchanged price ratio. Thus a balanced growth, if feasible, can be sustained. But of course in Kalecki's model it is not feasible because the supply of good 1 is, at least in the short run, fixed.

In this set up, Kalecki considers the effect of an increase in the production of capital goods, say to $\bar{X}_2$. Then (since p_2 responds only to changes in m, l_2 and w) p_1 rises in order to clear the markets, i.e. to satisfy (4). This immediately results in a rise in w (see (3))[4] which pushes up p_2 (see (2)). That a rise in p_1 raises p_2 can also be seen directly from (5). Now the rise in p_2 once again raises p_1 in order to clear the markets (see (4)); and the process continues.[5] p_1 and p_2 keep rising and their ratio remains within the segment AB. In brief, at $(X_1, \bar{X}_2)$ there is a *structural disequilibrium*, i.e. (4) and (5) are inconsistent – it is not possible that markets clear *and* the aspirations of different classes are satisfied. And it is this inconsistency which stokes the inflation.

We are now in a position to return to a question I had raised earlier. Are the ideas of Nurkse and Kalecki compatible? At first sight, the answer does seem to be no. After all, Nurkse's producer treats the price response to his output changes as well defined (by equation (5) in chapter 2) and chooses his output to maximise profit. On the other hand, Kalecki's firm does not seem to have a clear profit-maximisation objective. He responds to any increase in the price of inputs by raising the price of goods so as to maintain the same percentage cost mark-up. The hope of reconciling Nurkse and Kalecki must lie in the fact that though they talk about very different kinds of response, they do so in different domains. Thus, for instance, Kalecki is silent – at least in this context – on the output strategy of firms.

One interesting way of accommodating Kalecki into the framework of the previous chapter is to suppose that long-run stagnation occurs for reasons similar to the ones given by Nurkse and that what Kalecki describes is the short-run reaction of firms and workers to disturbances in prices. For an analysis of this kind we have to be very careful in interpreting the variables m and W in (2) and (3). At any point of time they are given *parametrically* but it is quite possible that they are determined, in turn, by the long-run state of the economy. Hence given that an economy has, for a long time, persisted at (X, p) we could use (2) and (3) as equations to determine the values of m and W. In other words, m and W are the mark-up and the real wage that, respectively, the producers and the workers are

---

[4] Scitovsky (1978, p. 223) provides an interesting practical reason for the upwards-only flexibility of wages: 'Labour's stake in wage bargaining is always greater than management's' because 'the change in labour earnings equals the change in wages; but profits always change by less if the firm has the upper hand in product markets and so can escape part of the cost of a wage increase by shifting it on to its customers' shoulders in the form of price increase.... There, in the firm's lesser self-interest in the outcome of the wage bargain, is the key to ... the downward stickiness or upwards-only flexibility of wages'.

[5] The process does not *follow* from the above equations but is a plausible description of what happens in disequilibrium.

used to and have come to treat more or less as rights. Now, after this long period of stagnation, if the system is disturbed, equations (2) and (3) play a different role. W and m are by now 'internalised', they are parts of the structure; so (2) and (3) are the equations for determining p_2 and w. They are the outcome of the producers' and workers' efforts to retain the profit margin and real wage that they are used to.

I should qualify the above discussion with the remark that while a Nurkse-type stagnation does appear to be quite widespread among LDCs, inflation of the kind suggested by Kalecki is less frequently encountered.

3   Structural disequilibrium

The need for a separate view of inflation in LDCs arises from the fact that the inflationary experience in many of these countries is strikingly different from that in industrialised nations. In the latter, inflation is usually an episode spanning at most a couple of years[6] – often despite the best efforts of governments! Also an inflation of about 25 per cent is considered very high. In some LDCs, on the other hand, it can be chronic and at astonishingly high levels, often hovering around a 100 per cent per annum, so that a period of 25 per cent inflation appears stable. It ought to be pointed out that the experience of LDCs is by no means homogeneous. Thus a sharp contrast to Argentina and Chile is provided by India, where, since independence in 1947, there have been only three inflationary *episodes*. It is also interesting to note that the highest inflations in this century have occurred not in LDCs. The record is held by Hungary, 1946, with Germany, 1923, as runner-up. Unlike in many LDCs though, these hyper-inflations were of short duration.[7]

Not surprisingly, some of the best research on inflation in LDCs has been by Latin American economists. The two main schools of thought are monetarism and structuralism. The former is the same as monetarism discussed in the context of developed countries and

---

[6] This was so at least till the early seventies.

[7] The Hungarian hyperinflation lasted for 12 months and during this period prices rose 3.8×10^{27} times. In Germany the hyperinflation lasted for 16 months and during this time prices rose 1.02×10^{10} times (Cagan, 1956). The ranking of hyperinflations according to intensity would depend on the kind of measure that is used but, I think, Hungary's supremacy would remain unchallenged.

since so much has been written on it, I make just a few brief comments here. In its bare essentials monetarism is the view that price
increases are caused by increases in the money supply. Since government and the central bank control money supply, inflation is not
caused by avaricious shopkeepers and mercenary workers but by
governments trying to procrastinate the day of reckoning by creating
money and spending. The time-lag between the increases in money
supply and prices can be anywhere between 6 months and 6 years
(Pandit, 1978; Behrman, 1973). Such time-lags imply that a price
stabilisation programme requires a longer period of austerity than
what most governments, with their eyes fixed on the coming elec-
tions, are willing to undertake (see Sheehey, 1980). Thus inflation
once started, tends to continue unabated.

Two remarks are in order. First, while most empirical studies look
for a specific time-lag, it is very likely that the lag itself is endogenous, depending on a variety of factors, including how sharply the
money supply increases. Consider first a doubling of the supply of
money, spread out from January to December. Suppose this results
in the price-level doubling, spread over January to December in the
following year. In that case the time-lag is one year. Now, if in the
same economy we consider a doubling of the money supply but very
sharply – all in the first week of January, then it is unlikely that the
price increase will start so late or occur so slowly as to be centred on
the first week in the following year. In other words, we would expect
the time-lag itself to be affected by the sharpness of the money-
supply increase.

Secondly, there is a widespread belief that while monetarism is
empirically sound it is not based on any theory. Reality is probably
quite the reverse, because while the basic thesis does stand up to
casual reason (even though there is no completely rigorous theory),
the verdict of the data is by no means unequivocal (see, in the context of India, Chakrabarty, 1977, and Pandit, 1978) and the early
simple econometric tests, which strongly supported the monetarist
thesis, have been challenged on grounds of econometric methodology
(Hendry, 1980).[8]

---

[8] Hendry shows that if one uses such simple methods then cumulative rainfall in the UK
turns out to be an even better explanatory variable for price movements than money supply.
He also brings our attention to the findings of Llewellyn and Witcomb who claim to have
established 'a higher correlation between annual inflation and cases of dysentery in Scotland
(one year earlier) than Mills obtained between inflation and the rate of change of excess
money supply (two years before)!' Let me emphasise that Hendry's paper is not a critique
of monetarism, as some have mistakenly taken it to be, but of some popular econometric
methods.

To the structuralists,[9] the basic cause of inflation is not money. They do concede that an increase in money supply is needed for inflation, but argue that money supply itself responds passively to other more basic factors which are the real cause of inflation (see Olivera, 1964). More specifically, inflation is the outcome of 'structural disequilibrium' (I elucidate this with a model below). In a situation where individuals have the power to strive towards their aspirations, inflation is the outcome of the market's attempt to mitigate these conflicts (Aujac, 1950).

Beginning with Sunkel's (1958) seminal analysis of inflation in Chile, the structuralist approach has been extensively used to analyse chronic inflation in LDCs, particularly in Latin America. After developing his own theory, Seers (1962) provides a good overview of the early literature in a brief appendix. The importance attached to this school of thought must increase considerably with the contributions of Hicks (1974) and Scitovsky (1978) which have a distinctly structuralist flavour.

The main tenets in a structural theory of inflation are the following. Money prices are assumed to be rigid downwards. Hence every change in relative price translates into a general price rise. But this alone would not cause an inflation, it would cause a one-shot price rise. A relative price change is transformed into inflation because of the 'propogation elements' (Sunkel, 1958) in the system, namely the workers' attempts to retain a fixed real wage and the producers' efforts to hold on to the existing profit margins. The picture is completed by isolating the factors which trigger off the process by causing changes in relative prices. The structuralists emphasise two alternative sources; (a) the inelasticity of supply of agricultural output and other rigidities in the presence of a growing industrial sector, and (b) the increasing import requirements which accompany growth and the secular decline in foreign demand for primary goods.

Before attempting a critical analysis of this doctrine, it is useful to present a formal model of structural inflation. It is possible to think of Kalecki's model described in the previous section as an illustration of this kind of inflation. But in this model there exists an output vector at which there is equilibrium and inflation occurs only

---

[9] Structuralism – usually without such a label – has also been discussed in the context of developed economies; and while there is much in common between the Latin American and European structuralists, the former with their focus on LDCs do comprise a distinct school (see Canavese, 1982). While the ensuing discussion concentrates on indigenous disequilibrium, there is a substantial literature relating inflation to chronic balance of payment problems and, more generally, to 'external disequilibrium' (see Furtado, 1964, chapter 5).

because of attempts to alter this output balance. This is, however, not the only kind of structural disequilibrium. In some economies the inconsistencies may be more fundamental, in the sense of there being no meeting point of aspirations, that is, there being no output balance which gives stability. Cardoso (1981) has recently tried to develop such a model. She presents her model as a formalisation of the Latin American structuralist view of inflation. It is an interesting piece of work and I briefly sketch it here. The only reason why this presentation looks different from hers is that it is logically more consistent.

There are two goods: agricultural, 1, and industrial, 2. People spend half their income on the former, a quarter on the latter and save the rest. The government buys G units of good 2. Hence using the same notation as before, the market clearing conditions are

$$X_1 = (p_1 X_1 + p_2 X_2)/2p_1$$
$$X_2 = (p_1 X_1 + p_2 X_2)/4p_2 + G.$$

These may be rewritten, respectively, as follows:

$$p_1/p_2 = X_2/X_1 \tag{6}$$
$$p_1/p_2 = 3X_2/X_1 - 4G/X_1. \tag{7}$$

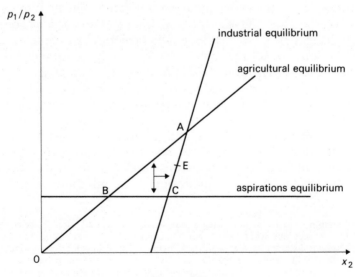

Figure 3.2

These are illustrated, assuming a fixed X_1, in figure 3.2. Making the same assumptions, as in the Kalecki model, that workers push up money wages to maintain real wage at W and p_2 is set to maintain a fixed mark-up, we get (5) as the condition which satisfies both these aspirations. This is shown in figure 3.2. as the 'aspirations equilibrium' curve.

It is obvious that barring the coincidental case in which the three curves meet at a point, there is no equilibrium, that is, it is not possible for markets to clear *and* for the aspirations of different classes to be satisfied.

Hence the behaviour of this economy depends crucially on our assumptions about the responses of the variables and agents to disequilibrium. It is assumed by the structuralists that agricultural production suffers from rigidities. For analytical convenience we make the extreme assumption of X_1 being fixed. So movements in p_1 clear the agricultural market. For instance if the demand for good 1, $(p_1 X_1 + p_2 X_2)/2p_1$, exceeds supply, X_1, that is if the economy is below the agricultural equilibrium curve then p_1 moves up. In sector 2, if demand exceeds supply, X_2 increases. So if the economy is to the left of the industrial equilibrium curve then X_2 increases. If p_1 rises, so that $W > w/p_1$, then workers push up w. To this the entrepreneur in sector 2 responds by pushing up p_2. The net effect is that if p_1 is too high, i.e. p_1/p_2 is above the aspirations equilibrium curve, then p_2 rises.

Cardoso shows that this economy will settle somewhere on the segment AC with a chronic inflation. Assuming that there exists a stationary point in this space, this is actually quite obvious. Consider any point in the interior of triangle ABC. From the above paragraph it is clear that three forces will be working on the economy at this point: p_1, p_2 and X_2 will be rising as shown by the three arrows. Since in the horizontal direction there is only one force, the economy will be drifting to the right. Hence, if there is a staionary point in this economy it must be on AC. Suppose E is such a point. At this point p_1 will be rising because of excess demand for agricultural goods. Here w will be rising and p_2 would be as well. Since this is a stationary point, the rates of increase in p_1 and p_2 will be the same. Thus the price ratios would remain the same though the economy would be continuously inflating. Even if a stationary point does not exist it is clear that there will be chronic inflation and the price ratio will be fluctuating between the values depicted by points A and C.

As Cardoso rightly observes, inflationary anticipation would soon make farmers raise p_1 faster and make industrialists raise p_2 faster, thereby making the inflation explosive. She does not, however, observe one important mitigating factor. *In reality*, not all groups have the power to bargain and satisfy their aspirations. As prices move up, the real income of the powerless gets eroded, while those who have the power gain. If the latter are interested in a certain amount of goods and not just in mark-ups, then after a few rounds of inflation they may feel satisfied and bargain with diminished verve and thereby bring the inflationary process to a gradual end. In short, inflation is brought to an end by the powerful workers and the entrepreneurs being subsidised by the pensioners, recipients of the dole and the thousands and thousands of civil servants. I wonder where we would be without our civil servants.

Of course, this cannot be repeated endlessly because then the real earnings of the fixed-income group would gradually head towards zero. So between successive inflationary episodes there must exist mechanisms by which some of the losses of this group are redressed. After all, pensions are updated from time to time, as indeed are the salaries of government employees.

Cardoso's analysis also suggests two kinds of price stabilisation policies; (a) a reduction in government expenditure and (b) a price and incomes policy for controlling real wages and the price mark-up. The former shifts the industry curve leftwards and the latter shifts the aspirations curve upwards. Note that the former, namely a fiscal policy, reduces the inconsistencies in the system only at the expense of reducing industrial production and, consequently, increases unemployment.

Many critiques and discussions of the structural approach have appeared in the literature.[10] Viewed in purely theoretical terms and given the broad methodological approach of the present book, one of the most important difficulties with the above kind of model is that there *seems* to be an element of irrationality in the behaviour of the agents. Consider a producer who is getting the profit margin that he wants. Now suddenly workers, for reasons that need not concern us here, raise wages. How does the producer respond? In a structuralist model, he simply raises the price of his product and passes on the cost increase to the consumer. This must, however, mean that we are assuming that producers have the power to raise prices (without losing so many customers as to make a loss). And here lies the crux of the matter. If the producer can raise his price, why does he wait to

---

[10] See Campos (1964) for a critique and an intelligent comparison of structuralism and monetarism.

do so only when workers raise wages? If he is rational, it seems that he should raise it anyway and earn some extra profit.[11]

This is a powerful critique, but it does not close all escape routes. It seems to me that there are two plausible defences. The first one entails abandoning the rationality precept and arguing that in reality human beings behave according to custom rather than to maximise profit. Thus if an economy remains stationary for a long time with the producers having a profit margin of $(m - 1)$ per unit of output, then they treat this margin as *customary* and try to retain it when disturbances occur, without bothering to compute the consequences.[12] This kind of explanation, however, has a rather fundamental open question. Even if we grant that people have a tendency to get accustomed to whatever prevails for a long time, it is not clear why the producer gets accustomed to the per unit profit margin and *not* to (a) the total profit, (b) the constancy of the price of his product, (c) not taking decisions, and one could go on. Each one of these assumptions would have very different implications for the model. One way out is to treat this as essentially an empirical question. Whether people do get accustomed to things and try to pursue these to the exclusion of other objectives and what it is that they get accustomed to (i.e. (a), (b), (c) or the profit margin), are questions that have to be ultimately settled empirically.

A second defence lies in showing how the raising of a price is profitable *and* possible only when the workers have just been granted a wage increase. This would make the producers' behaviour assumed in the structuralist model rational. It is, however, not clear to me how this can be shown. But since there is no proof of its negation either, this remains a possible route of defending the structuralist thesis. This is an interesting direction to pursue though it is likely to be theoretically terse.

While the formal model constructed above is well defined, structuralism in its full generality is extremely broad, encompassing a wide range of explanations, some of which are quite diffused. This turns out to be a weakness because it is not clear as to what would constitute a *test* of the structuralist thesis. Also, as it stands, structuralism fails to explain the great heterogeneity in the inflationary experiences of LDCs.

[11] The same method of criticism can be applied to Bhaduri's (1973) model of stagnation and, in fact, more pointedly. I do this in chapter 9.

[12] It is possible to think of this customary behaviour as rational in a deeper sense. If evaluation is costly, then taking this into account, it may be better to use a rule of thumb and to review this rule only at certain intervals. The existence of evaluation costs could, however, raise some rather complex problems, which I discuss elsewhere (Basu, 1980).

The upshot of this is clear. There is no generalised hypothesis which explains the inflationary experience of LDCs. This is not surprising at all given that so little is understood about inflation in general. It sounds hackneyed but is true that a more satisfactory theory has to absorb elements of both monetarism and structuralism. The aim of this chapter was the modest one of presenting the main existing points of view and their shortcomings and thereby to motivate research towards a more general theory of inflation in the less developed economy.

CHAPTER 4

Foreign Exchange and Trade: Some Considerations

1 Closed and open economies

Trade and development is often considered to be a subject in its own right and a vast amount has been written under this heading. The aim of the present chapter is a limited one – to comment on a few selective themes which are particularly relevant in today's world and which impinge on the issues discussed in this book. Thus we begin with some traditional arguments for trade and protection and discuss their relevance in the context of a LDC caught in a poverty trap such as the one discussed in chapter 2. Then we turn to the subject of foreign exchange which is often thought of as one of the most prominent factors constraining growth in LDCs. This is studied with the help of a two-gap model.

The optimistic results of a two-gap model could get destroyed once we allow the 'terms of trade' to be flexible. In section 3 below I discuss a recent result which shows how aid can diminish the *recipient* country's welfare because of an adverse movement in the terms of trade. Section 4 below examines the more long-run problem of a secular decline in the terms of trade faced by third-world countries: the so-called Prebisch doctrine.

The standard argument for trade is that it allows for specialisation. If country 1 is better at producing good x than y *relative* to country 2, then it would be efficient for 1 to specialise in the production of x, 2 to specialise in y and then for each to acquire both commodities through trading.[1] This way the two countries are better off than what they would be if each tried to produce its own requirement of

---

[1] Of course, specialisation would typically not be *total* as long as the countries have strictly convex production possibility frontiers.

41

x and y and did not engage in trade. The important point is that it is *comparative* advantage which leads to trade, *absolute* advantage being immaterial. This is best illustrated with the well-known example of a lawyer who is better than his typist not only in the practice of law but also in typing. But while in law he is ten times as good as his typist, in typing he is only doubly so. The lawyer has absolute advantage in both activities, but nevertheless it is obvious – or at least would be to anyone willing to ponder for a moment – that both are better off if the lawyer specialises in law and leaves the typing to the typist.

In brief, trade allows a country to step outside its autarkic production possibility frontier. Let me illustrate this with the example of a small price-taking country – particularly since I will in a moment consider such a country to discuss Nurkse's vicious-circle thesis.

There are only two goods and figure 4.1 shows the country's production possibility frontier, CD. Let the international prices of the two goods be p_1^* and p_2^*. Assuming no transport costs, the country can, through trade, move along any straight line parallel to AB, which has a slope of p_1^*/p_2^*. If this economy pulls down all its shutters, its feasibility space is given by COD. If, on the other hand, it follows a completely open door policy, the feasible set is AOB, because it can produce goods denoted by point E and, through trade, move to any point on AB.

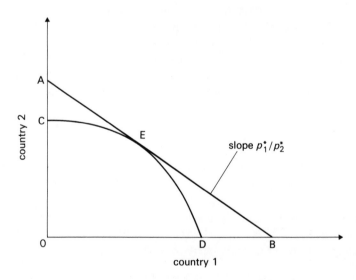

Figure 4.1

Turning to Nurkse's model of an LDC we find that trade can have an even more significant an impact than in the above case. Recall that a poverty trap, of the sort described in chapter 2, section 3, is an equilibrium in the *interior* of a production possibility set. But if the LDC is a small economy with free trade then it is possible that its prices are fixed by the international market place and they do not respond to its changes in production and trade. Under these circumstances, the country can never get caught in a poverty trap. The reason is obvious enough. In the poverty trap, that is at the Nurkse equilibrium with unemployment, every firm, when considering an expansion, worries about the fact that the market is limited, that its expansion will depress the price. But this cannot happen if the prices are fixed at the international levels. Hence, for the same reason why a Walrasian economy cannot be in a poverty trap, neither can a small open economy be in one. Thus if a small autarkic economy is in a poverty trap or a vicious circle, then the opening up of trade *could* lead the economy first *up to the production possibility frontier* and then beyond it (in the same way as shown in figure 4.1).

This neat theoretical result should not, however, be confused with Nurkse's views on trade policy which were much more involved. Indeed in turning to policy questions one has to be cautious not to jump to conclusions too hastily. The case for free trade is not axiomatic. Externalities, dynamic factors, equity considerations and the fact that economies are not always price-takers may call for governmental interference of some kind. On the other hand, the case for protection is made in government circles often for wrong reasons and by decision-makers who are unaware of the first principles. In the early eighties, there was a controversy in India concerning the import of soda ash. Many business houses (particularly the domestic producers of soda ash) and even government sources argued at length as to how the trade liberalisations, which had just taken place, were harmful for the economy and how the foreigners were 'dumping' their soda ash on India. An analysis of the situation, however, suggests that the real reason for the concern was that the domestic producers were, for the first time, finding themselves unable to charge the high prices that they could merrily impose earlier. And in any case, if it was true – as was being alleged – that the foreigners were consistently offering their soda ash below the cost price, there would be some merit in the simple advice: to take the soda ash and send them a thank you note.

There are many situations where trade barriers are desirable but the arguments for such barriers need to be a good deal more sophisticated than the ones popularly adduced. This may be illustrated with what is probably the best known case for protection: the infant industry argument.

The argument, very simply put, is that a new entrant to an industry can hardly be expected to survive unless it is protected for some time from competition from more expeinced producers. In other words, a nascent industry ought to be protected, if it is felt that once established, it will be able to fend for itself without governmental support.

Dating back to the works of John Rae (1834) and Frederich List (1841), the infant argument has had a long history.[2] Even today, it is very much the sacred cow among the many arguments for protection.

At first sight this case for protection seems quite sound but on closer examination it turns out to be vulnerable and other sophisticated props are needed to maintain it (see Little, Scitovsky and Scott, 1970; Friedman and Friedman, 1980; Corden, 1980). The Friedmans' critique of the infant industry argument is as follows. First note that it is worth protecting an industry if it is expected that its losses during infancy will be more than compensated later. But if that is true, then the industry should be willing to take the losses. Why then does it need protection?

This is a powerful critique but underlying it is the presumption that there exists a perfect capital market in the economy. Suppose that no such capital market exists and in fact that no credit is available. Now consider an entrepreneur contemplating a new export industry which will make large losses for two years (if it does not receive protection) and then earn profits which will in the long run far outweigh the losses. In this case the entrepreneur will be *willing* to undertake this project; but if he does not have enough money of his own he may, nevertheless, be *unable* to undertake it. Hence, there may be a good case for either providing him with protection or subsidising him for two years.

Thus the validity of the infant industry argument hinges critically on the condition of the capital market and whether the industrialist can raise his own finance or not. It is clear that the justification for protection (or for free trade) is much more complex and involved than ordinarily supposed and it is naive to make general recommendations without accounting for the specificities of a situation. Also

[2] It was also defended vigorously by John Stuart Mill (1848), though there is evidence that he was later dismayed by the way his argument had been misused. To quote Robbins (1968, p. 115): 'Poor Mill; such an admission from such an authority was made the pretext for all sorts of practices which he regarded as quite indefensible.'

in all questions of trade policy, e.g. liberalisation, protection etc., there is the important normative issue of how to weight the welfares of different people. The general presumption seems to be that the weight on the welfares of the citizens of the country being considered is one and the weight on foreigners zero. Clearly this is ethically quite unappealing. Unfortunately, many standard policy prescriptions hinge critically on this. A small lowering of weight on the income of a wealthy indigenous industrialist can demolish a case for protection. This also warns us against presuming that the proponent of autarky is necessarily a radical; he may be quite the reverse.

2 Foreign-exchange constraints and growth: a two-gap model

Trade, it was just argued, has the *potential* for raising the welfares of nations. Trade, suitably conducted, can also ease the foreign-exchange constraint faced by a country and this can have dynamic consequences. First of all, note that a greater foreign-exchange availability can be used by a less developed economy to rupture the small savings–small growth vicious circle. The economy can use the foreign exchange to either import capital goods or to import consumer goods while devoting domestic resources to the production of capital goods. In either case, investment and hence growth can be stepped up without cutting into consumption. So foreign exchange can be used to supplement savings which are typically quite inadequate in less developed economies.

Foreign exchange and exports have another role. They can enable an LDC to acquire essential capital equipment which it does not have the know-how or ability to produce indigenously. This second use was recognised, and received a lot of attention, in the sixties (Chenery and Bruno, 1962; Mckinnon, 1964; Chenery and Strout, 1966) and, in conjunction with the savings-augmenting role of foreign exchange mentioned in the above paragraph, gave rise to the so-called 'two-gap models' of growth. A vast amount has been written on this subject and some economies have actually tried to conduct planning exercises based on such models. These are fixed-price models and there has been some attempt recently to reanalyse them (Gunning, 1983a) using our newly acquired skills in fix-price equilibrium analysis (Drèze, 1975; Malinvaud, 1977).

I present here an adaptation of Mckinnon's model and use it to raise some issues in the dynamics of foreign exchange and trade.

There are two kinds of capital goods, domestic and foreign and these are required in fixed proportions to produce goods:

$$Y = \min[aK_d, bK_f], \tag{1}$$

where K_d and K_f are the amounts of domestic and foreign capital goods available, and Y is the national income (an aggregation of consumer goods and capital goods produced in the country).[3] Assuming that there is never any unutilised capital in the economy, we have

$$Y = aK_d = bK_f. \tag{2}$$

The total savings, S, undertaken in a year is given by

$$S = sY. \tag{3}$$

The maximum amount that the economy can export, E, in a year is given by

$$E = eY. \tag{4}$$

The presumption behind (4) is that Y is an index of the country's capacity to produce goods which are sophisticated enough to be considered exportable.

The total investment, I, is the addition to the total capital stock of the country that occurs over a year, that is,

$$I \equiv \Delta K \equiv \Delta K_d + \Delta K_f.$$

I shall also use the symbols I_d and I_f for ΔK_d and ΔK_f. Given that there is never any unutilised capital, that is, given (2), we get

$$I = I_f + I_d = \frac{b}{v} I_f \tag{5}$$

where $v = ab/(a + b)$ is the output-capital ratio.

Let F be the amount of foreign-capital transfer that takes place during the year. It is convenient to think of F more specifically as the volume of foreign exchange received as loan or aid. Clearly the *maximum* amount of foreign capital that can be acquired in a year is $(e + f)Y$, where $f \equiv F/Y$. Hence, given (5), the maximum value of I is given by $(b/v)(e + f)Y$. This therefore is the maximum value of investment possible given the *foreign-capital constraint*. Of course,

---

[3] There are many ways of justifying such aggregation. The simplest is to assume that a unit of output can, at any time, be willed into a unit of domestic capital. The fixed price assumption gives us the freedom to define a 'unit' as we wish.

this much investment may, nevertheless, not be possible because of inadequate savings. From (3) it follows that $(1-s)Y$ of the national income is consumed. Hence the total investment cannot exceed sY plus the amount that can be purchased with the foreign exchange, fY.[4] That is, investment must be less than $(s+f)Y$. This is the *savings constraint*. Putting the two constraints together[5]

$$I = \min[(s+f)Y, \frac{b}{v}(e+f)Y]. \qquad (6)$$

The growth rate of the economy, g, equals $\Delta Y/Y$ where ΔY is the change in income during the year. From (2) and (5) it follows that $g = (v/Y)I$. Substituting I from (6) we get

$$g = \min[v(s+f), b(e+f)]. \qquad (7)$$

So the growth rate depends on which constraint is binding. For instance, if it is the foreign capital constraint which is binding, i.e. $(b/v)(e+f)Y \leqslant (s+f)Y$, then $g = b(e+f)$.

The main result of this model can be captured in a diagram. In figure 4.2 let line AB partition the space between two zones: to the left of AB the foreign capital constraint is operative and to the right the savings constraint is binding. Clearly AB is the locus of all e and f which satisfies $v(s+f) = b(e+f)$. It is easy to check that the iso-growth curves in this space will look like the broken-line curves, which have a 45° slope to the left of AB, and are horizontal to the right. This means that if the savings constraint is effective, increased exports do not raise the growth rate. However, in an LDC suffering from a shortage of foreign capital, export and growth are positively related. An increase in F always raises the growth rate, though its effectiveness is greater to the left of AB. We must remember that unless it comes in the form of aid, typically F will have to be repaid in the future and so it is worthwhile trying to devise other mechanisms to raise the growth rate. From (7) it is obvious that one way of increasing the growth rate is to increase the country's capacity to export, e, and to simultaneously raise the rate of savings, s.

This model, despite its rigid assumptions, throws some very interesting light on the relation between the growth rate and savings. It shows that the relation is not an infallible one; and there is no

[4] It is being assumed throughout that domestic capital can be bought abroad if necessary.

[5] In this model investment can be smaller than savings (even *ex post*) because investment is here defined as the addition to capital stocks and *does not include inventories of consumer goods*.

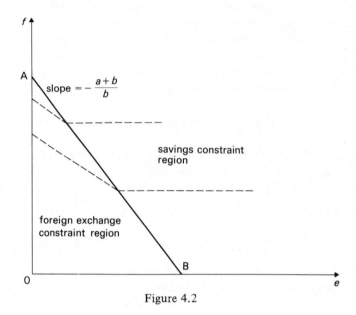

Figure 4.2

need to be mystified if growth rates stagnate, despite increases in s. For instance, in India, the savings rate hit the 20 per cent mark in the late seventies and has continued to persist at approximately this rate. However, the growth rate of national income has remained around a stubborn 3.5 per cent. The most plausible hypothesis is that the Indian economy was strangled by infrastructural bottlenecks, which indeed did assume unmanageable proportions during the late seventies.

Such a possibility can be illustrated with our two-gap model. Suppose that there is a bottleneck in foreign-capital equipment, then – as is obvious from (7) – g does not respond to increases in s. An increase in the savings rate causes a pile-up of inventories, while leaving g unaffected. So savings do not *guarantee* growth. Neither does capital. In the region where the foreign capital constraint is effective, if domestic capital is increased, it will remain unutilised and g will remain constant, with the capital–output ratio rising.

In the context of this model import-substitution is equivalent to producing the kind of capital goods which could earlier only be imported. This would shift the foreign-capital constraint and increase growth, or at least its potential. Industrialisation in this model amounts to a rise in e, the economy's capacity to export. As we saw above, if the foreign-capital bottleneck is effective, then greater industrialisation (by raising exports) increases growth. The argument in favour of industrialisation becomes stronger if it is true, as has been alleged, that the terms of trade between primary and industrial goods have a secular tendency to decline. The issue of terms of trade has not risen so far because of our assumption of fixed prices; but it is an important topic and I discuss it in the next two sections.

But before moving on, let me re-emphasise that the model of this section supposes that F is invariably used to enhance investment. Of course, in reality, no one has full control over such matters. If it so happens that the available foreign exchange is used to enhance consumption or is spent on non-productive capital, then it is possible, that in the next period more foreign exchange will be needed, first to repay the loan and then to buy consumption goods. In other words, the economy may well get into a debt-trap[6] the outcome of which is a general lowering of welfare. In poor countries the temptation to use aid to buy consumer goods is so high that the danger of a debt-trap is a real one. Increases in F do not automatically confer benefits on society.

In fact, once we allow the terms of trade to vary, we find that in some situations a greater foreign exchange availability can be harmful even in the absence of a debt-trap, because of adverse movements in the terms of trade. This is what we turn to now.

3   Aid and welfare: a paradoxical theorem

A recent paper by Chichilnisky (1980) has received a lot of attention and has generated much interest (see, e.g., Srinivasan and Bhagwati, 1983; Geanakoplos and Heal, 1983; and Dixit, 1983). Given the several mistakes in the paper, this is fair testimony of the appeal of its central result. Chichilnisky's paradoxical theorem asserts that there is a class of situations where a transfer of commodities or aid results in a decline in the welfare of the recipient nation, even when the world equilibrium is Walras stable. This last qualification is important in the light of Leontief's work where a similar result was proved but the validity of which hinged on the equilibrium being unstable (Mundell, 1968, p. 21). Chichilnisky's result is one in a class of a large number of paradoxical 'immiserisation theorems' in trade[7] in which a deterioration in welfare occurs as a consequence of

[6] I discuss the mechanics of a 'debt-trap' in a microtheoretic context in chapter 9.
[7] One of the earliest and best known being that of Bhagwati (1958).

some change which, on the face of it, appears to be desirable. The topical interest in Chichilnisky's theorem derives from the current North–South debates, in particular from the question of North–South transfers.

In this model there is a homogeneously poor country, South (S), and a rich country, North, consisting of two income groups: the high (H) and the low (L). Aid takes the form of a commodity transfer, from group H to S. What happens then is not difficult to see. Since the South has a higher propensity to consume basic goods, as its income rises, the price of basic goods rises. And, it can be shown that in a class of situations,[8] this price rise can be sufficiently marked to render the South worse off in the end. I shall, here, demonstrate this possibility with an example.

Let U_H, U_L and U_S be the welfares accruing to, respectively, the high-income group (in the North), the low-income group (in the North) and the South. There are two goods: basic (B) and non-basic (A). It seems reasonable to assume that group H has a stronger preference for good A than group L has, and that the South has a strong preference for B. In particular, assume

$$U_H = \min[2B_H, A_H]$$

$$U_L = \min[B_L, A_L]$$

$$U_S = \min[B_S, 2A_S].$$

Let the initial endowment vectors of the three income groups be $(\bar{A}_H, \bar{B}_H)$, $(\bar{A}_L, \bar{B}_L)$ and $(\bar{A}_S, \bar{B}_S)$. Let the price of good A be p and that of good B be 1. In other words, p represents the relative price of the two goods. The demand function for the basic good is easy to derive.

Consider group S. Its indifference curves and endowment vector is illustrated in figure 4.3. Clearly, the consumer equilibrium will always be on the ray 0R, which is the line joining the kinks of all the indifference curves and therefore is represented by the equation $A_S = B_S/2$. Substituting this in the budget constraint, $pA_S + B_S = p\bar{A}_S + \bar{B}_S$, we have

$$B_S = \frac{(\bar{B}_S + p\bar{A}_S)}{[1 + (p/2)]}.$$

---

[8] There was some ambiguity in Chichilnisky's specification of the class of situations where the theorem is valid. This has been pointed out and rectified by Gunning (1983).

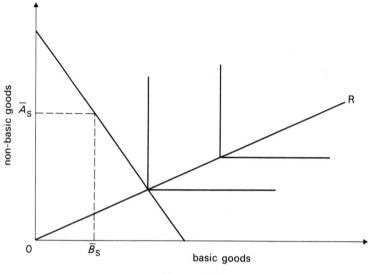

Figure 4.3

Going through a similar exercise for every income group, we get the following demand functions for the basic good:[9]

$$B_{\mathrm{H}} = \frac{\bar{B}_{\mathrm{H}} + p\bar{A}_{\mathrm{H}}}{1 + 2p} \tag{8}$$

$$B_{\mathrm{L}} = \frac{\bar{B}_{\mathrm{L}} + p\bar{A}_{\mathrm{L}}}{1 + p} \tag{9}$$

$$B_{\mathrm{S}} = \frac{\bar{B}_{\mathrm{S}} + p\bar{A}_{\mathrm{S}}}{1 + (p/2)}. \tag{10}$$

Hence the aggregate excess demand, D_{B}, for good B, is a function of p and is given by

$$D_{\mathrm{B}}(p) = \frac{\bar{B}_{\mathrm{H}} + p\bar{A}_{\mathrm{H}}}{1 + 2p} + \frac{\bar{B}_{\mathrm{L}} + p\bar{A}_{\mathrm{L}}}{1 + p} + \frac{\bar{B}_{\mathrm{S}} + p\bar{A}_{\mathrm{S}}}{1 + (p/2)} - \bar{B}_{\mathrm{H}} - \bar{B}_{\mathrm{L}} - \bar{B}_{\mathrm{S}}$$

$$\tag{11}$$

[9] These demand functions have one exception. If the price of either of the two goods happens to be zero, the budget constraint in figure 4.3 coincides with the indifference curve over a region. Hence demand in such a situation is set-valued and not unique. A failure to appreciate this led Chichilnisky to suppose that her axiom (C.1) rules out an equilibrium with the price of basic goods being zero; (C.1) does not achieve this. Since in my example we focus only on positive prices, (8), (9) and (10) are adequate.

A *Walras equilibrium* is a price p such that demand equals supply, i.e. $D_B(p) = 0$. By the Walras Law of Markets we known that if the basic-good market is in equilibrium, so must be the non-basic-good market.

Assume that the structure of endowment in the world is as follows:

$$\bar{A}_H = 75 \qquad \bar{B}_H = 35;$$
$$\bar{A}_L = 20 \qquad \bar{B}_L = 30;$$
$$\bar{A}_S = 15 \qquad \bar{B}_S = 20.$$

With this endowment structure, it is easy to check that $p = 1$ is an equilibrium.

Now consider a North–South transfer. Assume that $\frac{5}{9}$ units of A is transferred from H to S[10] (that is, foreign aid equivalent to about 0.5 per cent of the North's GNP). The endowment vector of H becomes $(75 - \frac{5}{9}, 35)$ and that of S becomes $(15 + \frac{5}{9}, 20)$. In this new situation $p = \frac{1}{2}$ is a Walras equilibrium.

In this new equilibrium South can be shown to be worse off than it was initially. Since prices are positive, if follows from South's utility function that its welfare level is equal to B_S. Using (10), we see that in the initial equilibrium $B_S = (20 + 15)/1\frac{1}{2} = 23\frac{1}{3}$ and after the transfer $B_S = 22\frac{2}{3}$. Hence the net effect of receiving aid is a fall in the welfare level from $23\frac{1}{3}$ to $22\frac{2}{3}$, that is, nearly 5 per cent!

What is particularly ingenious in this model is that the initial equilibrium can be shown to be *Walras stable*, which means that the above result is more than just an exercise in comparative statics: there is reason to expect the new equilibrium to be realised.

The stability of the equilibrium can be checked in different ways. Using (11) to differentiate $D_B(p)$ with respect to p and then inserting the values of the initial endowment vectors and also $p = 1$, we get

$$\frac{\partial D_B}{\partial p} = \frac{5}{18}.$$

Since this is positive, it means that as the relative price of B falls, the excess demand for B rises, thereby establishing the property of stability.

A more transparent method, in the present context, is as follows. Suppose p is held constant at the original level, that is $p = 1$, after

---

[10] The form of the transfer does not matter. As long as the transfer is 'equivalent' (in terms of the new price) to $\frac{5}{9}$ units of A, the discussion below would remain unaffected (see Gunning, 1983). This is a corollary of the fact that all endowment points which lie on the equilibrium budget hyperplane lead to the same equilibrium.

the North–South transfer. Then by inserting the new endowment values and $p = 1$ in (11) we get $D_B = \frac{5}{27}$. Hence, the new endowment structure at the old price results in an excess demand for basic goods. So we would expect the relative price of basic goods to rise, that is, for p to fall. So p does move in the direction of the new equilibrium price (which is $\frac{1}{2}$). This shows that the equilibrium is stable.

While I have demonstrated Chichilnisky's claim with an example, it is clearly possible to generalise its applicability to a wider class of situations. Chichilnisky (1980) and Gunning (1983) have tried to specify this class under the assumption of fixed coefficient utility functions. What would happen under more general utility functions remains to be explored.[11]

4   The terms of trade in the long run

The long-run behaviour of the terms of trade faced by less-developed economies is a subject of much controversy and emotion. Before delving into these issues it is useful to be a bit more precise about the meaning of 'terms of trade'.

Broadly speaking, a country's terms of trade is an index of the amount of foreign goods it can command. Assuming that an LDC exports one good and imports another, its *commodity terms of trade* or *net barter terms of trade*, N, is equal to P_X/P_M where P_X is the price of a unit of export and P_M is the price of a unit of import. If the country exports and imports more than one good, P_X and P_M should be interpreted as price indices. Clearly, since N depends on the choice of units, it has no significance in one period taken in isolation. What matters is the change in N. If the LDC's terms of trade improve, that is N rises, it means that the country can import more with each unit of export.[12]

[11] It can, however, be shown that with Cobb-Douglas utility functions a similar result would not be valid.

[12] There are many different kinds of terms of trade with each one having a different welfare significance. Some have distinguished between the net and gross barter terms of trade, the latter being the ratio of the volumes of imports and exports. This, however, does not have much significance if the balance of payments is not zero; and if it is zero, it coincides with N. Much more interesting are the income terms of trade ($= N . Q_x$, where Q_x is the volume of exports) and the single-factoral terms of trade ($= N . Z_x$, where Z_x is an export productivity index). If, as a result of an increase in N, the volume of exports fall too sharply then the net effect is undesirable. The income terms of trade captures this. The single-factoral terms of trade is also important because it shows how much a unit of resources can buy. Thus, if N falls but the domestic economy becomes more productive in that it now uses less resources for each unit of export, then there is no reason to believe that the trading conditions have deteriorated for the domestic economy. The single-factoral terms of trade takes this into account. In the ensuing discussion, however, I use the commodity terms of trade throughout, which allows me to drop the term 'commodity' without causing any confusion.

Fluctuation in the terms of trade or a deterioration in it is destabilising and harmful for an economy. Not surprisingly, a large part of the so-called North–South controversy centres around the terms of trade; and behind many international commissions and agreements is the desire to stabilize the terms of trade.

One of the most celebrated academic debates about the terms of trade and development emanated from what is known as the Prebisch doctrine.[13] In a short monograph written for the United Nations Economic Commission for Latin America (UNECLA, 1950) Raúl Prebisch argued that LDCs exporting primary products almost invariably face a secular decline in the terms of trade. His argument, however, was a purely empirical one, based on an analysis of the terms of trade of Great Britain from 1876 to 1938.

All through this period, Britain's terms of trade improved steadily and markedly; and inverting this finding, Prebisch hypothesised that during this period the terms of trade of LDCs worsened. Prebisch tried to generalise this purely empirical claim later (Prebisch, 1959) into the assertion that a long-run decline in the terms of trade of a LDC is an essential consequence of growth and trade between the North and the South, or the 'centre' and the 'periphery', to use Prebisch's terms. This was based on three assumptions. First the functioning of a global Engel's law which states that as growth occurs the relative demand composition in economies shifts away from primary products to manufactures. Secondly, manufacturing industries are not typically competitive; so increases in productivity are not passed on to consumers through lower prices, but are retained by the producing country as higher profits. Thirdly, new synthetic substitutes for primary products are bound to appear periodically, thereby diminishing the share of primary goods in the international market.

Much has been written on Prebisch's thesis and its weaknesses are now well-known (Haberler, 1961; Meier, 1963; Thirlwall, 1972; Elkan, 1973). First, there was the expected and valid criticism that Britain's terms of trade ought not to be treated as the inverse of the terms of trade of LDCs. For one, a substantial part of British imports came from other developed countries. Even primary imports were substantially from Australia and New Zealand. Also, during this period, freight charges and transport costs fell very sharply, which means that there is no reasons to treat an improvement in one country's commodity terms of trade as reflecting a deterioration in its trading

---

[13] Similar ideas have also been expressed by Singer (see Singer, 1950). A more recent discussion of Prebisch is contained in Bacha's (1978) paper.

partner's terms of trade; both could have improved. Finally, the terms of trade do not always take into account the quality of a product; and it is reasonable to assume that during the period studied by Prebisch the quality of manufactured items improved more than the quality of primary products, so that the improvement in Britain's terms of trade may well be a reflection of this.

So the particular empirical experience and statistics from which Prebisch attempted to derive his thesis is unsound and does not really support the thesis. But, of course, the theory may nevertheless be valid because the *reasons* which Prebisch gives in its support are not easy to dismiss, even if his empirical demonstration is. This means that the purchasing power of primary goods may indeed have a tendency to decline in the long run; and there may be some merit in Prebisch's advocacy of import-substitution and industrialisation in LDCs.

It is interesting to note, in this context, the remarkable performance of the 'Asian super-exporters', particularly South Korea and Taiwan, which, starting from a situation of low productivity and surplus labour in the fifties, have quite transformed themselves.[14] It would be naive to assume, as some do, that the Asian experience is definitive evidence of the virtues of *laissez-faire* and governmental non-interference.[15] In fact, I am inclined to believe that the economic success and politics of these countries are separable. What these countries do demonstrate is the potential of exports and labour-intensive production. Much of their growth originated in the success of exporting labour-intensive manufactured goods. Thus these countries benefited consistently from trade not because the Prebisch doctrine is wrong, but precisely because they did not put to test what Prebisch had warned against – the dangers of trying to grow, relying exclusively on primary goods exports.

[14] Even social statistics such as life expectancy and literacy, are impressive in these countries, though in these respects, Sri Lanka, with about one-fifth the per capita income of Korea, is clearly the most outstanding performer.
[15] Anyway these governments were not particularly non-interfering. It is true that by the late sixties both Korea and Taiwan had established virtual free-trade regimes, but the presence of the government has always been enormous. For instance, both countries have used elaborate licensing mechanisms. In Korea, a large part of organised banking has been controlled by the government which made it possible to implement important credit reforms (see Little, 1981; Datta Chaudhuri, 1981; Park, 1981).

PART II

The Dual Economy

CHAPTER 5

The Structure of a Dual Economy

1 Introduction

For many years, the crucial distinguishing feature of a less developed country was taken to be its dualism. A dual economy consists of two sectors: a small industrialised sector, and an agricultural sector. The industrialised sector is typically located in the few urban pockets and it operates, more or less, like any modern industrial economy. This sector may therefore be referred to also as the modern or urban sector. Surrounding this sector is the much larger agricultural sector. Here the modes of production are primitive, and a vast majority of the population are very poor – living at or near subsistence consumption. Consequently, in the literature, this sector has been referred to alternatively as the primitive, traditional, rural or subsistence sector. The labour market in a dual economy is, or at least appears to be, stratified into two parts, with the workers in the industrial sector earning higher wages than their counterparts in the rural sector. In fact, much of the formal literature on this subject has evolved around this particular feature of the larger idea of dualism.

This model has had its demurrers. It has been pointed out that labour markets are often fragmented into more than two parts and also that dualism is not the distinguishing feature of under development because there are traits of it even in developed economies. These are not disturbing criticisms. It is unlikely that any of the initiators of the dual economy model would deny that the labour market may in reality be fragmented into more than two sectors. The assumption of *duality* is merely for analytical convenience. If fragmentation – irrespective of the number of parts – in itself causes some problems and we wish to examine these, then the simplest

assumption to make is that of dualism. There is nothing methodologically disturbing in that. And anyway, *beginning* with a *dual*
labour market assumption, many economists have gone on to explore
the problems raised by the existence of sub-markets. The increasing
attention which the urban informal sector is receiving is an example
of this.

As defence against the second part of the criticism, it should
simply be noted that while developed countries may have traits of
dualism, the claim behind the dual economy literature is that such
dualism is much sharper in LDCs.

For much of the present-day literature on this subject, the starting
point is Lewis' classic paper (Lewis, 1954), but the origin of the idea
can be traced to earlier writings, of which particular mention should
be made of Boeke (1942, 1953) and Furnivall (1939). Furnivall, in
his work on India, develops the idea of plurality of which dualism is
a special case. He defines a plural economy as a society consisting of
'two or more elements or social orders which live side by side, yet
without mingling, in one political unit' (p. 447). While Furnivall does
speak of economic pluralism his view-point is usually much wider.
Economic dualism is assigned a much more central role in Boeke's
work. He explicitly rejects the idea of native–foreign dualism as of
any major significance. And when he speaks of the town–village
dichotomy he emphasises that a 'village' should not be interpreted
literally but in the sense of a 'pre-capitalistic' community.

However, it is only with Lewis (1954, 1958) that we really go
beyond description, to an analysis of the economic consequences of
dualism.

The reader should be warned at the outset that what is conventionally known as the Lewis model occupies a very small portion of
Lewis' (1954) long essay. It is essential to read the essay in its
entirety if one wishes to appreciate Lewis' sweep and breadth of
ideas. It is because of this that Lewis' work occupies a seminal place
in the literature despite its many analytical loose ends. And it is
precisely because of the absence of this that much of the literature
that followed turned out to be sterile and mechanical.

The Lewis model is a long-run analysis of the development of a
dual economy. It traces the path, over time, of a poor economy
getting gradually industrialised. There have been many attempts to
fomalise this long-run aspect of Lewis (1954), but the present book
adopts a different approach. After presenting the model, it examines
some narrower and less ambitious aspects – essentially short-run
microtheoretic ones. Such analyses, over the last decade or so, have

generated many fruitful discussions and insights. The works of Harris and Todaro (1970) and Stiglitz (1974) are two of the more important pieces in this neo dual economy analysis and we turn to these in the next chapters.

2   The Lewis model

Consider a closed economy consisting of two sectors: the industrial sector and the rural sector ('capitalist' and 'subsistence' sectors were the expressions used by Lewis). Lewis describes his model as a 'classical' one, meaning thereby that in the rural sector there is, for all practical purposes, an unlimited labour supply at the subsistence wage. More precisely, this means that at the subsistence wage there is an excess supply of labour and the excess supply is sufficiently large so that no employer – incumbent or prospective – has to worry, when considering employment expansion, about having to bid up wages or about getting rationed in the labour market.

If the capitalist sector wishes to draw on this unlimited supply of labour, it cannot, however, do so at the subsistence wage. It typically has to pay a higher wage, w, which is a mark-up on the rural subsistence wage, m. Lewis adduces reasons for the existence of this wage gap. Note first that a part of the wage gap is only apparent because the cost-of-living in the urban sector is almost invariably greater than that in the rural sector. But it is generally empirically true that even in real terms urban wages are above rural wages. This, according to Lewis, could be 'because of the psychological cost of transferring from the easy going way of life of the subsistence sector to the more regimented or urbanised environment' or 'it may be a recognition of the fact that even the unskilled worker is of more use to the capitalist sector after he has been there for some time than the raw recruit from the country'. While these explanations are not to be dismissed, they are clearly not completely convincing. For the time being, therefore, we shall do what has been the standard practice in the literature that followed Lewis (1954): that is, treat the rural-urban wage gap as exogenously given. The issue of how the wage gap actually emerges and is sustained is taken up in the next chapter.

To avoid as many loose ends as possible I make some more strong assumptions – no doubt deviating somewhat from Lewis' original formulation. Let L be the total amount of labour in the economy (thereby shelving the important issue of increasing populations aside). Let the rural marginal product curve of labour be horizontal

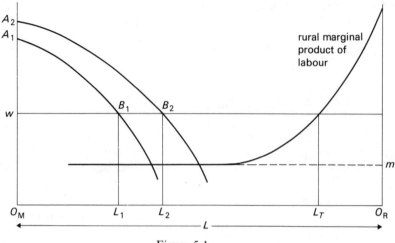

Figure 5.1

over a considerable stretch with the marginal product being more or less around subsistence level. This is shown in figure 5.1 in which O_R is the origin of the rural sector and O_M of the modern sector. The wage in the urban sector, w, is considerably above the subsistence level, and we assume it is rigid downwards for *exogenous* reasons. Assume, for the moment, that both sectors produce the same good. In the initial period the marginal product curve of labour in the urban sector is A_1B_1. Though I write as though there is only one employer in the urban sector this is not the case and that is obvious from our assumption that the urban employer is a wage-taker. Clearly, in order to maximise profit he employs O_ML_1 units of labour. The remaining labour $L - O_ML_1 = O_RL_1$ remains in the rural sector, with the marginal worker earning m.

This may be referred to as a *snapshot view* of the Lewis economy and this has been, in many ways, the starting point for much of the literature on dual-economy analysis. As far as Lewis was concerned, the central theme was the dynamics of the system. For this, it was assumed that workers do not save because they are too poor. Rural landlords do not save because they prefer the joys of conspicuous consumption. Only the modern sector capitalists save and invest and for simplicity it was supposed that they save their entire profit. Saving in this 'classical' model is not distinguished from investment. So the capital stock with the urban employer in period 2 gets augmented by the profit in period 1, which is equal to A_1B_1w in figure 5.1 (assuming for simplicity that depreciation is zero). In accordance with standard theory it is supposed that the marginal product of labour rises as the capital stock increases. Hence the marginal product curve of labour in period 2 lies above A_1B_1. Let the marginal product curve in period 2 be A_2B_2. Then urban employment rises to O_ML_2 and rural employment is O_RL_2. The profit in the urban sector is given by A_2B_2w. As before this is invested causing a further shift in the urban marginal product curve of labour. This relentless cycle of surplus, reinvestment and growth continues and steadily the industrial sector absorbs the rural one.

The process continues with the urban wage remaining constant, up to the point where O_ML_T labour is employed in the urban sector. At that point the character of the economy changes in an important way. From here onwards the wages in the two sectors begin to move upwards and they maintain parity. Also at this point the rural marginal product ceases to be below the urban wage. This is the famous 'turning point' and from here onwards the economy begins to look very much like a developed economy and the classical assumption of unlimited labour ceases to hold.

While what is known as the Lewis model ends at this point, Lewis' own canvas was much larger and he used this model to bear upon a wide range of political and economic issues. Thus it may be argued that capitalists recognise the potential of the subsistence sector as a source of cheap labour and therefore have a vested interest in keeping rural wages low. To quote Lewis (1954, p. 149): 'Thus, the owners of plantations have no interest in seeing knowledge of new techniques or new seeds conveyed to the peasants, and if they are influential in the government, they will not be found using their influence to expand the facilities for agricultural extension'.[1]

The basic model can also be extended to the international sphere. At the end of the process described above, it is natural that employers would begin to look for cheap labour beyond the borders of their country. They then face two options: they could bring in cheap immigrant labour or base their factories in poor countries where labour is plentiful and cheap. Both these developments have of course taken place with profound impact on the world economy and both these matters are subjects of much research and analysis.

---

[1] This is borne out well by recent experience in India. The 'food for work' programme, which was started by the Government of India in 1977 as a small step to alleviate abject rural poverty, has been vigorously lobbied against by landlords under various pretexts. The actual reason, however, is that the programme was having a certain measure of success in preventing wages in some regions from declining to abysmal levels.

The Lewis model generated a lot of interest among development economists and in the sixties there were many attempts to restate it more formally (among the more interesting being Ranis and Fei, 1961, and Jorgenson, 1967). The main concern of this literature is to examine the turning points in the long-run process described by Lewis. It is clear, in retrospect, that this direction turned out to be a *cul de sac*.

A more fruitful and exciting direction of research was the one which focused on the short-run aspects of the dual-economy model of Lewis. And it is to these that we turn in the next two chapters. In a sense, what we do and what much of the literature in the seventies has been implicitly doing is to take a slice of time out of the entire process and examine it with care. Do things work out the way Lewis envisaged?

3   Critiques

The Lewis model has been subjected to criticism from various perspectives. This section critically examines the decision-making of the capitalists and workers.[2] It is argued that if capitalists are granted a limited rationality then the Lewis process might begin to stagnate before running its full course.

Before that, let us get a possible methodological objection out of the way. It may be claimed that my mode of examining the Lewis model violates the very spirit of Lewis' enquiry which is classical in nature. Whosoever agrees with this claim, my suspicion is that Lewis would not, because his model is not classical in this sense. In fact, it is quite evident from his paper that he was greatly concerned about the motivations of individual agents. In this respect, therefore, he was neoclassically inclined.

Regarding capitalists, Lewis assumes – what at first sight appears quite straightforward – that they maximise profit. But while the objective of profit-maximisation is well defined in a static context, it can be quite ambiguous in a dynamic model such as this. On reflection, it becomes clear, that by this assumption what he means is that in *each* time period the capitalist maximises profit. It follows that in each period the capitalist chooses his labour input such that the marginal product of labour is equal to the wage. Clearly this assumption cannot tell us how much the landlord invests because

---

[2] Some of these same issues are examined by Enke (1962) though from a different point of view.

that is an intertemporal decision. So Lewis' assumption that capitalists invest their entire profit is a separate and distinct assumption.

Hence instead of assuming a single grand objective function for the capitalist and deriving various behavioural postulates, Lewis *begins* by assuming two behavioural rules. This in itself is not objectionable,[3] but it is important to check the implications of such behaviour. Are we denying the capitalist even a limited rationality?

The trouble arises when we relax the assumption of a single good. Let us assume, as does Lewis, that the industrial sector produces a good which is distinct from the product of the agricultural sector. With this, the question of terms of trade between agriculture and industry comes into play. This places serious obstacles in the path of development described above. Lewis was aware of some of the difficulties that arose from the question of terms of trade but he dealt with these rather cursorily. Others have discussed the matter at greater length (see for example, Chakravarty, 1977).

Here I take up an interesting and pointed issue. Suppose there are many producers in the industrial sector and they are all price-takers (the argument is strengthened if we assume a monopoly). Let the price of the industrial good in terms of the agricultural good be p. A representative producer's output, X, is a function of capital, K, and labour, L. Within each period, K is fixed. Given that w is expressed in terms of agricultural goods, the amount of labour employed is given by

$$pX_L(L, K) = w.$$

This is depicted in figure 5.2. The curve $a_1 b_1$ shows the *value* of marginal product curve (i.e. $pX_L(L, K)$ as a function of L). L_1 is the equilibrium employment.

In reality p is formed as the outcome of a complex general equilibrium and a definitive analysis would have to be quite detailed. For simplicity, it is reasonable to assume that p falls as the total urban output increases relatively to the rural one.

If in period 1, each firm invests its profit, $a_1 b_1 w$, then the marginal product curve will shift to the right, true. But the value of marginal product curve need not shift similarly, because with the higher industrial output, the price p will be lower. In fact it is quite possible that the value of marginal product curve (at the new equilibrium price) will lie to the left of $a_1 b_1$.

---

[3] In a different context I have argued that there are situations where it is better to begin from direct behavioural postulates rather than from a utility function (Basu, 1981).

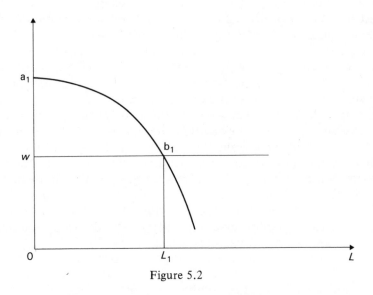

Figure 5.2

This highlights two important difficulties. First, there arises a question of capitalists' rationality. If investment in the first period diminishes profits in the second period, would it not be more reasonable for the capitalists to consume more (instead of investing) in period 1 *and* to earn more profits in period 2? Lewis is not unaware of this difficulty, and he discusses it, somewhat tangentially, in terms of some ideas of Malthus, Ricardo and Marx. While his discussion is interesting, he dismisses this criticism for reasons which are not too convincing. There is, however, a good argument which neutralises the above criticism. If the urban sector is composed of a sufficiently large number of capitalists then the fact that the *total* urban investment causes a deterioration in terms of trade in the next period would not enter into any individual capitalist's calculations. Thus investment would not be held back for *this reason*.

While this is true, this criticism nevertheless draws our attention to the question of investment criterion. Surely a capitalist would pay some attention to the rate of return that his investment will fetch him. If it drops too low, he might be tempted to consume more instead of putting away all surplus as investment. It is therefore important to recognise that the proportion of profit that is ploughed into investment is a *variable* controlled by the capitalist and is liable to change depending on the rate of profit and other signals in the economy. And it is possible that an adverse movement in these signals may lead to a short-circuit in the Lewis process because of the capitalist's refusal to invest adequately.

In order to focus on the second difficulty let us assume away the above problem by supposing that capitalists mechanically invest all their profits. But as we have already seen, this will cause a deterioration in the terms of trade. And this may be so sharp as to cause an inward shift in the value of marginal product curve for labour.

This implies the interesting possibility that even if capitalists behave exactly as postulated by Lewis and invest all their profit, urban employment may fail to grow.[4] The general upshot of this analysis and some of the literature on this seems to be that beginning from a primitive dual economy the forces which Lewis wrote about are likely to be present and are going to move the economy in the direction suggested. But the process is not an inexorable one leading an economy to the turning point and into a 'developed' state. Instead it is likely that the process itself generates forces which leads to stagnancy well before such a happy state emerges. The experience of underdeveloped countries does not seem to controvert this position.[5]

Finally, let us consider one slice of time in the whole process described above, for instance, period 1 as depicted in figure 5.1: $O_M L_1$ workers are employed in the urban sector at a wage w and $O_R L_1$ workers are employed in the rural sector at a considerably lower wage, m. But then, this should attract more workers from the rural sector into the urban one. It is true that they would not find jobs in this period but certainly some workers would like to be present in the urban sector in the hope of finding a job. This means that at each point of time there would exist some urban unemployment. This is precisely the starting point of the well-known Harris–Todaro model. What Harris and Todaro (1970) do is to assume a dual economy not dissimilar to the Lewis one but in their analysis the labourers' decision to locate themselves in the urban or the rural sector is based explicitly on expected earnings maximisation. The model they construct, therefore, could be thought of as an elaboration of a short-run segment in the Lewis process. Their model throws interesting light on the functioning of labour markets, migration and the consequences of urban employment policies – matters which go unnoticed as too microscopic in Lewis' ample canvas.

[4] Lewis discusses the possibility of employment declining with mechanisation. But his reasons are different. It should be emphasised that the present argument is different from the standard one – that automation displaces labour.

[5] There are many other aspects of growth in dual economies which have been discussed by econonists but which I have chosen not to dwell upon here. A relatively important omission is the analysis of the distributional impact of growth. For this, the interested reader may be referred to Taylor (1979, pp. 149–60).

CHAPTER 6

Migration and Unemployment

1 Migration and urban unemployment

While the problem of underemployment in the agrarian and subsistence sectors has for long been a major focus in the economic analyses of LDCs, the subject of urban unemployment has been relatively neglected – at least till recent times. In fact, urban unemployment cannot occur in the Lewis model and in others of that genre. Yet the problem demands serious theoretical attention because here conventional remedies have often surprised governments by accentuating rather than curing the problem. For example,[1] in 1964 the Kenyan government, in an effort to reduce urban unemployment, particularly in Nairobi and its outskirts, had entered into a pact with capitalists and trade unions which, among other things, entailed both the private and public sectors to increase their employment by 15 per cent. However, when this was implemented the consequence turned out to be quite the reverse of what was expected. The *possibility* of new jobs caused migration from the rural regions to Nairobi in such numbers that the end result was a higher urban unemployment. This experience is not unique. It has been observed many times that an attempt to remove urban unemployment *directly*, by creating more jobs, has had the opposite consequence.

For these reasons it is important to try and construct a realistic theory of rural–urban labour distribution, which could be used for policy purposes. Clearly such a theory would have to be based on some hypothesis of migration. The literature on migration goes back almost a hundred years, to two papers by the British demographer, Ravenstein (1885, 1889) – the first paper being based on the British census of 1881. This was followed by a long period of silence after

---

[1] This is taken from Todaro (1969).

which the subject was once again taken up by demographers and sociologists, one of the best-known works being that of Lee (1966). Lee reviews Ravenstein's 'Laws of migration' and proposes his own.

This literature, however, turns out to be of little use to the economist for the kind of questions his discipline raises. One basic difficulty with the literature is a tendency to state too many and too general causes, with the consequence that the theories verge on being unfalsifiable. Also the conclusions are often no less self-evident than the assumptions. What is of interest to the economist is that one cause identified repeatedly in this literature is the human urge for the betterment of his economic state. As Ravenstein (1889, p. 286) writes: 'but none of these currents can compare in volume with that which arises from the desire inherent in most men to "better" themselves in material respects'.

This economic motivation is the corner stone of the Harris–Todaro (HT) model which derives its name from the papers of Todaro (1969) and Harris and Todaro (1970). These papers provide an interesting analysis of migration and unemployment in LDCs and the HT theory is what we turn to now.[2]

The essence of this model is easy to convey by making some strong assumptions. The ensuing paragraphs present such a model leaving a fuller version for the next section and some readers may prefer to go directly to that.

Suppose there are L workers in the economy with L_M and L_R being the numbers employed in the modern and rural sectors. The urban wage is fixed at w and the rural marginal product of labour (which is assumed to be equal to the rural wage) is fixed at w_R, and $w_R < w$. Assume that the number of urban jobs available (L_M) is exogenously fixed. So if there are more labourers than L_M in the urban sector some would have to be unemployed. In the rural sector workers can always find work. Hence the total urban labour force (i.e. employed plus unemployed workers) equals $L - L_R$, with $(L - L_R) - L_M$ being unemployed. The crucial assumption of the HT model is that workers base their migration decision on their *expected* incomes. Since finding a job in the rural sector is ensured, the expected rural income is w_R. But the expected urban income is got by multiplying w by the probability of finding a job there, which, it is supposed in the HT model, is equal to the rate of urban employ-

---

[2] Given that the economic motivation is an important one, it is quite reasonable that economists should concentrate on it. But one should be cautioned that the decision to migrate is based on a variety of complex issues and the belief that it can be understood *entirely* within the realm of economic analysis betrays either naivety or a vacuously broad definition of what constitutes 'economic analysis'.

ment, $L_M/(L - L_R)$. Hence as long as

$$w \frac{L_M}{L - L_R} > w_R$$

there will be rural–urban migration (with a reverse inequality implying an urban–rural migration). Since L, L_M, w and w_R are fixed, as
people migrate from the villages to the modern sector, i.e. as L_R
falls, the left-hand expression falls as well. Equilibrium is reached,
i.e. there cease to exist any tendencies to migrate, when

$$w \frac{L_M}{L - L_R} = w_R.$$

The 1964 Kenyan experience mentioned above is captured well
even by this simple model. Rewrite the equilibrium condition as
follows:

$$L_R = L - \frac{w}{w_R} L_M.$$

Hence,

$$\frac{\partial L_R}{\partial L_M} = -\frac{w}{w_R}.$$

Therefore, if the number of urban jobs is raised by one unit, rural
employment falls by w/w_R units. In other words, creating one additional job in the urban sector induces w/w_R people to migrate into
the urban sector, which mean (since $w > w_R$) that urban unemployment instead of declining, rises.

While this simple version of the HT model makes the central point
of Harris and Todaro's thesis forcefully, its reach is quite limited. For
instance, in this version, creating jobs *invariably* increases urban unemployment. Fortunately the complete model is more flexible in this
respect. Also, L_M and w_R are endogenously determined in the actual
HT model, though w continues to be exogenously fixed. The latter
is relaxed in chapter 7. The next two sections present the complete
HT model and discuss some fiscal policy issues relating to employment and production.

2   The Harris–Todaro model

There are two sectors: the rural (R) and the urban or modern (M).
They produce X_R and X_M units of output and employ L_R and L_M
units of labour. This is a short-run model with fixed capital endow-

ment in each sector. Hence, output in each sector is supposed to be a function of labour:

$$X_R = f_R(L_R) \qquad f_R' > 0; f_R'' < 0 \tag{1}$$

$$X_M = f_M(L_M) \qquad f_M' > 0; f_M'' < 0. \tag{2}$$

The total labour units[3] available in the economy is fixed at L. Hence,

$$L_R + L_M \leqslant L \qquad L_R; L_M \geqslant 0. \tag{3}$$

I shall assume, for simplicity, that both sectors produce the same good (though by different techniques). This leaves all the major HT results unaltered. This assumption can be viewed in an alternative way. We could think of X_R and X_M as different commodities in a small open economy. Then assuming constant world prices, we may redefine the units of X_R and X_M such that both their prices are equal to unity.

Let w be the urban market wage expressed in real terms. The urban capitalist is a wage-taker[4] and his objective is to maximise profit, which implies

$$f_M'(L_M) = w.$$

In this economy, however, the urban wage has a political or institutional lower bound at $\bar{w}$:

$$w \geqslant \bar{w}.$$

This is an important assumption and will be referred to as the *wage rigidity axiom*. It is assumed that $\bar{w}$ is above the wage that would prevail if wages were flexible. This ensures that, for wages $\bar{w}$ and above, there is an excess supply of labour in the urban sector which implies that competition will drive w down to $\bar{w}$. Hence the profit-maximising condition above may be written as[5]

$$f_M'(L_M) = \bar{w}. \tag{4}$$

[3] In this model we do not distinguish between labourers and labour units.

[4] I write as though there is only one urban capitalist. This assumption is easy to relax. But the assumption of the employers being 'wage-takers' is important.

[5] Actually profit maximisation in the urban sector gives us two conditions

$$(w - \bar{w})[(L - L_R) - L_M] = 0 \tag{i}$$

$$f_M'(L_M) = w. \tag{ii}$$

Condition (i) asserts that at equilibrium it cannot happen that wage is above the institutional minimum and there exists urban unemployment. It can be shown that at the HT equilibrium $(L - L_R) - L_M > 0$. Hence by (i), $w = \bar{w}$. This is what allows us to write (ii) as (4). This formulation has the advantage that we do not need to assume that $\bar{w}$ is above the *laissez-faire* wage. If $\bar{w}$ is less than such a wage, it simply ceases to be effective. I have refrained from discussing this in the main text because this is quite transparent in the diagram developed below.

In the rural sector wages are flexible and equal to the rural marginal product $f_R'(L_R)$. This flexibility ensures that there is no rural unemployment. Therefore, the total labour force (employed plus unemployed workers) in the urban sector is equal to $L - L_R$, and the probability of a migrant finding urban employment is supposed to be $L_M/(L - L_R)$. Workers maximise *expected* earnings. Hence if

$$f_R'(L_R) < \bar{w}\, \frac{L_M}{L - L_R},$$

workers would migrate from the rural to the urban sector. Migration equilibrium is attained when

$$f_R'(L_R) = \bar{w}\, \frac{L_M}{L - L_R}. \tag{5}$$

This completes the description of an HT economy. Unlike in the simpler version, condition (5) alone does not ensure equilibrium in the entire economy. A HT equilibrium is a situation satisfying (1)–(5). It is possible to solve for L_M, L_R, X_M and X_R from (1), (2), (4) and (5). Denote the solution vector as $[L_M^o, L_R^o, X_M^o, X_R^o]$ which, for brevity, will be referred to as E^o. It is possible to show, and is obvious from figure 6.1 below, that $L_M^o + L_R^o < L$, i.e. E^o satisfies (3). Hence E^o satisfies all the five conditions and depicts the HT equilibrium.

Before illustrating this equilibrium on a diagram, let us characterise the 'optimum' in this economy. As in Harris and Todaro (1970) and in many related papers, assume that social welfare, U, depends on the output produced,[6] i.e. X_R and X_M. Since in the present version both sectors produce the same good, we may write

$$U = X_R + X_M. \tag{6}$$

Suppose we have a command economy in which the government can distribute labour between sectors R and M as it wishes and the only constraints it faces are (1)–(3). How should the government choose L_R and L_M? This is answered by maximising (6) subject to (1), (2) and (3). Since X_R', $X_M' > 0$, unemployment is never desirable. Hence (3) holds as a strict equality. Hence, the maximisation is a simple Lagrangian exercise which yields the following first order conditions:

$$L_R + L_M = L \tag{7}$$

---

[6] For other assumptions and their policy implications see Anand and Joshi (1979).

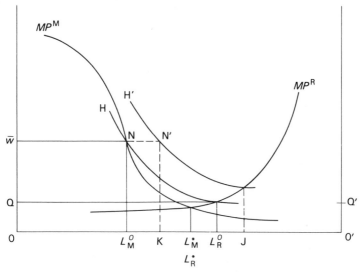

Figure 6.1

$$f'_M(L_M) = f'_R(L_R).\tag{8}$$

Let L_R^*, L_M^* be the solution of (7) and (8). By inserting these values in (1) and (2) we get the optimum sectoral outputs, X_R^* and X_M^*. Let E^* denote the optimum vector $[L_M^*, L_R^*, X_M^*, X_R^*]$. It is not difficult to see that if the wage rigidity axiom was not present then the *laissez-faire* outcome would coincide with E^*.

We compare the HT equilibrium and the optimum, with the help of a simple diagram (see Corden, 1974; Corden and Findlay, 1975; Basu, 1980a) which may be used to depict both E^o and E^*. Let MP^M and MP^R in figure 6.1 be the marginal product curves of labour in sectors M and R. These are drawn with origins 0 and 0', respectively, where the length of 00' is equal to the total labour force, L.

Clearly, output is maximised by breaking up the labour force between the two sectors at the point where MP^M and MP^R intersect. Hence the optimum entails employing $0L_M^*$ in the urban sector and $0'L_R^*$ is the rural sector.

In the HT model the urban sector has an institutionally fixed minimum wage $\bar{w}$. If $\bar{w} > f'_M(L_M^*)$, the optimum is unattainable, because the urban sector will then employ less than $0L_M^*$. As shown in the figure, urban employment will be equal to $0L_M^o$. What is the level of rural employment? To derive this we draw a rectangular hyperbola H, through point $N = (L_M^o, \bar{w})$. The point of intersection between H and MP^R gives the rural equilibrium. $O'L_R^o$ is the level of rural employment and $0'Q'$ $(= 0Q)$ the rural marginal product of labour.

Why this is so, is easy to see. Since H is a rectangular hyperbola, $(\bar{w})(0L_M^o) = (0Q)(0L_R^o)$. This implies that

$$(\bar{w}) \frac{(0L_M^o)}{(0L_R^o)} = 0Q.$$

This is the same as (5) and hence L_M^o and L_R^o in figure 6.1 represent the HT equilibrium. Urban unemployment consists of $L_M^o L_R^o$.

The rectangular hyperbola is a handy instrument for describing an HT equilibrium. The general rule for using it is as follows: Given the equilibrium urban wage and employment level, draw a rectangular hyperbola through the urban wage-employment point (N, in the above case), and the point of intersection of this rectangular hyperbola with the rural marginal product curve gives us the level of rural employment.

This diagrammatic method allows us to see very easily why the direct policy of curing urban unemployment by employing more people in the urban sector may accentuate the unemployment problem. Let the urban sector, in figure 6.1, employ $L_M^o K$ more at the fixed wave $\bar{w}$ because of governmental pressure. Then the urban sector wage-employment point is depicted by N′ and hence the relevant rectangular hyperbola is the one through N′. This is labelled H′ in figure 6.1. It is obvious that rural employment drops by $L_R^o J$. Hence urban unemployment, instead of dropping by $L_M^o K$, drops by $L_M^o K - L_R^o J$. This may be positive or negative, and hence unemployment could decrease or increase.

It is now possible to compare this model with what I earlier referred to as a snapshot view of the Lewis process. This may be done directly by comparing figure 6.1 above with figure 5.1. Unlike in the HT model, in Lewis' theory there is no urban unemployment in each period. When new urban jobs are created, just the right number of people migrate from the rural sector to fill in the new vacancies. Also note that in the HT theory rural–urban migration could continue (as indeed it often does in reality) despite the existence of urban unemployment. It is not surprising that the theory of this chapter describes a short period with greater realism than the analysis of the previous chapter. This is for the obvious reason that the HT model attempts precisely that – to analyse a short-run equilibrium; on the other hand the Lewis model provides a rather inadequate picture of what happens in the short run because Lewis' canvas is much wider. It describes the progress of society over long periods.

It is therefore possible to combine the two models with the HT model being used to depict what happens in each time period and then using Lewis-type dynamics to explain changes over time.

Over the last decade Harris and Todaro's work has given rise to a substantial literature, criticising and modifying the basic model (Corden and Findlay, 1975; Fields, 1975; Todaro, 1976; Mazumdar, 1976; Neary, 1981; to mention just a few). Mazumdar makes the interesting observation that the use of the urban employment rate as the probability of finding an urban job amounts to an overestimation of the likelihood of a migrant finding a job. Let L_M be the number of jobs in the urban sector and $L - L_R$ be the number of workers in the urban sector. If L_M people are chosen for employment from the $L - L_R$ workers *by a random process* then the probability of each person finding a job is $L_M/(L - L_R)$. In reality, however, a person who is presently employed would have a greater probability of finding a job than this in the next period because employers do not typically sack all their employees at the beginning of each period and choose new workers by a random process. This in turn means that a new arrival in the urban sector has a smaller probability of finding a job than $L_M/(L - L_R)$. Having observed this there are two possible courses of action, (a) we may treat the probability as a *function* of the urban employment rate rather than equal to it, and (b) a more sophisticated approach would be to treat the probability as determined by the rate of labour turnover, the number of new jobs and the size of urban unemployment. While I do not pursue these here, both these approaches have been attempted (see Stiglitz, 1974 and Mazumdar, 1976).

There has also been a considerable amount of empirical research in this area and in the context of the present model one of the most interesting findings has been the 'discovery' of the urban informal sector. In the HT model it is supposed that in the urban sector people either find jobs in the formal sector at a wage w or they remain unemployed. Of course, it is recognised that this is a stylised fact and is not an exact description of reality. But what a series of empirical studies in Latin America and Asia have revealed is that this stylised fact differs from reality in one respect in a rather *marked* way. It has been observed that many who do not find employment in the urban formal sector end up working (often on poorly paid odd jobs) in the urban 'informal' sector. Indeed the informal or unorganised sector can be quite large. There has been a vast amount of empirical research in recent years on the nature and effect of the informal sector (e.g. Joshi and Joshi, 1976). And clearly for actually designing policy, knowledge of this sector is essential.

However, from a theoretical point of view, the existence of the urban informal sector need not be particularly disturbing. There has been work incorporating this in the HT theory. The standard procedure is to think of the urban sector as offering two wages, the formal sector wage, w, and the informal wage, $\hat{w}$ (this may be stochastic) and while w is above the rural wage, $\hat{w}$ is below. If a worker fails to find a job in the limited formal sector, he is absorbed in the informal sector. As before, the probability of a migrant finding a formal job may be taken to be equal to the proportion of the urban labour force employed in the formal sector. The decision to migrate is based on the expected incomes in the rural and the urban sectors. It is not difficult to see that one can proceed along these lines and construct a model which will be a more sophisticated version of what is essentially the HT model.

Theoretically a more vexing difficulty concerns the formation of the urban wage. In the HT model, as in most early dual economy models, the problem is averted by simply assuming that urban wages are rigid downwards. This assumption is crucial. It ensures that at equilibrium $\bar{w} > f'_R(L^0_R)$, i.e. there exists a rural–urban wage gap. And this, in turn, implies that there will exist urban unemployment.[7] This is easy to see: if there does not exist any urban unemployment, the probability of finding an urban job equals 1. Hence, the expected urban earning is equal to $\bar{w}$ and this exceeds the expected rural earning, $f'_R(L^0_R)$. But that is incompatible with equilibrium.

Given the crucial nature of the wage rigidity axiom, the question obviously arises as to how we can explain it. This is a difficult problem and there have not been too many attempts to answer this. But one extremely interesting approach based on a labour turnover model of firms has been explored by Stiglitz (1974). What Stiglitz tries to establish is not the *absolute* rigidity of the urban wage (in any case that is not necessary for the main theorems of an HT-type model) but merely to show why the urban wage may equilibrate *above* the rural one.

In the next chapter the labour turnover model is presented and subjected to some scrutiny. Chapter 8 also looks at the problem of

---

[7] In the case of a theory with an informal sector, the rural–urban wage-gap ensures the existence of an urban informal sector *or* urban unemployment.

wage rigidity though from a different perspective. But first a brief look is taken at some policy questions which arise from the HT model.

3 Policy issues

We have seen that equilibrium in an HT economy is a 'sub-optimal' one: not only is it characterised by unemployment but the marginal labour in the urban sector is more productive than the marginal worker in the rural sector. What policy measures can be adopted to shift the economy towards the optimum, E^*?

Consider first the use of employment subsidy to the urban sector. At first sight it appears that this ought to work. Such a policy would induce urban firms to employ more workers. Since it is the urban sector that has unemployment and it is also the more productive sector, one would expect this policy to redress some of the imbalances in the economy.

But there is an obvious flaw in this argument. In figure 6.2, consider the effect of an urban employment subsidy. If a subsidy of S is given to a firm for each person employed, the per worker cost to a

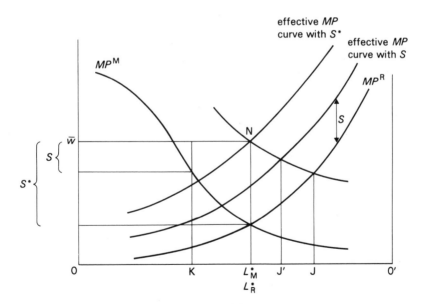

Figure 6.2

firm becomes equal to $\bar{w} - S$. This means that urban employment is equal to OK. Hence, for the same argument as adduced earlier, the desirability of such a subsidy is doubtful because, the total unemployment may increase as a consequence of this subsidy.

It is easy to see that $E^* \equiv [L_M^*, L_R^*, X_M^*, X_R^*]$ is unattainable by any urban employment subsidy: To induce urban firms to employ the optimum amount, L_M^*, a subsidy of S^*, as defined below, is needed:

$$S^* \equiv \bar{w} - f_M'(L_M^*). \tag{9}$$

S^* is shown in figure 6.2. Given this subsidy, the urban wage-employment point is depicted by N. To find the equilibrium rural employment we have to pass a rectangular hyperbola through N, as shown. Hence rural employment settles at $0'J$ which is less than the optimal $0'L_R^*$. Hence an urban subsidy which ensures optimal employment in the urban sector, necessarily implies sub-optimal employment in the rural sector.

From this, Harris and Todaro went on to argue that no *single* policy could correct the aberrations of an HT economy. So we need to look for policy *combinations*. For instance, one possibility is to give a subsidy of S^* to the urban sector and to simultaneously restrict migration so that all workers, other than those who find jobs in the urban sector, are forced to settle in the agricultural region. But clearly a policy such as this is bound to be politically unpalatable and even otherwise is ethically not the most appealing.

What Harris and Todaro did not observe was that one way of preventing rural–urban migration without coercion is to give a subsidy to rural workers. If a subsidy of S is given to each rural worker then *to the rural worker* his effective marginal product curve is an upward displacement of MP^R, the height being given by S, as shown in figure 6.2. Therefore, if urban workers are given a subsidy of S^* and rural workers a subsidy of S, then rural employment is at $0'J'$. It is now obvious as to how to attain the optimum E^*. Give all workers, rural and urban, a subsidy of S^*. This is, in fact, the central result of Bhagwati and Srinivasan (1974). This was the basis of their claim that there does exist a single policy which can direct the HT economy to the optimum. Even if we leave aside the rather philosophical question as to whether a *uniform* subsidy (to both sectors) of S^* is a 'single' policy or not, it is clear that this is a theoretically interesting possibility, which had earlier been overlooked.

There are, however, some serious difficulties with these prescriptions. First there is an information problem with the optimal subsidy $S^* \equiv \bar{w} - f_M'(L_M^*)$. To be able to compute S^* we need to know $f'_M(L^*_M)$, i.e. the marginal product of labour that would prevail *at the optimum*. Hence, it is reasonable to suppose that at the time of implementing this policy, S^* will be an unknown.[8]

It is interesting to observe, however, that this information hurdle is not insurmountable. This is so because the Bhagwati–Srinivasan subsidy is, fortunately, not the only one whch ensures optimality. It can be shown that any uniform subsidy, S, which is equal to *or greater than* S^* is optimum, i.e. even if a subsidy of $S > S^*$ is given, a labour distribution of $[L^*_M, L^*_R]$ is attained. The only difference is that the urban wage, w, now rises above $\bar{w}$. In fact w exceeds $\bar{w}$ by the same magnitude as the one by which S exceeds S^*. I have discussed these issues formally in Basu (1980a) but it is possible for the reader to check these results using the above diagram. This is particularly easy if we think of the urban subsidy as one which shifts the *effective* marginal product curve of labour in sector M upwards (in the same way as was done for the rural sector).

This generalisation makes the information problem less acute since now we are required to pick any subsidy in the interval (S^*, ∞) rather than precisely S^*. And it can be shown that this can always be ensured (Basu, 1980a).

While the information problem is possible to solve, its solution highlights a serious practical shortcoming of this class of policy prescriptions based on the central idea of an employment subsidy. This concerns the funding of these subsidies. In the literature cited above this problem is kept aside by assuming that there exists sources from which funds may be raised without distortionary consequences. But as is clear from the above discussion, an optimal subsidy may be quite large and since it is to be given to both the rural and urban sectors the total bill to the government of such a policy can be enormous. As Kesselman (1979) shows, in some situations, the total subsidy bill may exceed the national income! It is therefore unlikely that it will be possible to fund the entire subsidy from 'non-distortionary' sources.

Hence no policy discussion is complete without directly taking into account the problem of subsidy finance. But there has been very little work in this direction and therefore the ensuing brief discussion is merely indicative.

[8] This problem does not arise in a partial equilibrium analysis. In such an analysis it is typically assumed that the rural sector is very large compared to the urban sector with the consequence that rural marginal product of labour is (for all practical purposes) constant. Assume that it is constant at m. It is easy to see that the optimum occurs when urban marginal product of labour becomes equal to m. Hence $S^* = \bar{w} - m$. Since m remains unchanged, it is observable in the initial situation and hence S^* is computable.

Before venturing into this, it is useful to be armed with a simple but not obvious result. It is possible to show with the help of calculus (see Appendix 1) that for all $S < S^*$, if S is raised a little, social welfare, U, defined by (6), necessarily rises. We already know that for all $S \geqslant S^*$, U remains stationary at its optimal value U^*. Hence the relation between S and U is as shown in figure 6.3. The theorem, that for all $S < S^*$, $(\partial U / \partial S) > 0$, will be referred to as the *monotonicity proposition*.

There are broadly two ways of coming to grips with the problem of subsidy finance in these models. First, we could assume that there exists a maximum amount of money that can be raised without distortionary effects and that no subsidy which exceeds this maximum amount is feasible. Secondly, we could assume that every rupee raised has some distortionary effect which increases in magnitude as the subsidy bill becomes larger.

Assume that the government can impose a certain maximum amount of non-distortionary, lump-sum tax and that some amount of external assistance is available. The sum of these two is the maximum amount of subsidy than can be doled out. How much subsidy should be given in this situation? While the answer can be complex in a relatively sophisticated model – like that of Blomqvist (1979) – it is straightforward in the simple HT model. It is clear from the monotonicity proposition that additional subsidies can do no harm. Hence, the entire amount of money raised may be doled out as subsidies.

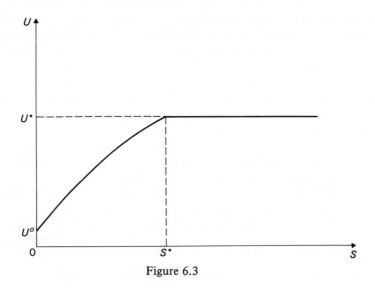

Figure 6.3

This does not appear to be a very reasonable solution and for a good reason. This approach supposes that *within* the maximum limit, money given out as subsidies has no opportunity cost. But clearly governments typically would have a variety of alternative openings for using money beneficially. Moreover in reality it is highly unlikely that any fund will be available which has no non-distortionary effects. External assstance typically has to be repaid in kind or otherwise. Lump-sum taxes in practice are seldom non-distortionary. This makes the second approach mentioned above the more serious one. Here again Blomqvist (1979) has made some enquiries but the scope for further research remains immense. The general principle is obvious enough: the point, at which the distortionary effect of raising one more rupee becomes as large as the benefits of an additional rupee's worth of subsidy, is the optimum point. This principle coupled with the monotonicity proposition (and assuming that U is a continuous function of S) implies that the optimum subsidy (once we include the question of its financing in the model) is smaller than the Bhagwati–Srinivasan subsidy S^*. Of course the exact magnitude would depend on – among other things – the exact relation between distortion and the subsidy bill.

The last argument is strengthened by introducing savings into the objective function. The sub-optimality of savings is a chronic problem in many LDCs and received much attention in the dual economy models of the sixties (see Sen, 1968). But for some reason this problem has been ignored in the context of dual economy models of the HT type. In the light of the emphasis on savings in the development economics literature, it may be reasonable to incorporate savings generation as an explicit objective in formulating optimum subsidies. Then, in case a larger subsidy bill is met by taxing profits, it is likely that the level of savings will drop and the optimum subsidy would be even smaller than suggested above.

Finally, there is a case for looking beyond simple subsidy measures to cure the ailments of an HT economy. Unemployment exists in the HT economy because, (a) the urban sector has a fixed minimum wage, and (b) to find employment in the urban sector a labourer has to be present there. It immediately follows that most of the policies can also be classified into two groups: those which lower the rural-urban wage-gap (I) and those which improve the availability of information and mobility in labour markets (II).

Most of the existing policy discussions occupy a subcategory in (I). This is probably explained by the fact that subsidies are more amenable to elegant theorising than some other more realistic policies. But even within (I) there are other possibilities like investing in rural infrastructure to raise rural productivity, and 'food for work' programmes. A large number of developing nations and international agencies have been emphasising the importance of this option. Under (II) would figure measures like the creation of rural employment exchanges and regular recruitment programmes and efforts to improve communication between rural and urban regions. (The interested reader may refer to Fields (1975) for some preliminary dicussion of such measures.)

Appendix 1   The monotonicity proposition

The monotonicity proposition mentioned and utilised in section 3 above is formally established here.

Consider the HT model of section 2 above. Let S be the wage subsidy given to all workers. Then condition (4) becomes[9]

$$f'_M(L_M) = \bar{w} - S \tag{4'}$$

and condition (5) becomes

$$f'_R(L_R) + S = \frac{\bar{w}L_M}{L - L_R}. \tag{5'}$$

This is the algebraic equivalent of what was diagrammatically discussed in sections 2 and 3 above.

Now for each level of subsidy S, (1), (2), (4') and (5') can be solved to find the equilibrium $[L_M, L_R, X_M, X_R]$ vector.[10]

The *monotonicity proposition* asserts that if S is the subsidy given to both sectors and S is less than S^* (defined by (9)) then if S is increased, social welfare U (defined by (6)) also increases. This may be proved as follows. Since

$$U = f_M(L_M) + f_R(L_R),$$

and L_M and L_R depend on S,

$$\frac{dU}{dS} = f'_M \frac{dL_M}{dS} + f'_R \frac{dL_R}{dS}. \tag{10}$$

---

[9] Since we shall only consider subsidies which are smaller than S, there will be no occasion for w to rise above $\bar{w}$. Hence the use of $\bar{w}$ (rather than w) in (4') and (5').

[10] It is easy to check, that since in this appendix we only consider $S \leqslant S^*$, (3) is automatically satisfied.

From (4'),

$$f_M'' \frac{dL_M}{dS} = -1,$$

i.e.

$$\frac{dL_M}{dS} = \frac{-1}{f_M''}$$

From (5')

$$Lf_R' + LS - L_R f_R' - SL_R - \bar{w}L_M = 0.$$

By differentiating with respect to S:

$$Lf_R'' \frac{dL_R}{dS} + L - L_R f_R'' \frac{dL_R}{dS} - \frac{dL_R}{dS} f_R' - S \frac{dL_R}{dS} - L_R - \bar{w} \frac{dL_M}{dS}$$
$$= 0.$$

By grouping and substituting for dL_M/dS, we get

$$\frac{dL_R}{dS} = \frac{(L_R - L - \bar{w}/f_M'')}{[(L - L_R)f_R'' - f_R' - S]}$$

By substituting for dL_M/dS and dL_R/dS into (10), we get

$$\frac{dU}{dS} = -\frac{f_M'}{f_M''} + \frac{f_R'(L_R - L - \bar{w}/f_M'')}{(L - L_R)f_R'' - f_R' - S}$$

$$= \frac{-f_M'(L - L_R)f_R'' + L_R f_R' f_M'' - Lf_R' f_M'' + f_R'(f_M' - \bar{w}) + Sf_M'}{f_M''[(L - L_R)f_R'' - f_R' - S]}$$

$$= \frac{(L_R - L)f_R'' f_M' + (L_R - L)f_R' f_M'' + S(f_M' - f_R')}{f_M''[(L - L_R)f_R'' - f_R' - S]},$$

since

$$f_M' - \bar{w} = -S,$$

by (4').

Since $L_R + L_M \leqslant 1$, $f_M', f_R' > 0$, $f_M'', f_R'' < 0$ and $f_M' > f_R'$ (this is easily checked), it follows that $dU/dS > 0$.

CHAPTER 7

The Rural-Urban Wage Gap

1 The labour turnover model

Labour turnover is costly to employers. This is particularly true in the industrial sector. Because of specialisation, till a new worker gains the rhythm of the others, a whole assembly line could be disturbed. Also, in industry, workers typically work with instruments which require getting used to. So with new employees the pace of work may slow down and breakage increase. While these factors are present also in the rural backward regions, there they have a more minimal role and for simplicity we may suppose that labour turnover is costly only in the urban sector. If we couple this with the assumption (not at all unrealistic) that a firm paying a higher wage faces a lower labour turnover rate, then we are on the verge of an explanation of why urban employers may not lower their wages despite the existence of unemployment.

This is the intuitive basis of a very interesting contribution of Stiglitz (1974), which tries to provide an endogenous explanation of the rural–urban wage gap. This paper has received less attention than it deserves and one reason for this must be its rather confusing style. I present here a simplified version of the labour turnover theory. With this I try to show that the conceptual basis of this theory is extremely rich and it ought to be explored further, but also that its formalisation has important flaws. Some of these I try to resolve but some loose ends remain which demand further research.

The annual labour turnover rate or the quit rate faced by a firm depends on a variety of factors of which Stiglitz considers three: (a) the wage paid by the firm *vis-à-vis* the average industrial wage, (b) the wage paid by the firm *vis-à-vis* the rural wage, and (c) the urban unemployment rate.

84

Given imperfect information among workers it is reasonable to suppose that the average industrial wage, the rural wage and urban unemployment serve as signals of general labour market conditions; and as any of these deteriorate workers become more hesitant to quit a secure job in order to search for a better one. Hence (a), (b) and (c) are realistic, but it is possible to simplify further. The interaction between urban firms raises interesting issues but these are not central in the context of dual economy analysis. So I shall assume that there is only one urban firm, relegating to section 3 below a brief discussion of inter-firm interaction in the presence of labour turnover. Also, while the urban–rural wage ratio and urban unemployment are factors which determine the quit rate, in this model it turns out (as in the HT model) that these two factors are causally related. Hence one of these may be omitted and it is therefore assumed that only (b) determines the quit rate, q:[1]

$$q = q \left(\frac{w}{w_R} \right) \qquad q' \leqslant 0, \tag{1}$$

where w is the urban wage and w_R is the rural wage (which is equal to the marginal product of rural labour).

The production function in the urban sector is as before:

$$X_M = f_M(L_M) \qquad f_M' > 0, \; f_M'' < 0. \tag{2}$$

The firm faces two costs: the wage cost (wL_M) and the labour turnover cost ($Tq(w/w_R)L_M$, where T is the cost incurred by the firm every time a worker quits and a new person is employed[2]). The firm chooses w and L_M so as to maximise profit, π, given by

$$\pi = f_M(L_M) - wL_M - Tq \left(\frac{w}{w_R} \right) L_M$$

which may be rewritten as

$$\pi = f_M(L_M) - \left[w + Tq \left(\frac{w}{w_R} \right) \right] L_M. \tag{3}$$

---

[1] There are more sophisticated models of labour turnover. A particularly interesting contribution is that of Salop and Salop (1976). In this they argue that firms use wage increment clauses to cut down turnover, because a firm which offers a low starting wage but promises sharp increments in future would attract only those who do not intend quitting soon. However, since in the present analysis the labour turnover is a small part of a much larger framework it is reasonable to use simpler assumptions.

[2] It is assumed throughout this model that a quit is immediately replaced, i.e. the firm never faces a shortage of labour. I comment on this in a while.

It is obvious from (3) that the firm first chooses w to minimise $w + Tq(w/w_R)$ and then chooses L_M to maximise π. This is clear also from the first-order conditions:

$$1 + \frac{T}{w_R} q' \left(\frac{w}{w_R}\right) = 0 \tag{4}$$

$$f'_M(L_M) = w + Tq\left(\frac{w}{w_R}\right). \tag{5}$$

(4) and (5) can be solved to get w and L_M as a function of w_R (and, of course, also T but since T remains unchangèd it may be suppressed):

$$w = w(w_R) \tag{6}$$

$$L_M = L_M(w_R). \tag{7}$$

Hence once the rural wage is known, we know what the level of urban employment and wage will be.

In order to keep the analysis simple assume that the marginal product of labour in the rural sector is constant at m.[3] It is easy to generalise this. Since wage equals marginal product in the rural sector, w_R is constant. Therefore, by (6) and (7), w and L_M are given. The only variable which remains to be explained is the level of rural employment, L_R.

In keeping with the Harris–Todaro (HT) tradition, suppose that workers migrate to whichever sector offers a higher expected income and the urban employment rate represents the probability of finding an urban job (in the rural sector jobs are assured). Thus the migration equilibrium condition is, as before,

$$w_R = w \frac{L_M}{L - L_R} \tag{8}$$

where L represents the total available labour in the economy. There is one qualification though. Clearly (8) is meaningful if and only if $w \geqslant w_R$. If $w_R < w$, then everybody would flock to the rural sector, that is, $L_R = L$. So the full statement of the migration equilibrium condition is: if $w \geqslant w_R$, then (8) is valid, and if $w_R > w$, then $L_R = L$.

However if $w_R > w$, then some rather fundamental questions arise regarding Stiglitz's formulation. I turn to these later. In the meantime, let us steer clear of complexities by *assuming* that $w \geqslant w_R$ in the final equilibrium.

---

[3] In other words, the rural production function is as follows: $X_R = mL_R$.

Having solved (6) and (7) for w and L_M (8) can be solved for L_R (recall that w_R is constant). Let $[\tilde{w}, \tilde{L}_M, \tilde{L}_R]$ be the solution of (6), (7) and (8). Since $\tilde{w} \geqslant w_R$ (by assumption), hence $\tilde{L}_M + \tilde{L}_R \leqslant L$. Therefore, $[\tilde{w}, \tilde{L}_M, \tilde{L}_R]$ is the equilibrium vector in this model.

Before subjecting the model to a critical analysis, it is useful to represent the Stiglitz equilibrium on a diagram. The diagrammatic approach helps us understand the kind of assumptions needed on the quit function and the production function to ensure the existence and uniqueness of a solution.

Figure 7.1 represents Tq as a function of w, for a given w_R. It is assumed that if w/w_R is very high, greater than, say θ, then $q'(w/w_R) = 0$. In other words, $q(\theta)$ is the 'natural' quit rate determined by retirement and death. Once that quit rate is reached, q cannot be lowered any further by raising w. But for all $w/w_R < \theta$, $q'(w/w_R) < 0$. Also assume that as w/w_R goes to 0, $q'(w/w_R)$ goes to (negative) infinity. It is convenient to assume that q is twice differentiable and, for all $w/w_R < \theta$, $q''(w/w_R) > 0$. The graph in figure 7.1 captures all these assumptions. These assumptions guarantee the existence and uniqueness of an optimum (w, L_M) for the firm, for every given w_R.

The same graph is reproduced in the left-hand panel in figure 7.2, assuming that $w_R = m$. Clearly for different w_R we would have different graphs. In particular as w_R rises, the graph shifts up. Fortunately, because of our assumption of m being a constant, this graph remains unchanged throughout.

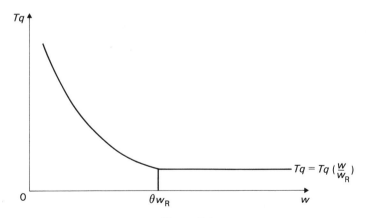

Figure 7.1

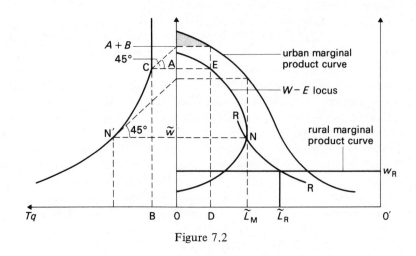

Figure 7.2

The centre piece of this analysis is the urban wage-employment locus (*W–E* locus, in brief). To derive this consider any urban wage, for instance, *A*. Then *Tq* is given by *B*. Then $w + Tq \; (= A + B)$ may be represented on the vertical axis by drawing a 45° line through point (B, A), denoted by C in the diagram. Now, given the marginal product curve for labour, the firm would employ those people such that the marginal product for labour equals the per worker cost, i.e. $A + B$. Hence, *given* a wage of *A*, the optimum employment from the firm's point of view is 0D. Hence point (D, A), denoted by E, depicts one possible wage-employment combination. By starting from other wages, we could, by a similar process, compute other such wage-employment points and by connecting all these we get the *W–E* locus. This curve depicts the following: if the firm is *given* a wage, it shows the level of employment optimal for the firm. Therefore to know the firm's optimum (w, L_M) we simply have to find out which point on the *W–E* locus maximises the firm's profit.

Consider any point, e.g. E, on the *W–E* locus. What is the total profit at this (w, L_M) combination? This is given by the area between the marginal product curve and the per worker cost line. The per worker cost to the firm corresponding to any point on the *W–E* locus is got by drawing a vertical line from that point to the marginal product curve. Hence for the (w, L_M) combination depicted by point E, the profit is given by the shaded area.

Clearly then profit is maximised at point N. Hence the firm should pay a wage of $\tilde{w}$ and employ $0\tilde{L}_M$ people.[4] To find the equilibrium rural employment we have to repeat the technique used in the diagrammatic depiction of the HT equilibrium: through the urban wage–employment point, i.e. N, draw a rectangular hyperbola (denoted RR in figure 7.2). The point of intersection between this and the rural marginal product curve (assumed to be a constant function) gives the rural employment. Hence $0'\tilde{L}_R$ is the equilibrium in the rural sector.

At first sight, the Stiglitz equilibrium is like a standard dual-economy equilibrium; but there is an important difference. The gap between the urban and rural wages arises endogenously. That is, it is quite possible that $w > w_R$ at equilibrium without any assumption of wage rigidity. It is important to appreciate the reason for this. If $w > w_R$, the urban employer would have workers coming to him who would be willing to work for a lower wage than w. In conventional analysis it is taken for granted that in such a situation a rational employer would in fact lower the wage. And if he does not it must be because of political reasons or trade-union pressure. This is not so in the labour turnover model. Here the employer may *prefer* not to lower wages. This is because, if the employer does lower the wage then indeed his wage bill (for the same number of employees) would fall but with a lower wage he could face a higher labour turnover and its associated cost. And the latter may offset the gains from a smaller wage bill. Hence, the urban wage may not fall despite the existence of involuntary unemployment.

2 Extensions and critique

Let us begin by getting one relatively minor difficulty out of the way. If it is possible for firms to hire labourers under the enforceable

---

[4] Since N is the highest point on the W-E curve viewed horizontally, the 45° line at N' must be tangential to the curve in the left panel. Hence at the optimum, the slope of the $Tq\,(w/w_R)$ curve is equal to -1. That is

$$Tq'\left(\frac{w}{w_R}\right)\frac{1}{w_R} = -1.$$

This is precisely what our algebra had given; see (4).

Since $\tilde{L}_M$ is that level of employment where the marginal product of labour in the urban sector is equal to the per worker cost, $\tilde{L}_M$ is the solution of

$$f'_M(L_M) = w + Tq\left(\frac{w}{w_R}\right)$$

which is the same as (5).

contract that they will not quit, then the above theory ceases to be relevant. In that case if there are people willing to work for a firm at a wage below what the firm is currently paying, then the firm could offer a lower wage and demand guarantees of 'no quitting'. At equilibrium, the firms would make the terms unattractive up to the point where the labour market just clears. The possibility of contractual employment not only disturbs the last remark in section 1 above, but it opens up a vast area and issues which are important but tangential to the motivation of this monograph. Hence we stay clear of this problem by assuming that firms cannot enforce 'no quit' contracts.

Observe that what this model shows is that there is no reason to expect a rural–urban wage equalisation. But is there any reason why $w \geqslant w_R$ is a more likely outcome than $w < w_R$? This is an important question since in reality the urban wage is seldom below the rural wage.

Up till now I had ruled out $w < w_R$ by assumption. The question here is, what conditions on the primitives of this model ensures this result? Consider the following condition on the quit function and the turnover cost:

$$w = w_R \to q'\left(\frac{w}{w_R}\right) \cdot \frac{1}{w_R} < -\frac{1}{T}. \tag{9}$$

(9) says that if $w = w_R$ then the slope of the graph in the left panel of figure 7.2 is less than -1 (remember the slopes are given in negative numbers).[5] Since we have assumed that the set above this graph is convex $[q''(w/w_R) > 0]$, it is clear that the slope cannot be equal to -1 where $w < w_R$. Recalling that the firm's optimal wage is where the slope of the graph equals -1 it becomes clear that (9) ensures that $\tilde{w} \geqslant w_R$.

While condition (9) does solve the problem of the direction of the rural–urban wage gap, it is a purely technical condition. Hence the question must arise as to whether there is a conceptual justification for using (9) or there is some alternative explanation of why the urban wage exceeds the rural one.

[5] Note that

$$q'\left(\frac{w}{w_R}\right)\frac{1}{w_R} < -\frac{1}{T}$$

is equivalent to

$$\frac{\partial Tq(w/w_R)}{\partial w} < -1.$$

Before attempting to answer this notice that this model has one important loose end. While the behaviour of the firms is presented in detail, the workers' decision-making is left obscure. It is not explained with any rigour what motivates a worker's decision to quit. Clearly in the background of the theory lies some kind of labour-market uncertainty. Otherwise it is difficult to see why a labourer working for a firm would quit his job when the only two other options are to be unemployed or to work in the rural sector for a lower wage. In reality labourers may quit in order to search for a better job, and a search is necessary because a typical economy is characterised by an array of wages about which the worker has very incomplete information. The present model with its assumption of labour turnover mimics this reality without bringing it formally into the model. This in itself should not be a basis of criticism. In fact semi-rigorous approaches such as this do have an important role in the development of ideas.

With the above explanation in the background, consider the firm paying a wage lower than w_R. Then there will be no unemployment and so working for the firm is the worst option open to a worker. Even if workers do not have full information to know this, they will observe that the labour market conditions are very favourable for them. This means that there would be reasons to expect a 'very high' quit-rate faced by the firm. Condition (9) – given the other assumptions about the quit function – may be thought of as approximately capturing this idea.

There is, however, one important objection to this against which we have to guard ourselves. This relates to the observation in footnote 2 (p. 85). In Stiglitz's model a firm may face a higher or a lower turnover but never a shortage of labour. The quit rate is assumed to be exactly matched by the 'replacement' rate and moreover between a quit and a replacement there is no time-lag.[6] It is this assumption that allows Stiglitz to speak of the 'quit rate' and the 'labour turnover' as synonyms. If we adopt this dual perspective, the difficulty becomes quite transparent. We had assumed that as the firm lowers its wage, the quit rate rises. But by the above argument this means that the replacement rate rises as well. This may be realistic up to a point, but when the wage drops sufficiently, the assumption that each quit can be immediately replaced becomes grossly unrealistic. Hence, the assumption in the previous paragraph that as

---

[6] There is however a disturbing dichotomy in Stiglitz's characterisation of a firm and a sector. I comment on this below.

w drops below w_R the labour turnover becomes 'very high' is unrealistic.

While this criticism is no doubt valid, what is fortunate is that, rather than weakening, it strengthens the conclusion that firms would prefer to pay a higher wage than w_R. This is for the following reason: as the firm lowers w towards (or below) w_R, the quit rate rises, but between each quit and replacement a time gap emerges (a possibility that is implicitly denied in Stiglitz's formulation) which inflicts an additional cost on the firm. So if it was not worthwhile for the firm to lower the wage to w_R because of a high turnover, now with the introduction of this new element, the argument is merely strengthened.

Finally, there is a serious dichotomy in Stiglitz's assumption about worker response to a firm and to a sector. As far as a firm is concerned (as already noted), a quit is immediately matched by a replacement so that quits are really turnovers. On the other hand as far as each sector goes (e.g. the urban sector), it is labour *supply* which changes and not merely the turnover rate. If the urban expected earnings rise, the workers leave the rural sector. The quits are not matched by a reverse stream. This difficulty takes the form of a direct inconsistency if $w < w_R$. In that case $L = L_R$. But according to (1), the turnover is very high, which is absurd in a sector without any labourers. Assumption (9), or the direct one of $w \geqslant w_R$, prevents this direct inconsistency, but the essence of the problem remains.

These are some of the open questions which remain and need to be answered before we can claim to have given a completely rigorous formulation of Stiglitz's theory of dualism. And clearly an important clue must lie in distinguishing between the quit rate and the rate of replacement.

3   Labour turnover and duopsony: a digression

The interaction between firms in the Stiglitz (1974) model was omitted from the analysis in section 1 above because it does not add much to our understanding of *dual* economies or underdevelopment. But nevertheless it gives interesting insights into the functioning of labour markets. Here I construct a simple example to illustrate this. This should also help dispel a possible misunderstanding that involuntary unemployment and multiple wages can exist only in economies where the labour turnover cost varies between sectors, as in the model of section 1.

Suppose there are only two firms, denoted 1 and 2, in an economy. Stiglitz assumed that the labour turnover faced by firm i is a function of the ratio of w_i and the average wage, i.e. $(w_1 + w_2)/2$. There is no harm in supposing instead that the annual labour turnover, q_i, faced by firm i is a function of w_i/w_j, where $i \neq j$. That is

$$q_i = q \left(\frac{w_i}{w_j}\right), \qquad i \neq j, \; i = 1, 2. \tag{10}$$

As in section 1 above, the firm chooses w_i so as to minimise the per worker cost, i.e.

$$w_i + Tq \left(\frac{w_i}{w_j}\right). \tag{11}$$

In this model involuntary unemployment and wage rigidities might arise at equilibrium. Intuitively this is easy to see. Consider firm i's problem. By raising its wage, the wage component of the cost goes up but the turnover falls and so does the cost associated with it. Thus it might be advantageous for the firm to raise wages, even though there might exist workers on the labour market who are willing to accept jobs for a lower wage. So wages will be pushed up, up to the point where additions to the wage component of the cost is no longer redressed by diminishing turnover cost.

An example could be used to highlight the salient features of such inter-firm interaction. Suppose that the quit function, (10), has the following special form:[7]

$$q_i = \frac{w_j}{w_i}, \qquad i = 1, 2.$$

Let $T = 1$. Hence the per worker cost, (11), takes the following form:

$$w_i + w_j/w_i. \tag{12}$$

Firm i chooses w_i to minimise this and so we get the following first-order condition:[8]

$$1 - w_j/w_i^2 = 0.$$

Rearranging this we get firm i's *reaction function*, $w_i = \sqrt{w_j}$, which shows what is the best wage for firm i given firm j's wage. More

---

[7] In the equations that follow, it is assumed throughout that if $i = 1$, $j = 2$ and if $i = 2$, $j = 1$.

[8] The second-order condition is obviously satisfied.

explicitly, the *reaction functions* for firms 1 and 2 are, respectively,

$$w_1 = \sqrt{w_2},$$

and

$$w_2 = \sqrt{w_1}.$$

By solving these we get $w_1 = 1$, $w_2 = 1$. So this is the equilibrium wage configuration. This is in fact a *Nash equilibrium*. A wage configuration (w_1^*, w_2^*) is a *Nash equilibrium* if and only if the following is true: if firm 2 sets its wage at w_2^* then w_1^* is optimal for firm 1, and if firm 1 sets its wage at w_1^* then w_2^* is optimal for firm 2. That is, it is a configuration from which no agent can benefit by deviating.

Given that $[1, 1]$ is the equilibrium wage vector, the per worker cost faced by each firm at equilibrium equals 2. This is got by substituting the equilibrium values in (12). What is interesting is that both firms are worse off at the equilibrium than they would be if they both agreed to pay a smaller wage. For instance, if they both agreed to pay a wage of $\frac{1}{16}$ then for each firm the cost of employing one labourer would be $1\frac{1}{16}$ which is better than the situation at the equilibrium. But of course the wage vector $[\frac{1}{16}, \frac{1}{16}]$ is not a Nash equilibrium. For example, consider firm 1. It will soon realise that if $w_2 = \frac{1}{16}$, it could cut down its cost (by curbing its labour turnover) by setting $w_1 = \frac{1}{4}$. This is obvious from the reaction function given above. And if $w_1 = \frac{1}{4}$, firm 2 clearly does best by setting $w_2 = \frac{1}{2}$. And so the process continues, converging towards the only[9] Nash equilibrium, $[1, 1]$.

As long as the quit functions take the form of $q_i = w_j/w_i$ and $T = 1$, the wage vector of $[1, 1]$ will not change even if there is involuntary unemployment. Suppose labour supply is inelastic and equal to 3 and the marginal product of labour of firm i is given by

$$MP^i = \frac{2}{L_i}, \qquad i = 1, 2$$

where L_i is the amount of labour employed by firm i. The equilibrium employment is clearly equal to 1, since at equilibrium MP^i must be equal to the per worker cost. Hence aggregate labour demand at equilibrium is 2 and therefore the equilibrium is characterised by involuntary unemployment of magnitude 1 ($= 3 - 2$).

Two final warnings are in order. First, note that in the above analysis the 'quit rate' is equated with the labour 'turnover', i.e. each

---

[9] Assuming that $w_1, w_2 > 0$.

quit is immediately replaced. This does not cause any problems in the above example. But if labour supply has some elasticity then it is quite possible that there exists a wage where the labour demand exceeds aggregate supply. Then the above assumption runs into logical difficulties and it would be necessary to distinguish between quits and turnover.

Secondly, it should be emphasised that in this analysis, as in Stiglitz (1974), the quit function is a 'primitive'. This causes no *logical* problems; but for a theory to be more complete, it is desirable that the decisions to quit and join firms (or sectors) be explained from more basic and better-known facts of human behaviour.

CHAPTER 8

The Efficiency Wage Hypothesis

1 The basic theory

Wage rigidity is one of the key factors behind dualism in backward economies. It is also a cause of labour market fragmentation in general and of unemployment. Despite this, attempts to explain wage inflexibilities are few and far between.[1] One important contribution, the labour turnover theory, was examined in chapter 7. Another widely discussed explanation is the efficiency-wage hypothesis. The seminal work on this subject appeared in the late fifties (Leibenstein, 1957, 1957a, 1958) and recent years have witnessed a resurgence of interest in this area (Mirrless, 1975; Rodgers, 1975; Stiglitz, 1976; Bliss and Stern, 1978; Agarwala, 1979).[2]

The basic axiom of this model[3] is that a worker's productivity is positively related to his level of consumption. By considering extreme examples it becomes clear that the axiom must have at least some limited validity. One qualification has often been pointed out which I think is reasonable: that such a positive relation exists only at low levels of consumption. Fortunately that is all that the theory needs.

Assume, in addition, that the link between wages and consumption is fairly stable. This is clearly tenable for low-income groups and this, in conjunction with the basic axiom, implies that a worker's productivity depends on his wage.

---

[1] The reason for this is quite clear. The explanation of price rigidities is an extremely vexing theoretical problem. We know this not only from development economics but from research in pure theory.

[2] The period in between was not totally barren. Ezekiel (1960), Wonnacott (1962), and also parts of Myrdal (1968) discuss this problem.

[3] The model in this section is based on Mirrlees (1975).

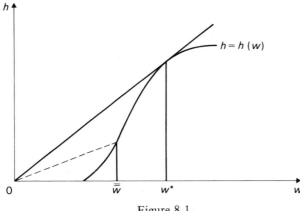

Figure 8.1

The concept of productivity can be made formal in many ways. In the existing literature it is assumed that output depends not on the *hours* of labour but on the number of *efficiency units* of labour used; and the number of efficiency units that a worker can produce per hour is a function of the wage he receives. Assume that each labourer works for a fixed number of hours; h is the total number of efficiency units produced by each labourer and w is the wage rate. Hence the above statement may be written as

$$h = h(w) \qquad h'(w) > 0 \qquad\qquad (1)$$

Since total output, X, depends on the number of efficiency units used:[4]

$$X = f(nh(w)) \qquad f' > 0, \ f'' < 0, \qquad\qquad (2)$$

where n is the number of labourers.

It is reasonable to assume that (1) has the shape illustrated in figure 8.1. It means that when consumption is very low, increases in consumption have a sharp effect on productivity but the effect becomes less pronounced at higher levels of consumption.

Let us first take up a partial equilibrium problem. A single owner is trying to decide on how many workers to employ, n, and what wage to pay, w. His objective is to maximise profit, π, which is equal to $f(nh(w)) - nw$ (w being given in real terms). Suppose $\tilde{w}$ is the prevailing reservation wage or the supply price of labour. This means

[4] This is a short-run model. So the amount of capital used is treated as a constant and therefore ignored in the production function.

that if he offers less than $\tilde{w}$, no workers would be forthcoming but if he offers more he could have as many workers as he wishes. It should be emphasised that while $\tilde{w}$ could be the prevailing market wage, it is not necessarily so. For instance, if there is no proper labour market and workers are willing to work for any wage above the subsistence level, then $\tilde{w}$ would be the subsistence wage. Hence the employer's problem is the following:

$$\max_{\{n, w\}} f(nh(w)) - nw \tag{3}$$

subject to $w \geqslant \tilde{w}$.

In standard theory if an employer was free to pay any wage equal to or above $\tilde{w}$, he would opt for the lowest, i.e. $\tilde{w}$. But in the present context this is not necessarily so, because a higher wage ensures a larger number of efficiency units from each hour of labour and therefore from each labourer. This means that the inequality constraint cannot be converted into an equality, as is permitted in related standard problems.

The solution to the above maximisation problem is best worked out in two steps. Consider first the hypothetical case where there are no constraints on w. Then the maximisation of profit yields the following first-order conditions:

$$f'(nh(w)) \cdot h(w) - w = 0 \tag{4}$$

$$f'(nh(w)) \cdot h'(w) - 1 = 0. \tag{5}$$

It is easy to check that these are sufficient conditions. (4) and (5) imply

$$\frac{w}{h(w)} = \frac{1}{h'(w)}. \tag{6}$$

Let $w = w^*$ be the solution to (6). Then w^* is known as the *efficiency wage*. It is quite obvious that to depict this on figure 8.1, we have to draw a straight line through the origin tangential to the wage-efficiency curve. The point of contact represents w^*, as shown.

There are many ways of interpreting the efficiency wage. The following is probably the most useful: note that $w/h(w)$ is the cost of one efficiency unit. Thus while w is the cost of buying one labour unit, $w/h(w)$ is the cost of buying one efficiency unit. Now note that if the wage is $\tilde{w}$, the cost of each efficiency unit is given by the slope (its inverse, to be more precise) of the broken line in figure 8.1. Therefore, w^* is the wage which minimises $w/h(w)$, i.e. the cost of efficiency units; and hence it is christened 'the *efficiency* wage'.

Now consider the employer's actual problem, which is to maximise (3) *subject to* $w \geqslant \tilde{w}$. If $\tilde{w} \leqslant w^*$, then w^* is feasible and so that is precisely what would be paid. If $w^* < \tilde{w}$, then w^* is no longer feasible. It may be checked that the employer maximises profit by giving a wage as close to w^* as is feasible.[5] Hence in this case he will pay $\tilde{w}$. Therefore, the optimal wage, w, depends on the supply price of labour, $\tilde{w}$, in the following way:

$$w = w(\tilde{w}) = \begin{cases} w^* & \text{if } \tilde{w} \leqslant w^* \\ \tilde{w} & \text{if } \tilde{w} > w^*. \end{cases} \tag{7}$$

Once w is chosen, n is determined by inserting w in (4). Since w is a function of $\tilde{w}$, the optimal n must be a function of $\tilde{w}$ as well. Clearly, as long as $\tilde{w} < w^*$, n does not respond to $\tilde{w}$; and if $\tilde{w} \geqslant w^*$, $\partial n / \partial \tilde{w} < 0$.[6] Thus

$$n = n(\tilde{w}). \tag{8}$$

Equations (7) and (8) are illustrated in the left and right panels, respectively, of figure 8.2. Equation (8) is a kind of demand curve for labour. It depicts the labour demand corresponding to every reservation wage rate. However, the reservation wage is not always equal to the actual wage. For example, if the reservation wage is w_1, the actual wage is w^*. This means that though the employer can get workers as long as he pays them w_1, he *prefers* to pay them the higher wage w^*.

This completes the partial equilibrium analysis. The model can explain the existence of wage rigidities and involuntary unemploy-

---

[5] Note that the profit function may be rewritten as follows:

$$\pi(n, w) = f(nh(w)) - nh(w) \frac{w}{h(w)}.$$

Suppose initial wage and employment are at w and n and $w > w^*$. Consider a lowering of w to $\hat{w}$, which is still above w^*. It is clear from figure 8.1 that $\hat{w}/h(\hat{w}) < w/h(w)$. Let n' be such that $n'h(w) = nh(w)$. Clearly, $\pi(n', \hat{w}) > \pi(n, w)$. Hence if $w > w^*$, the employer can always do better by lowering w and suitably amending n.

[6] This is easily explained as the outcome of two effects, (a) as $\tilde{w}$ rises, w rises, and (b) as w rises, n falls. (a) is obvious from (7). In fact $\partial w / \partial \tilde{w} = 1$. (b) follows from (4), which may be rewritten as

$$f'(nh(w)) = \frac{w}{h(w)}.$$

It is clear from figure 8.1 that as w rises (recalling $w \geqslant w^*$) so does $w/h(w)$. Since $h'(w) \geqslant 0$ and $f'' < 0$, a rise in w has to be accompanied by a fall in n for the above equality to be valid.

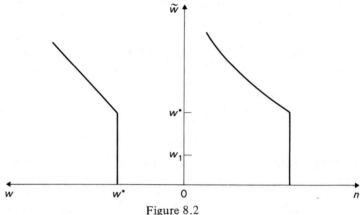

Figure 8.2

ment. But to see this properly the partial equilibrium model needs to be fitted into a general equilibrium frame.

In the partial equilibrium analysis we worked out the wage that an employer would pay *given a fixed reservation wage*. The purpose of a general equilibrium model is to show what the reservation wage will be and therefore what will be the actual wage paid.

Suppose, for simplicity, that there are l identical employers – each like the one described above. Then the aggregate demand for labour, N^D, for each reservation wage is given by:

$$N^D = ln(w).$$ (9)

Assuming that the aggregate labour supply, N, depends on the wage paid, we have

$$N = N(w).$$ (10)

Let S and S' in figure 8.3 represent two alternative supply schedules. If there exists a wage $\hat{w}$ greater than w^* such that

$$N(\hat{w}) = ln(\hat{w}),$$

i.e. demand equals supply, then $\hat{w}$ is the equilibrium reservation wage and also the actual wage paid. If on the other hand at w^*, supply exceeds demand, that is

$$N(w^*) > ln(w^*),$$

then w^* will be the actual wage paid in the market. The reservation wage is less than w^* (in fact it is less than or equal to w^{**}).

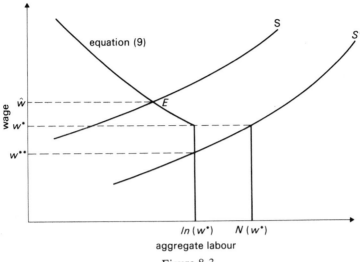

Figure 8.3

This second case arises if the supply curve is like S'. This is the interesting case, because here the equilibrium is characterised by involuntary unemployment equal to $N(w^*) - ln(w^*)$. Competition among the unemployed to find jobs fails to lower wages because employers *prefer* giving a wage of w^* to giving a lower wage.

This theory explains quite a few widely observed features of backward economies. Most importantly it explains the persistence of involuntary unemployment while at the same time explaining wage rigidity in labour surplus economies. This has already been demonstrated above. A special case of this is where labour supply is so excessive that, for all practical purposes, labour supply is infinite at the subsistence wage, w^s. This is the kind of assumption used in the Lewis model. Then despite the infinite supply at w^s, wages would be rigid at w^*,[7] thereby providing one possible explanation of the wage mark-up discussed by Lewis (1954).

A second important contribution of this theory is that it can explain the existence of wage dispersion (Mirrlees, 1975). Note first that it is very possible for the function $h(w)$ to be different for different kinds of jobs with the likely implication that w^* – the efficiency wage – would differ from one job to another. Now, if

---

[7] I am assuming, quite realistically, that $w^* > w^s$.

there is a great excess of labour supply, e.g. infinite supply at w^s, then each employer would pay the efficiency wage relevant to him. This would result in a range of wages and also involuntary unemployment, which is a rather realistic picture.

These are sufficiently important implications for the theory to be treated seriously and subjected to empirical scrutiny. A thorough empirical test of the hypothesis is difficult to devise and remains to be attempted. One of the best existing empirical studies is that of Bliss and Stern (1978).[8] They look at several kinds of indirect and interesting evidence. The verdict is a mixed one, though the existing nutritional evidence supports the view that there is a relation between calorie intake and the ability to work.

Claims have been made on behalf of this theory that it can explain two other salient features of underdevelopment, (a) surplus labour, and (b) dualism. In the two remaining sections of this chapter I try to confute the claim concerning surplus labour and defend the other.

2   Surplus labour and the efficiency wage

A sector is characterised by *surplus labour* if it is possible to remove a fraction of the labour force without causing any reduction in output. Such a situation is also described as one having *disguised unemployment* because, of the employed population, a part is redundant though not visibly so.[9]

It has been claimed by many (not without others contesting it) that surplus labour is widespread in overpopulated backward economies: 'most businesses in underdeveloped countries employ a large number of "messengers", whose contribution is almost negligible; you see them sitting outside office doors, or hanging around in the courtyard' (Lewis, 1954). The persistence of surplus labour is the source of some puzzlement to economists and a number of explanations have been suggested. One predominant view used to be that in LDCs, for a variety of reasons, marginal productivity of labour is zero over certain ranges. This has the consequence that the withdrawal of a part of the labour force has no effect on the output (Nurkse, 1953). This approach, however, raises doubts about the rationality of labourers or employers. If it is a family farm, why do

---

[8] Some piecemeal evidence is to be found in Leibenstein (1957, 1957a).

[9] The concepts of disguised unemployment and surplus labour have been interpreted in many different ways in the literature (Robinson, 1937; Navarrete and Navarrete, 1951; Sen, 1968, 1975, chapter 4).

they work so much if their efforts are not productive? If they are employed workers, why do their employers employ and pay them? In attempting to answer these questions, Sen (1966, 1975) showed that zero marginal productivity of labour is neither necessary nor sufficient for the existence of surplus labour. This argument is easy to demonstrate with a slightly simplified version of Sen's (1975) model.

Consider a family farm with $\bar{n}$ working members. Output, Q, depends on the hours of labour used. So if x denotes the number of hours that each member works, we have:

$$Q = f(\bar{n}x) \qquad f' > 0, \ f'' < 0.$$

Let the cost of each hour of labour expressed in terms of the output be fixed and equal to c. Assuming that the family objective is to maximise total production net of total leisure cost, they will work up to the point where

$$f'(\bar{n}x) = c. \tag{11}$$

Let the x which solves this be denoted by $\bar{x}$. Suppose that x^* is the maximum number of hours that a person can work. Then, surplus labour exists if $\bar{x} < x^*$. This is easy to see. Define n^* such that $n^*x^* = \bar{n}\bar{x}$. This means that if the farm had n^* members, then each of them would be working for x^* hours because clearly $f'(n^*x^*) = c$. Since $\bar{x} < x^*$, hence $\bar{n} > n^*$. Therefore, if from the family with $\bar{n}$ working members, $\bar{n} - n$ were withdrawn, then this would result in each member working $x^* - \bar{x}$ hours more and since $n^*x^* = \bar{n}\bar{x}$, hence $f(n^*x^*) = f(\bar{n}\bar{x})$, which means that output remains undiminished. This argument hinges on the assumption of constancy of the cost of leisure. The assumption as used above can be weakened in many ways as long as this essence is retained.

Turning now to the efficiency-wage hypothesis it seems that a similar argument for surplus labour should be possible. If the withdrawal of some labour results in an increase in wages, then the productivity of the remaining labour will increase and it seems possible that the total output will not fall. I show here that this explanation is not tenable.

Return to the general equilibrium model of section 1 above. If the equilibrium wage is w^* and $N(w^*) > ln(w^*)$, then there is unemployment but it is open. Hence the interesting case in this context is one where there is no excess supply of labour. Let me make the simplifying assumption of a completely inelastic labour supply curve, i.e. $N(w) = N$, for all w. Assume that the supply curve is a vertical line through E in figure 8.3. Then $\hat{w}$ is the equilibrium wage because $ln(\hat{w}) = N$.

Suppose now a part of the labour force is withdrawn and $\bar{N}(<N)$ remains behind. Clearly the new equilibrium wage, $\bar{w}$, is greater than w. Given that productivity is positively related to the wage rate, $h(w)$ must rise. Is it possible that there *exist* cases where $h(w)$ rises sufficiently for total output to remain undiminished? The answer is no and for the following reason.

Since $\bar{w} > \hat{w}$ and both $\bar{w}$ and $\hat{w}$ are greater than w^*, it follows from the shape of the $h(.)$ function that

$$\frac{\bar{w}}{h(\bar{w})} > \frac{\hat{w}}{h(\hat{w})}. \tag{12}$$

From (4) we see that at equilibrium n and w must be such that

$$f'(nh(w)) = \frac{w}{h(w)}. \tag{13}$$

Let the initial and new equilibrium n be denoted by $\hat{n}$ and $\bar{n}$ respectively, i.e. $\hat{n} = n(\hat{w})$ and $\bar{n} = n(\bar{w})$. (12) and (13) imply that

$$f'(\bar{n}h(\bar{w})) > f'(\hat{n}h(\hat{w})).$$

Since $f'' < 0$, this implies $\bar{n}h(\bar{w}) < \hat{n}h(\hat{w})$. Therefore, $f(\bar{n}h(\bar{w})) < f(\hat{n}h(\hat{w}))$, i.e. the output after the withdrawal of labour is smaller. Since all the functional forms were unspecified, it follows that surplus labour cannot be explained from the axiom that productivity depends on consumption.

The above argument is really quite straightforward and, not surprisingly, Leibenstein does not make any claims which contradict it. Leibenstein's (1957, p. 75) own explanation of surplus labour in the context of the efficiency wage theory hinges on some rather unrealistic institutional assumptions. But even with these assumptions, there are difficulties in constructing a valid argument, as shown in a lucid and interesting paper by Agarwala (1979).

3   Dualism and the efficiency wage

The basic theory of section 1 above in conjunction with some ideas from the labour turnover model of the previous chapter provides an interesting additional reason for the large rural–urban wage gap.

To see this, we must first appreciate that the relation between wage and efficiency described in equation (1) is not an instantaneous one. In fact, from the evidence listed in Bliss and Stern (1978), it seems likely that the relation is a fairly long-run phenomenon. If the food intake drops, for short periods people can keep up their level of work by reducing body weight. They cite a study of a woman who had a weekly cycle of losing on average one pound per day on week-days and replacing during week-ends. They also quote Haswell's (1975) research in a Gambian village which showed that the workers had a yearly cycle in body weight which allowed them to maintain a certain level of work despite seasonal fluctuations in the availability of food. This tendency of the human body to act as an energy store is one of the underlying causes of the time-lag between food intake and efficiency.

This has one immediate implication: in jobs with a high labour turnover the impact of raising wages on efficiency is likely to elude the employer because it is probable that a worker would quit before the wage affects his productivity. This means that in such jobs wages would not be as high as in more permanent jobs where the employers can reap the benefits of increased efficiency. This is in conformity with some evidence from South Africa and Brazil, noted in Bliss and Stern (1978), which shows that slaves (the most permanent type of labour) have a higher calorie intake than other 'free' workers.

It was argued in the previous chapter that labour turnover in the industrial sector is generally more costly to the employer than such turnover in the agricultural sector. Hence, as seen in chapter 7, in the industrial sector employers would pay a higher wage and thereby reduce turnover. Having done so, they will find (for reasons discussed in the above paragraph) that wages now affect productivity. Hence there will be an additional reason to raise wages. So the rural–urban dualism would be sharper than suggested in the above chapter, and the actual wage gap could be thought of as having two components: one part as a response to turnover costs and the other for reasons of productivity. It ought to be possible to introduce this turnover argument formally in the 'basic theory'. This might enable us to devise new tests of the basic hypothesis and also to measure the actual role of the two factors in the emergence of rural–urban wage gaps in backward economies.

PART III

The Rural Economy

CHAPTER 9

Stagnation in Backward Agriculture

1 Introduction

Some of the most significant innovations within development economics in the last decade or so have occurred in the analysis of rural
markets and agrarian relations. The ongoing research in this area has
two antecedents. First, there are the works of agricultural economists
and the early studies of land tenure which can be traced back through
Cheung (1968) and Johnson (1950) to Marshall (1920), Mill (1848)
and Smith (1776). Secondly, the studies of sociologists and social
anthropologists have had a limited but undeniable impact. What is
interesting is that some of the most engaging empirical findings have
come from the direct observation technique of these social scientists
rather than from the stacks of hurried questionnaires of economists.

What has emerged from this confluence is interesting and different.
It is becoming clear that the analysis of backward rural regions and
agrarian relations cannot be thought of as simply a special case of
standard general equilibrium theory. New concepts are often needed
and some of the conceptual categories which are sharp in the context
of industrialized economies are arbitrary and hazy in backward
agriculture. This has left the agrarian economist with two options:
to use old concepts and talk in imprecise terms or to develop new
ones and conduct more precise discussions. Tentative efforts to
adopt the second option have been made in many recent works.

When it is claimed that the new theories are not special cases of
standard theories, one need not go to the other extreme and maintain that the two sets of theories are in conflict. If by a theory one
means an analytical proposition then clearly two theories can never
conflict. If they do, they constitute a philosophical paradox. If on

the other hand one interprets a theory as an explanation, then indeed
two theories may conflict; but here also they *need* not.

The features of a traditional economy which are confounding are
many. Of these, stagnation and lack of innovation in the rural sector
are the most stark. There are villages and large regions which have
remained unchanged for centuries. How does one explain this? In
terms of human traits which are exogenous to an economist's
domain? In terms of institutions and tenurial relations?

Tenurial arrangements themselves are puzzling because of their
large diversity often even within a single district. Economists have
been curious to find out why so many forms exist and whether one
form is more efficient than another. Moreover, interlinked with the
tenurial relations one often finds credit agreements between landlords and peasants. The issue of rural moneylending has received a
large amount of well-deserved attention from writers and social
workers. The theoretical economists' interest in the subject is
relatively recent.

One particular characteristic of backward agriculture which is
receiving considerable attention in current research is the 'interlinked' nature of exchange. It is becoming increasingly clear, and
here social anthropologists have played an important role, that it
could be misleading to analyse labour and credit markets and tenure
relations in isolation. This is because in backward regions exchanges
are often based on multiple deals. It has been suggested that 'interlinkage' could be the key to understanding the multiplicity of rural
wages and interest rates observed in empirical studies.

These are issues addressed in this and the next three chapters,
beginning with an analysis of the causes of stagnation and non-
innovation. The perspective here is microtheoretic and the subject
of economy-wide stagnation, as discussed by Nurkse and Kalecki, is
discussed elsewhere in the book.

Briefly covering some early ideas, the next section goes on to
expound on the relatively new hypothesis of Bhaduri (1973). This
hypothesis has received very wide attention (Griffin, 1974; Newbery,
1975; Mukherji, 1975; Ghose and Saith, 1976; Rahman, 1979;
Srinivasan, 1979; Braverman and Stiglitz, 1981; Desai, 1981 and
others). And also, though I shall argue that as an explanation of stagnation Bhaduri's model is inadequate, his *perspective* has been
influential in recent research in agrarian relations. His theory also
raises questions which motivate the next chapters.

From this hypothesis we go on to discuss other explanations of
non-innovation, some with origins in economics and, more cursorily,
others with origins beyond.

2   A theory of stagnation

That certain tenurial arrangements could dampen innovation and generate inefficiencies has been appreciated by economists for some time now. Both Smith (1776) and Marshall (1920) examined different land tenure systems and came out on the same side, preferring a fixed rental system to share tenancy. In a fixed rental system the landlord gives the land to a tenant for a constant annual rent. Thus in this system the landlord gets a fixed income from land and the tenant earns the residual. In share tenancy the landlord gives his land to a tenant with the agreement that he will receive a fixed *proportion* of the output. We may for the time being assume, as is often the case in reality, that this proportion is half. Now consider a tenant thinking of an innovation which will raise output by a certain quantity. Is the innovation worthwhile to him? It is worthwhile only if the cost of innovation is less than *half* the increase in output. This is because only half the increase in production would accrue to the tenant in a share tenancy system. In a fixed rental system, however, the entire increase in output is received by the tenant (so goes the traditional argument). Hence innovations are much more easily acceptable to a tenant in a fixed rental system and share tenancy would be relatively stagnant. This, in a nutshell, is the argument associated with Marshall (1920, Book VI, Chapter 10; see Griffin, 1974, for discussion).[1]

Observe that in Marshall's approach as in most earlier ones (Mill, 1848; Smith, 1776; see Johnson, 1950, for discussion) the onus of innovation is thought to be on the tenant. Bhaduri's model contrasts itself to this tradition by treating the landlord as the one who takes the decision whether to innovate or not. He then goes on to show how in a semi-feudal society it is usually not in the landlord's interest to innovate. At the risk of oversimplicity his argument may be summarised as follows: in semi-feudal agriculture a landlord has two sources of earnings. He earns as rental a proportion of the total output. This could be thought of as his *property income*. But that is not

---

[1] While this was Marshall's principal argument, the earlier economists were never too niggardly in their explanations. Marshall (1920) had adduced a variety of other non-economic reasons, including (p. 538): 'And among the causes which have fostered this enterprise [which lead to change and innovation], none is more important than the absence of temptations to wait for a petty inheritance, and to marry for the sake of property rather than in the free exercise of individual choice ....' While one may be pardoned for not agreeing with this particular argument, it is interesting to contrast Marshall's *approach* to that of the present-day economist with his over enthusiasm for treating amorphous explanations as no explanations at all.

all. He typically loans money to his tenants at an exorbitant interest rate, and from this derives a regular income which comprises his *usurious income*. With a technological innovation, the tenant's income goes up, his need for consumption loans comes down and as a consequence the landlord's income from usury goes down. Hence, it is *possible* that an innovation lowers the *net* income of the landlord and is therefore undesirable to him.

The model is now developed formally. For the sake of simplicity assume that there is only one commodity, paddy. All transactions, including borrowing, are done in terms of this good. Therefore, money does not appear in the picture. The predominant tenurial form is share tenancy. A tenant or a peasant produces x units of paddy each year and keeps a proportion α for himself and pays $(1-\alpha)$ to his landlord as rental. It is assumed that x is technologically given, while α is given by custom; of course, $0 < \alpha < 1$. So in the short run both these variables may be treated as constants. Let b_t be the amount borrowed by the peasant in year t, and let c_t be the amount consumed by him. The interest rate is i. A peasant does not save. Hence,

$$b_t = c_t - [\alpha x - (1 + i) b_{t-1}]. \qquad (1)$$

All loans in this model are consumption loans.

The concept of equilibrium used here is that of a *stationary state*. Since we wish to analyse a rural economy which has settled into a pattern for many years, this is quite apt. A *stationary state equilibrium* is supposed to be achieved when the values of the variables cease to change from one year to another. Hence in a stationary state $c_t = c$ and $b_t = b$ for all t. By substituting the *stationary values* in (1), we get

$$b = \frac{\alpha}{i} x - \frac{c}{i}. \qquad (2)$$

Let $\bar{x}$ be the yearly output which is fixed as long as technology does not change. Assume that in the initial equilibrium, consumption is fixed at the minimum subsistence level, $\bar{c}$. It is now possible to solve (2) for b. Denoting the solution by $\hat{b}$, we have

$$\hat{b} = \frac{\alpha}{i} \bar{x} - \frac{\bar{c}}{i}. \qquad (3)$$

Since the purpose of the model is to examine a situation of indebtedness, it is asumed that $\hat{b} > 0$.

The most interesting feature of Bhaduri's model is this initial equilibrium depicted in (3). Even though quite limited in scope, it does characterise a particular reality well. The equation illustrates a *debt-trap* in which the peasant, once caught, cannot get out. An example could be helpful in clarifying this.

Let $\bar{x} = 100$, $\alpha = \frac{1}{2}$, $\bar{c} = 30$ and $i = 1$ (i.e. 100 per cent interest). Then (3) implies $\hat{b} = 20$. Consider any year. Harvest yields 100 units of paddy. After paying the rent the peasant has 50 units, but he still has to repay his debt. Since $\hat{b} = 20$, his debt is 20, which, given 100 per cent interest, implies that he has to pay his landlord 40 units of paddy. Thus after paying his rent and repaying his debt he has only 10 units left. But for subsistence he needs 30. So he borrows 20 to survive. In the next year, after harvest and after paying his rent, he brings home 50 units. But again he has to pay 40 units as debt repayment. So once again he is left with 10 units; and the cycle continues.[2]

The landlord's yearly income in the above example is 70. He gets 50 as rental income and 20 as interest on the 20 units he lends every year. There is another way of looking at this. The total output being 100 and since the peasant's consumption is 30 and he does not save, the landlord's income is 70.

The above situation is described as a debt-*trap* because there is nothing in the model which ensures this particular equilibrium. If the peasant could somehow heave himself out of the groove he could increase his consumption. In fact any consumption between 30 and 50 *could* have been an equilibrium. But once a value is fixed, it keeps recurring. How the initial equilibrium evolved is not explained in the model. That in itself need not worry us. It is futule to try and do away with historicity by explaining all. But there are other important questions regarding this equilibrium which are taken up in the next section.

Reverting back to the algebra and the initial equilibrium, consider a landlord who has the option of making an innovation which will raise the yearly output, i.e. x, from $\bar{x}$ to $\bar{x} + \Delta x$. In order to trace the consequences of such an innovation it is necessary to specify the peasant's consumption behaviour when the initial equilibrium, to which he is accustomed for years, is disturbed by some exogenous shock.

---

[2] 'At harvest time in a Mandinko village rice is sold at 2d. a cigarette tin, but in the rains price rises to $3\frac{1}{2}$. The repayment of debts after the sale of groundnuts makes a considerable inroad into the average income; this leaves the people short of money; and the vicious circle is ready to be repeated', Gamble (1955, p. 78). Quoted in Ames (1962, p. 52).

I shall assume a very simple consumption function which illustrates the main point and does not in any way hamper the spirit of the model. The *paddy balance* with the peasant in year t after harvest and after repayment of debt is $\alpha x - (1 + i) b_{t-1}$. In the initial equilibrium this fell short of $\bar{c}$ by $\hat{b}$. If the equilibrium is disturbed favourably (from the tenant's point of view), he will find that his paddy balance is higher. It could, of course, still be short of $\bar{c}$ but it is possible that it crosses the subsistence mark. The following consumption behaviour is assumed

$$\alpha x - (1 + i) b_{t-1} < \bar{c} \to c_t = \bar{c}$$

$$\alpha x - (1 + i) b_{t-1} \geq \bar{c} \to c_t = \alpha x - (1 + i) b_{t-1}.$$

These two cases may be referred to as, respectively, case I and case II. In words, this means that as long as the peasant finds that his paddy balance is below his subsistence requirement (even though it may be higher than the paddy balance in the initial equilibrium), he borrows just enough to give himself a subsistence consumption. If on the other hand he finds his paddy balance is above $\bar{c}$, he consumes the entire paddy balance, implying a zero borrowing and zero savings.

After the innovation $x = \bar{x} + \Delta x$. It is possible to conceive of stationary state equilibria such that both cases I and II occur. But if we study the dynamics of our system it becomes clear that case II is the one that actually emerges.[3] Though it is easy to conduct a similar exercise for case I, we restrict our attention to case II only. Hence in a stationary state the peasant's consumption is given by

$$c = \alpha x - (1 + i) b. \tag{4}$$

Equations (2) and (4) comprise the equilibrium system given the innovation. Since $x = \bar{x} + \Delta x$, these two equations may be solved for c and b. Let the equilibrium values be denoted by c^* and b^*. It is clear from (2) and (4) that

$$b^* = 0$$

$$c^* = \alpha(\bar{x} + \Delta x).$$

The main question is whether the landlord benefits from this innovation or not? What is interesting is that there cannot be an uncondi-

[3] It is easy to see intuitively why this is so. In the initial equilibrium, paddy balance each year is $\alpha \bar{x} - (1 + i) \hat{b}$. The year in which the innovation takes place the paddy balance is $\alpha(\bar{x} + \Delta x) - (1 + i) \hat{b}$ which is larger than usual. Thus the peasant takes a smaller than usual loan which means that his balance in the following year will be even larger (since loan repayment is smaller). Hence the left-hand expression in case I keeps increasing and it is not difficult to see that it must at some points cross $\bar{c}$.

tional answer to this. Let z represent the landlord's income. Since peasants do not save

$$z = x - c.$$

Using $\hat{z}$ and z^* to denote the landlord's income in the initial and the post-innovation[4] equilibrium, we have

$$\hat{z} = \bar{x} - \bar{c}$$

$$z^* = \bar{x} + \Delta x - \alpha[\bar{x} + \Delta x].$$

The innovation is worthwhile if and only if

$$z^* \geqslant \hat{z}$$

$$\leftrightarrow (1 - \alpha)\,\Delta x \geqslant \alpha\bar{x} - \bar{c} \tag{5}$$

$$\leftrightarrow \qquad \Delta x \geqslant \frac{i\hat{b}}{1 - \alpha},$$

by using (3).

(5) is easy to interpret; $(1 - \alpha)\,\Delta x$ is the additional income from the innovation. But the technological change helps the peasant escape indebtedness, thereby causing the landlord to lose his usurious earnings, $i\hat{b}$. Whether the innovation is desirable for the landlord or not depends on the magnitudes of these two terms.

Let Δx^* be the critical value of Δx which makes the innovation desirable. Then

$$\Delta x^* = \frac{i}{1 - \alpha}\hat{b}. \tag{6}$$

Figure 9.1 plots this relation.

Δx has to be above the critical frontier for the innovation to be profitable to the landlord. Also, the larger the initial indebtedness, i.e. $\hat{b}$, the larger the innovation has to be for the landlord to find its adoption worthwhile.

What the model demonstrates is that there exists a class of technological advances which would not be in the interest of the landlord to adopt. These are the smaller innovations and therefore the ones more easily available. If these are rejected, stagnation becomes a great likelihood. This is the essence of the hypothesis of stagnation in backward agriculture.

[4] The expression 'post-innovation' could be misleading. The way we have modelled we could have an economy with innovation or without. By 'post-innovation' is meant the former.

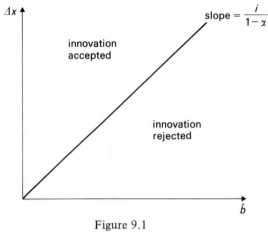

Figure 9.1

It may be noted in passing that

$$\frac{\partial \Delta x^*}{\partial i} > 0; \quad \frac{\partial \Delta x^*}{\partial \alpha} > 0; \quad \frac{\partial \Delta x^*}{\partial \hat{b}} > 0.$$

That is, the critical size of innovation, Δx^*, varies directly with i, α and $\hat{b}$. This is reasonable. Both i and $\hat{b}$ reflect earnings from usury. Naturally, the larger these are, the greater the loss in interest earnings (caused by innovation) and hence the bigger the innovation needed for the net income of the landlord to rise. α represents the other side of the coin. It is inversely related to the rental earnings of the landlord. Hence a larger α needs a larger Δx for the innovation to be worthwhile.

3   The debt-trap: by chance or by design?

One of the most interesting features of the model is the low-consumption trap. The *description* is realistic: poor people are often caught in a trap where indebtedness leads to indebtedness via the repayment burden and subsistence needs. But the *explanation* of the persistence of indebtedness suggested by the model is not adequate. As Newbery (1975) correctly observes, in this theory the trap exists without the exercise of any power on the part of the landlord. Hence it is very simple for the peasant to get out of the trap. A good year with a slightly better than usual harvest could set the peasant on his way to freedom.[5] Alternatively the peasant could get himself freed through a simple manoeuvre.

Return to the example on page 113. Recall that the peasant was borrowing 20 units every year. Now let him resolve to borrow 5 units less than usual in one year. He could manage this by consuming 5 units less that year or by getting alms from friends or by any other means.[6] In the next year his paddy balance after paying the rent (50) and repaying his debt (30) is 20. Thus to consume 30 he needs to borrow 10. Then in the following year his paddy balance is 30 and he needs no loan. Hence in all following years he can consume 50. Therefore his consumption pattern over time is

$$25 \qquad 30 \qquad 30 \qquad 50 \quad \ldots 50 \ldots \qquad \text{(stream 1)}$$

If on the other hand he chooses not to borrow less in any year his consumption pattern is

$$30 \qquad 30 \qquad 30 \qquad 30 \quad \ldots 30 \ldots \qquad \text{(stream 2)}$$

It seems reasonable to suppose that stream 1 is superior to stream 2. Hence if stream 2 persists we are forced to conclude that the peasant is abnormally short-sighted. Note that this argument does not depend on the fact that he cuts down his borrowing by *five* units. Even a one unit less debt in one year could ensure that he is on the road to freedom and higher consumption.

To model a peasant as an agent relentlessly maximising a well-specified utility function, as economists often do, is somewhat contrived. But that is not what is being done here to criticise the model. Instead, it is being argued that by a very simple and obvious move the peasant can (given the rules of the game specified in the model) get out of perpetual indebtedness and that it is surprising that he does not opt for this. Therefore we have two options, (a) assume that peasants do not have even a limited rationality, or (b) treat the model as inadequately specified.

Option (a) is not an uncommon assumption. The urban dweller is frequently heard criticising the peasant for his crass stupidity. The

---

[5] This, of course, relates to the question of stability of the initial equilibrium (Mukherji, 1975).

[6] Given that he was consuming at subsistence level, it may be difficult to conceive of him consuming 5 units less. But note that Bhaduri's (1982) assumption is not that stringent. He supposes that consumption is 'somewhere near the minimum subsistence level'. Also, to construct the kind of example I do below, it is not necessary that he consumes less. He simply has to borrow less from the landlord in one year. One way of doing this, while keeping consumption constant (which would allow us to construct a similar example), is to take a small interest-free loan from a relative.

sentiment of, 'If only he would have the sense to do this ...', is a very common one. I am, however, inclined to adopt option (b).

Though on the surface of it a peasant seems to be in the trap only because of a mishap or a lack of minimal rationality, his predicament is much more inevitable. Because of the abundance of unskilled labour, the options open to peasants are very poor and the landlords find it easy to keep their tenants pushed against a subsistence or near-subsistence consumption. In reality, if a peasant was about to free himself from indebtedness a landlord would raise i, or lower α or charge some arbitrary fines and push him back to the state of low consumption and bondage. Over time the peasant learns this and ceases to make efforts to free himself; and we see the pattern described in the initial equilibrium repeating itself inexorably from year to year. The situation described in the initial equilibrium is therefore accurate. But the suggestion that another equilibrium with a higher consumption was equally possible is erroneous.

Breman's (1974) excellent social anthropological study of southern Gujarat, in India, provides direct evidence supporting the above position. Breman studies the bonded labourers of the *Dubla* caste. For the *Dublas*, bondage usually begins at the time of marriage when they take a loan which they are never again able to repay. But Breman warns that to think of the initial loan as the *cause* of lifelong servitude is a mistake. '[T]he loan is concomitance rather than cause' (p. 194). To a casual observer it appears that with some effort the *Dubla* can repay and get out of bondage. But that impression is false.

> For that matter, the landlords have it in their own power to prevent repayment, and they do not shrink from wrongfully adding all kinds of expenses to the debt.... A striking instance is that of a master who went to the hut of a *dubla* servant to lecture him about his absence. On the way there he hurt his foot on a thorn, with the result that the *Dubla's* account was debited with 5 rupees, the amount the master had spent on medicines. Another *Dubla* entered into marriage at the same time as his brother, and together they obtained 275 rupees from an Anavil [i.e. *brahmin* of the landlord class]. When, after three months, one of them died, the master charged the remaining brother with the total amount. (p. 194)

Since occurrences like this are usual why do the *Dublas* get into such deals and what gives the landlords the power to keep them in such misery? Breman's findings are in accordance with the suggestions in the above paragraph. 'Without a doubt, the large majority wishes, for lack of a better alternative, to remain in servitude' (p. 194).

Once we accept that the peasant consumes $\bar{c}$ not because he is caught in a fragile trap but because the landlord exercises his power and keeps him there (a venture in which he succeeds only because the large supply of labour ensures that the peasant's alternative is no better than $\bar{c}$), a monkey wrench gets thrown into the stagnation hypothesis. If in the first situation the landlord keeps the peasant at $\bar{c}$, he could do the same after the innovation. He could do this by altering i or α, or by hurting his foot and imposing a fine on the tenant. Then his income would rise by the full measure of the innovation, i.e. Δx. Hence when a single landlord considers an innovation it is to his advantage to adopt it.

The above argument in no way precludes the possibility that if all landlords innovate together they all become worse off. This possibility arises if the innovation is such as to raise the landlords' demand for labour. Then when all landlords innovate the minimum consumption at which tenants are available could rise above $\bar{c}$ (because of competition among landlords for labour) and the landlords could be worse-off as a consequence. This does not, however, change the fact that *each* landlord would nevertheless prefer to adopt the innovation.

It may at first appear that the stagnation thesis can be defended by pointing out that the decision to innovate is a concerted decision of all landlords, and given the argument in the previous paragraph, innovation will be resisted. But this is not a robust proposition because if all landlords form a cartel to decide about innovation, surely they can use the same cartel to refrain from competition among themselves and maintain the peasants' consumption at $\bar{c}$.

Therefore it appears that we have to forgo either the assumption that, as long as the economic situation at large is unchanged, the landlord can ensure that the peasant is held at his initial income level or the stagnation hypothesis. If we eschew the former, then it becomes almost impossible to explain the persistence of the initial equilibrium. Since the initial equilibrium described by Bhaduri captures a particular reality well, I would be inclined to sacrifice his explanation of stagnation instead.

There remains, however, a slender third option of explaining stagnation by relating innovation to a slackening of the landlord's grip over the tenant. This is precisely what Newbery (1975) attempted and it is what we turn to presently.

4   Alternative explanations of stagnation

A share tenant, as we shall see in greater detail in the next chapter, has a tendency to put in a smaller amount of labour on his plot than the amount of labour expended by an owner working on his own plot. Newbery assumes that, to begin with, there is a fixed coefficient technology (or, alternatively, because of the simplicity of technique, the landlord can supervise the tenant's labour input) and so the tenant cannot under-supply labour. Now an innovation takes place which changes the production function to one where substitution between land and labour is possible (or, alternatively, the technique becomes more complex and the supervision of labour is no longer possible). Then the tenant, given the above-mentioned tendency of a share tenant, will put in a smaller amount of labour. It is then possible that innovation entails a net loss for the landlord and the landlord will resist innovation.

The above explanation is analytically sound but its purpose is clearly illustrative. What Newbery shows is how a technology, which allows for greater substitution possibilities or greater moral hazards, may be undesirable from the landlord's point of view. But to treat this as a hypothesis of non-innovation we must first adduce good reasons or evidence as to why innovation would lead to greater substitution possibilities. As long as this lacuna remains, this line of enquiry cannot be claimed to be completed.

Turning to empirical studies, there seems to be some agreement that one of the most critical obstacles to innovation has been the unavailability of credit (Byres, 1972; Griffin, 1974; Newbery, 1975). According to Griffin, farmers rarely reach the point where they have to decide whether to implement a new technique or not. Most new techniques entail a considerable amount of initial spending and, therefore, barring the very rich, credit availability is a prerequisite for innovation. Stagnation is then explained as a consequence of the widely observed credit shortage in the rural sector. Griffin goes on to argue that the landlords in primitive sectors are often small-scale farmers with hardly any access to credit. Hence, unlike in Bhaduri's (1973) model, the absence of innovation 'may be due not to the landowners' *reluctance* but to their *inability* to innovate' (p. 91, my italics). By this argument the few rich landowners with their own liquid money and greater access to urban credit are the only ones prone to innovate (Byres, 1972). This also implies that growth and equality are antagonistic in a primitive economy.

Credit is therefore a necessary condition for innovation but to the extent that even rich farmers in many areas show a penchant for the status quo, the need for further explanation remains;[7] and for that it may be useful to look beyond economics.

---

[7] Is it at all possible for a *single* theory to accommodate the experiences of countries so diverse as, for instance, India on the one hand and Brazil on the other? This popular debate

There are many sociological and anthropological studies of stagnation. It is true that the arguments of sociologists are often amorphous, providing lists of reasons instead of well-structured hypotheses. Theoretical economists, on the other hand, have been much more elegant. The fact that the latter have met with such limited success, makes it possible that in this case reality is not amenable to elegant explanations. While we ought to be wary of platitudes, it would be foolish to dismiss an explanation just because it is amorphous.

Sociological theories range from the commonsensical to the complex. To go into these systematically would be beyond both the scope of this monograph and its author's ability. Instead I briefly review Epstein's (1967) interesting hypothesis. Her analysis bears closely on the issues discussed above and it also exposes the economist's 'trained incapacity' to look at obvious but non-economic explanations.

Based on her study of rural South India, Epstein contrasts two alternative systems for organising economic activities in a rural economy: the *customary system of rewards and obligations* (CSRO) and *the contractual system*. The contractual system is akin to what economists typically concern themselves with. In this, exchanges take place after agreement between the agents concerned and the agents are free to weigh the benefits and costs of the exchange before agreeing to it. The agreements or contracts cover relatively short periods and are therefore responsive to changing supplies and demands. In the CSRO there are agreements given by custom. For instance, a 'peasant master' could have an obligation to provide subsistence or a fixed 'customary' payment to his 'Untouchable labourers' who in turn have fixed chores to perform. The system of payments and duties could even be hereditary, being passed on from generation to generation.

While economists have concentrated on the contractual system – with some through habit believing that that is the only one existing – Epstein argues that in primitive societies the customary system is widely prevalent. She shows that this system is fundamentally inimical to innovation and thus societies with a greater dependence on the CSRO are more prone to stagnate. This is not difficult to see. Typically, for a new technology to be implemented effort is required not only from the landlord, but also from his tenants. To take Epstein's

---

appears to me to be basically a semantic one, since it is not at all clear as to what is meant by a 'single' theory. It is likely that once the terms used in the debate are properly defined, it will either be trivially true that a single theory can be used, or that it cannot. Only in fairly remote senses can this debate be thought of as a substantial one (see Basu, 1981).

own example, the adoption of the Japanese method of paddy cultivation in South India meant that the workers would have to undertake 'a more laborious way of spacing plants properly'. But the tenants or workers have neither any customary obligation to provide the additional effort nor any incentive to do so, since under the CSRO the landlord cannot pay them more. Similarly in this system, landlords do not have the incentive to adopt labour-saving innovations since they have to make their customary payments anyway.

Epstein gives many examples of the CSRO thwarting innovation. Thus in the village of Wangala when the Agricultural Department 'tried to introduce a cheap and most efficient weeding hook, the use of which would have considerably reduced the cultivation labour required, Wangala farmers were not prepared to employ the new tool'. This is readily explicable in terms of 'hereditary relationships' which 'make them responsible for providing a minimum of subsistence for their [fixed number of] Untouchable labourers' (p. 239).

What is interesting is the contrast between Wangala and another village Dalena where customary relations were weak. Dalena was much more receptive to innovations because its inhabitants had the flexibility to work out new agreements which would make the innovations beneficial to all those who would have to provide more effort.

While there are loose ends in Epstein's theory, it would be wrong to confuse it with the more commonplace belief that peasants do not like innovations because innovation implies change.[8] Her analysis is sophisticated and it would be interesting to try and give it more rigorous shape.

5 Remarks

The aim of this chapter was to discuss rural stagnation, but there was another side objective – to emphasise that competition works *within* certain limitations, defined by custom, barriers to entry and the law. As Sen (1981, p. 166) writes 'market forces can be seen as operating *through* a system of legal relations (ownership rights, contractual obligations, legal exchanges, etc.)'. Agrarian relations are governed by a combination of market forces, custom and power. Competition and subsistence needs determine the minimum consumption acceptable to a peasant, irrespective of the nature of the contract. And it is the

[8] Compare Mendras' (1970) quizzical observation explaining the absence of innovation in primitive agriculture: 'the peasant really accepts an innovation only if it is taught to him by his father along with the most traditional techniques' (p. 37).

structure of power which tends to ensure that he gets just this minimum, though custom may tamper with this outcome. What Mill argues in his chapter on share tenancy (Mill, 1948, Book II, chapter IV) is close to this, though he is not as definite in his views as Johnson (1950) makes him out to be.

In chapter 12 an equilibrium model of interlinked markets is constructed. It is argued in chapter 13 that in such models power does play a small role. But before going to interlinked markets we examine the nature of its components in isolation in the next two chapters.

There were two key elements in the stagnation hypothesis: tenancy and credit. In this chapter there were several comments on tenancy. The literature on this subject is, however, vast and theoretically advanced. Chapter 10 gives an outline of the traditional view of tenancy and discusses some of the recent advances.

In this chapter credit played an important role but the interest rate was treated as exogenously fixed. The first question in the analysis of usury concerns the determination of interest rates. Another question which relates to the discussion in the previous section is: if credit shortage is what is strangling innovation, then why do money-lenders not lend money for innovation and siphon back some of the returns through interest charges? What is it that prevents such free flow of credit and fragments the credit market? These are the kinds of issues taken up in chapter 11.

CHAPTER 10

Tenancy and Efficiency

1 Forms of agricultural land tenure

A person owning some agricultural land can organise production in a number of ways. He may, if it is a small plot, depend entirely on his family for the required labour. The *family farm*[1] is particularly suitable where the joint family system is prevalent and where labour-market transactions costs are high.

Secondly, he could act as an *owner-operator* (or a capitalist farmer) and hire workers at a fixed wage from the labour market to work on his farm. The analysis of this unit is analogous to the standard theory of the firm.

In both these cases the owner of the land also acts as an entrepreneur. If he wishes to absolve himself of this responsibility, he could opt for a number of different tenurial arrangements of which the two best known ones are *fixed-rent tenancy* and *share tenancy*. In the former, the tenant takes charge of cultivating the land and pays the landlord a fixed amount in each period. In share tenancy the tenant pays the landlord a fixed proportion of the output. These broad features can be coupled with a variety of specificities. For instance, in share tenancy the landlord may or may not share the costs of inputs (Adams and Rask, 1968) and he may or may not specify in the contract the amount of labour the tenant has to use on the land (Cheung, 1968).

While each of these institutions are well understood once it is assumed to exist, why a particular tenurial system comes into existence remains an open and a controversial question. This problem is particularly acute with share tenancy, which is perhaps the most interesting land-tenure system. Not only has this institution existed

---

[1] Two of the best-known analyses of this are Chayanov (1966) and Nakajima (1970).

124

in many parts of the world for many years,[2] it has inspired a vast amount of theoretical research.[3]

An empirical solution of the problem of why share tenancy exists is made difficult by the role of history. It is quite possible that share tenancy emerged in a certain region for economic reasons; but having persisted for many years, it became a part of society and continues to persist though its economic rationale may have disappeared. But let us begin by assuming that share tenancy exists, whatever the reasons, and examine its effects on the use of inputs, production and efficiency.

2 Share tenancy

Throughout the eighteenth and nineteenth centuries, share tenancy was a subject which inspired passionate responses, whether favourable or unfavourable. Thus to the Marquis of Mirabeau share tenancy was a 'deplorable method of cultivation, the daughter of necessity and mother of misery'. Arthur Young described it as follows: 'This subject may be easily despatched; for there is not one word to be said in favour of the practice and a thousand arguments can be used against it.' These are quoted from Higgs (1894) whose own views on share tenancy are the opposite. This is obvious from his description of the ethos of a region where share tenancy was prevalent: 'The standard of morality is high, and a sentiment of religion is generally diffused. The very few cases of illegitimacy which exist are viewed with reprobation.'

Marshall's analysis of share tenancy or *metayage*[4] is lucid and simple.[5] Assume that a landlord gives a plot of land to a tenant on the agreement that he must give the landlord fraction r of the total

---

[2] It existed in France for 500 years beginning in the thirteenth century. It is currently prevalent in many less developed economies.

[3] Smith (1776), Marshall (1920), Johnson (1950), Cheung (1968), Stiglitz (1974a), Newbery (1975a, 1977), Currie (1981), Rakshit (1982), to mention just a few.

[4] The French word *metayage* was used originally to describe a share tenancy in which the output is shared in halves, though now it is treated more or less as a synonym for share tenancy in general.

[5] For Marshall's analysis of tenancy see book VI chapter 10 of the 1920 edition of his *Principles*. While the model that he presented, which I discuss below, is indeed very simple, Marshall showed a remarkable awareness of the many pitfalls which one has to avoid in modelling share tenancy. Bliss and Stern (1982) rightly assert that Marshall had anticipated many of the subsequent developments and that much of Cheung's (1968) criticism of Marshall is untenable. It would, however, be unfair to overlook that Cheung (in footnote 2) did draw our attention to Marshall's footnote 2 (book VI, chapter 10, p. 536).

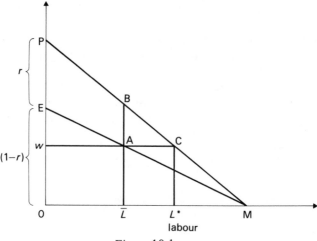

Figure 10.1

output each year. Assume also that labour is the only factor of production and that the tenant is not allowed to lease in any more land. In figure 10.1, PM depicts the marginal product curve of labour. Let EM be so drawn that its height at each point is $(1-r)$th the height of the marginal product curve of labour. This curve shows the additional amount the tenant earns with each additional unit of labour use. This will be referred to as the *marginal earnings curve*.

Now assume – and this is a rather strong assumption – that the opportunity cost of labour is fixed at w (which is expressed in real terms). This may be justified in two ways: by supposing that the subjective trade-off between labour and leisure is fixed or that there exists a labour market from where the tenant can always hire and sell labour at the fixed wage w. Given these assumptions, it is easy to see that the tenant will use $0\bar{L}$ units of labour (irrespective of whether it is his own or hired).[6] He will have a gross income of $0EA\bar{L}$ and the landlord will get a rent of PEAB.

Note that if the tenant had sold $0\bar{L}$ labour on the labour market (the only option open to him) he would have earned $wA\bar{L}0$. Hence his *net* income is EAw. Clearly, as long as the net income is positive it is worthwhile for him to be a share tenant. I spell this out because it is the crux of Cheung's criticism of Marshall. But before turning to that it is useful to take note of a few aspects of the Marshallian model.

[6] From here on I speak *as though* he uses his own labour. I do this only so that the language does not become too cumbersome.

First, observe that if the landlord had instead acted as an owner-operator, directly hiring labour from the labour market, he would be employing $0L^*$ units of labour and making a profit of PCw. Not only would he be better off but the total production in the economy would be more. This was the basis of Marshall's and even Adam Smith's critique of share tenancy: it is an institution which results in suboptimal use of inputs. At this point, the economist's perennial dilemma raises its head. Should we, given the above analysis, recommend that share tenancy be discouraged? Or, should we adhere to the assumption that individuals are rational, and search for the explanation which eluded Marshall and which makes share tenancy the best tenurial system for an individual who has chosen it? Newbery (1977) explicitly pursued the second line: 'If landlords and tenants choose a share contract in preference to a fixed-rent contract it can reasonably be inferred that a share contract has advantages which outweigh its drawbacks' (p. 585). I return to the question of the choice of share tenancy later.

In the above analysis it was assumed that a tenant cannot lease land from more than one landlord. If we relax this assumption a serious problem can arise because it is worthwhile for each tenant to lease in as much land as possible. This is easy to see. For every given amount of labour input, it is profitable for the tenant to rent more land and spread the labour over it as long as the marginal product of land is positive. Hence at equilibrium the marginal product of land would get driven down to zero (Johnson, 1950). It is to avoid this absurd conclusion that we assumed that the tenant cannot rent land from more than one person. While I continue to use this assumption in the ensuing analysis, all we really need to assume is that there is a restriction on the maximum amount of land that a person can rent.

Finally, let us return to a problem already noted. At equilibrium the share tenant earns more than he would earn by hiring out an equivalent amount of labour at the market wage w. Hence, there would exist an excess supply of people wanting to be share tenants. From this Cheung inferred that, (a) the above situation cannot be described as an equilibrium, and (b) the landlord can extract more from his tenant without fearing that the latter will desert him. In particular, he argued that a landlord would typically specify in the contract the amount of labour that is to be used on the land. Before questioning these, let us go along with Cheung and formalise a model with the assumption that input contracts can be enforced without cost.

Assume, as before, that a landlord leases out his land to a tenant who does not have any other land. The output, X, from this land depends on the amount of labour used, L:

$$X = X(L) \qquad X'(L) \geqslant 0, \ X''(L) < 0. \tag{1}$$

Let r be the landlord's share of the output. The landlord chooses r and also specifies the amount of labour input, L. He must, however, make sure that the tenant does not do worse than what he would do elsewhere, that is, $(1-r)X(L)$ must be at least as much as wL. Otherwise he would quit. Therefore the landlord's problem is:

$$\underset{\{r,L\}}{\text{Max}} \ rX(L),$$

subject to $\qquad\qquad\qquad\qquad\qquad\qquad\qquad\qquad\qquad\qquad\quad$ (2)

$$(1-r)X(L) = wL.$$

Though the constraint is actually a weak inequality, I write it as an equality because we know that the landlord would not give the tenant more than just enough to prevent him from quitting (since in this model, unlike in the Marshallian one, the landlord has the means to ensure this).

Forming the Lagrangian

$$Z = rX(L) - \lambda[wL - (1-r)X(L)],$$

we get the first-order condition by differentiating Z with respect to r, L and λ, and setting these equal to zero.

$$\frac{\partial Z}{\partial r} = X(L) - \lambda X(L) = 0$$

$$\frac{\partial Z}{\partial L} = rX'(L) - \lambda w + \lambda(1-r)X'(L) = 0$$

$$\frac{\partial Z}{\partial \lambda} = wL - (1-r)X(L) = 0.$$

These imply

$$\lambda = 1 \tag{3}$$

$$X'(L) = w \tag{4}$$

$$r = \frac{X(L) - wL}{X(L)}. \tag{5}$$

Since $X'(L) = w$, share tenancy of the kind envisaged by Cheung implies an 'optimal' use of labour. In fact, if we solve the constraint in (2) for r and substitute it in the objective function, the landlord's maximisation problem, (2), can be rewritten as

$$\underset{\{L\}}{\text{Max}}\, X(L) - wL.$$

But this is the objective function of the capitalist farmer. Thus a landlord who lets out his land to a share tenant with an input contract earns the same profit as a capitalist farmer.

A diagrammatic representation of the equilibrium r and L is revealing. Let PM in figure 10.2 be the marginal product curve of labour, as in figure 10.1. Since (4) and (5) comprise a recursive system, we can first determine the value of L without paying any attention to r. From (4) it is clear that $0L^*$ labour will be used. From (2) we know that r must be such that the share tenant's gross income, i.e. $(1-r)X(L)$, equals wL. Hence $E^*DL^*0 = wCL^*0$, which implies $E^*A^*w = CA^*D$. Therefore the landlord's income PCDE* may alternatively be represented by PwC. This has an interesting implication. Consider hypothetically that the landowner had given the same land out to a tenant on a *fixed*-rent basis? What is the maximum rent that he would be able to charge? The answer is PwC.

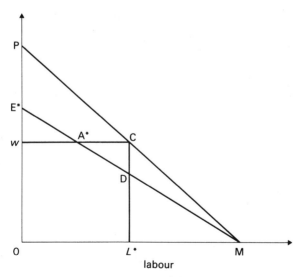

Figure 10.2

This is quite obvious. Note first that a fixed rent does not affect the marginal product curve of labour. Thus a tenant paying a fixed rent will apply $0L^*$ labour (if he does not quit) no matter how much the rent is. His income will be PCL^*0 *minus* the rent. Since the tenant has the option of quitting and working as a wage labourer, the minimum income he would find acceptable is wCL^*0. Thus the rent can be at most PwC. The landlord (being a profit-maximiser) would therefore be charging a rent of PwC if he decided to give out his land on a fixed-rent basis.

Hence share tenancy *a la* Cheung and fixed-rent tenancy are indistinguishable. This is the main problem with Cheung's analysis. One is left wondering whether it is at all a theory of *share* tenancy. Also, if the two systems are identical, why would any landlord opt for share tenancy with its complex contract and attendant problem of enforcing a labour input agreement which the tenant would prefer to violate?

Another problem relates to the determination of r. Cheung treats r as the outcome of the landlord's profit-maximisation exercise. Now a curious empirical feature of share tenancy is the remarkable tendency for this share proportion to cluster around 0.5 (Bardhan, 1983). This would be rather difficult to explain in Cheung's framework[7] where r depends on the nature of the production function, $X(.)$, and the value of w and would therefore vary between regions and also from one landlord to another. It seems more reasonable to treat r as given by institution or custom and L as the endogenously determined variable, exactly as was the case in Marshall's analysis. In fact, Marshall's model is probably closer to reality than that of Cheung.

Cheung's initial dissatisfaction with Marshall, based on the fact that in Marshall's model the tenant earns more than the opportunity cost of labour, is misplaced. Cheung argues that this feature of the Marshallian model makes it inconsistent with an equilibrium. This arises from treating an equilibrium as identical to an absence of excess supply (and demand). This is not at all necessary, as modern fix-price analysis demonstrates. As a purely logical exercise suppose that a landlord has only one option: (he is required by law) to let his land out to a share tenant; and that labour input contracts are impossible to enforce. In that case, even if the landlord chooses r to maximise profit, and gives out his land to a tenant, the tenant will be earning a surplus. This means that there will be other people

---

[7] Bell and Zusman (1976) have tried to explain this by setting up the landlord–tenant interaction as a bargaining game.

offering to become his tenant. There is an excess supply of tenants. This would nevertheless be an equilibrium and persist because the landlord in this case has no instrument to extract the surplus and make the tenant's position sufficiently unattractive to wipe out the excess supply of tenants. Excess supply is not, therefore, automatically inconsistent with the idea of an equilibrium. We have encountered excess supply equilibria in chapter 7 and in chapter 8.

If we do accept the Marshallian analysis, the important question which arises is why a landlord does not switch to fixed-rent tenancy or capitalist farming. Stiglitz (1974a) and Newbery (1977) have tried to answer this in terms of uncertainty and risk. Suppose first that the only kind of risk is in production. Output depends, not only on the inputs, but on the weather. In the owner-operator system the entire risk is born by the landowner because labourers earn a *fixed* wage and the owner earns the residual. In a fixed-rent system the tenant bears the entire risk. Thus, given risk-aversion, share tenancy may be optimal since it allows for risk-sharing.

Newbery, however, proved that if a landlord was free to partition his land between fixed-rent tenancy and capitalist farming then, by a suitable partition, he could always earn as much as he would by giving the entire land to a share tenant. Thus the domination of share tenancy seems to be threatened even in this case. There are, nevertheless, two arguments that we can fall back on. First, Newbery established his result under the assumption of constant returns to scale. So it is possible that if there are increasing returns to scale, then a partitioning of land may turn out to be sufficiently inefficient to make it unattractive. So production risk coupled with increasing returns may be a possible explanation of sharecropping.

Secondly, Newbery has shown that if along with production risk, labour markets are risky then even with constant returns an economy with only fixed-rent tenancy and (risky) wage contracts would not achieve production efficiency. Share tenancy is essential.[8]

There have also been some attempts to explain share contracts as a 'screening device' in a market where prospective tenants are endowed with different amounts of entrepreneurial skills but these are not observable. One such attempt was by Hallagan (1978). While Hallagan, it appears to me, fails to establish what he claims, he constructs a framework which is interesting and has the potential for further development.

---

[8] See Bardhan (1983) for a number of other explanations for the existence of share tenancy.

3   Screening and entrepreneurial ability

It has been argued by some that tenurial arrangements comprise an 'agricultural ladder' in which the individuals with the greatest entrepreneurial ability become fixed-rent tenants, those with no such ability become wage-earning workers, and the intermediate cases become share tenants (Spillman, 1919, see also Rao, 1971). This suggests that different tenurial arrangements may be devices for screening individuals with different degrees of entrepreneurial skills.

Let us assume, following Hallagan (1978), that society consists of landowners and workers and each worker possesses one unit of labour and a certain amount of entrepreneurial ability, E, which can range from 0 to 1. Land comes in indivisible units and each landlord possesses one or more units of these. Each unit of land has to be combined with exactly one unit of labour for it to be productive. The total output, X, from one unit of land depends on the amount of entrepreneurial effort that goes in (i.e. after one unit of labour has been put in):

$$X = f(E) \qquad f(0) > 0, \; f'(E) > 0, \tag{6}$$

$f(0)$ is the output when one unit of labour is used with no entrepreneurship.

The landlords know the production function but cannot distinguish workers in terms of the amount of entrepreneurial skills they possess. It is also assumed that workers use their entrepreneurial skills only if that helps increase their earnings.[9]

Assume that to start with there is only a wage-contract system. That is, there is a wage W (assumed to be less than $f(0)$) at which landlords employ workers. In a wage system it is clearly not in the workers' interest to apply their entrepreneurial skills. Hence, using Y and Z to denote the landlord's income per unit of land and the worker's income, respectively, we have:

$$Y = f(0) - W \tag{7}$$

$$Z = W. \tag{8}$$

Is this an equilibrium?[10] The answer is no. In fact, there is no wage

---

[9] More explicitly, a worker tries to maximise his earnings and between two options offering identical earnings he prefers the one requiring a smaller use of his entrepreneurial skills. In other words, his preferences are *lexicographic*.

[10] The notion of equilibrium used here is that of *contractual* equilibrium which is defined as a set of contracts such that no other contract exists by which a landlord could increase his earnings.

which would bring about an equilibrium. This can be shown by demonstrating how, starting from this situation, at least one agent can improve his condition. This a landlord can do by offering a rental contract, i.e. a worker has to pay the landlord a fixed amount of rent, R, for using each unit of land and any output above this accrues to the worker.

Since $f(1) > f(0)$, there must exist a real number R which satisfies the following inequalities:

$$R \geqslant f(0) - W \tag{9}$$

$$f(1) - R \geqslant W. \tag{10}$$

Let a landlord offer a rental contract with R satisfying the *strict* inequalities in (9) and (10). Then some workers, definitely those with $E = 1$, will prefer to take up such a rental contract (and earn $f(1) - R$) rather than a wage contract. The landlord also benefits from this since $R > f(0) - W$.

Defining E^* as $f(E^*) - R = W$, it is clear that workers would, on their own, segregate themselves, with those possessing $E \leqslant E^*$ prefering wage contracts and the others prefering rental contracts.

At this point, Hallagan overlooks an important condition. Consider a system in which wage *and* rental contracts exist. Would any (W, R) satisfying (9) and (10) suffice? Clearly no, because if (W, R) is such that (9) is a strict inequality, then why should any landlord offer a wage contract? Hence if we find both wage and rental contracts prevailing, then the following condition must hold:

$$R = f(0) - W. \tag{11}$$

This implies that $f(E) - R > W$, if $E > 0$. Therefore, barring the completely unendowed workers (i.e. those with $E = 0$), all would prefer rental contracts. And the unendowed workers would be indifferent between wage and rental contracts.

The interesting proposition which emerges from the above analysis is that if the entrepreneurial abilities of workers vary, then a fixed-rental system is bound to emerge; and it will be the dominant tenurial system.[11]

Contrary to Hallagan's claim, this framework cannot explain the emergence of share tenancy or the 'agricultural ladder'. Actually, the 'agricultural ladder hypothesis' as discussed by Spillman is a very different idea from the one explored by Hallagan. Spillman's paper is a rather Shakespearean account of the *stages* of a farmer's life. It

[11] A recent formal model of tenancy and screening – on which I am as yet unable to comment – is that by Allen (1982).

focuses more on the development of farmers' skills over time than on inter-farmer differences in one situation. More relevant are the findings of Brown and Atkinson (1981) and to the extent that they do find a correlation between entrepreneurial skills and tenure systems as discussed in the beginning of this section, there remains a need for constructing a theory which would explain this.

4 Scale, productivity and tenancy

An empirical observation about agriculture noted in many studies – Bauer (1946) for Malaysia, Sen (1962) for India and Okhawa (1972) for Japan – is the alleged *inverse relation* between farm size and productivity. These studies claim that in general the output per acre decreases with the size of the farm. The standard explanation is in terms of variability in the cost of labour. It is argued that a family working on its own land imputes a smaller cost to labour than the market wage. Hence small farms, which typically employ family labour, use more labour per unit of land than large farms with hired labour. Sen (1975) calls this a 'labour-based explanation' and differentiates it from a 'fertility-based explanation'. The latter asserts that small farms produce more not because more labour and other inputs are used but because the land is more fertile. In going from the empirical observation of the inverse relation to policy prescriptions, it is important to distinguish between the 'labour' and 'fertility' explanations, because it is quite likely that the causalities in these two run in the opposite directions. For instance, one plausible fertility-based argument is that more fertile land means a higher family income. This encourages larger families, which in the long-run implies a greater subdivision of land. So it is the greater fertility of land which causes farms to be smaller.

The reason why I discuss the inverse relation here is in order to comment on an interesting connection it has with tenancy. A large number of works in tenancy treat the *number* of tenants to whom a landlord leases out his land as a 'choice' variable, that is, an instrument which the landlord *chooses* in order to maximise his earnings (Bardhan and Srinivasan, 1971; Bagchi, 1973; also, Cheung, 1968).

We have already seen that in share tenancy there is a tendency on the part of the tenant to use less labour than the landlord would like. Signing contracts is not a sufficient guarantor of the landlord being able to extract this additional labour. One way of achieving this, therefore, may be through a suitable parcelisation of land. Consider a situation – not at all uncommon – where there are no labour markets and so the tenant has, for all practical purposes, no other options, if he leaves his present job. Then the landlord by allotting sufficiently small pieces of land to his tenants may be able to force them to work harder to ensure their survival: 'If the unit is small and the sharecropper is restricted in outside earnings, he must apply his labor and that of his family until he has achieved at least some minimum level of income' (Johnson, 1950, p. 119). The landlord being aware of this, his choice of size of farm to be leased out to each tenant would depend not only on the degree of the returns to scale but also on his desire to ensure that more labour is applied on each acre of his land.[12]

This hypothesis, apart from being of interest in itself, provides a new fertility-based argument for the inverse relation. Let us describe a plot of land on which a tenant by putting in all his labour can just extract a subsistence income for himself as a *subsistence plot*.[13] We have just seen that, given some assumptions, a landlord will parcel out his land in subsistence plots. It follows that a landlord with more fertile land would lease out smaller-sized farms. Thus the more fertile land would get more fragmented. This provides an explanation of the inverse relation in regions where tenancy is prevalent.

To conclude, it is worthwhile emphasising that the above hypothesis is not self-evident. In fact, it requires some rather strong assumptions. Consider the assumption that a tenant will work as much as necessary in order to earn his subsistence. This is treated as axiomatic by many (e.g. Johnson, 1950; and, more emphatically, Bagchi, 1973). I feel, however, that this view stems from a mistaken conception of leisure – a tendency to equate leisure with luxury. In reality, for people working long hours at low wages, leisure is an essential requirement. Hence subsistence (notwithstanding the common practice among economists) should really not be defined as a certain level of consumption, but as a downward sloping curve in the consumption-leisure space. Hence the claim that as the plot size is decreased and the tenant is impoverished he will work harder to reach a fixed level of consumption is not necessarily true. The value of leisure will also rise and he may aim for a different point on the subsistence *locus*.[14]

---

[12] This argument is formalised in Basu and Roy (1982) and Bose (1982).

[13] I am assuming that r is exogenously given.

[14] This conclusion is reinforced if we assume that a worker's productivity depends on his consumption in the same way as in chapter 8.

CHAPTER 11

Isolation and Usury: An Analysis of Rural Credit Markets

1 The lender's risk hypothesis

The unusually high interest rates in many backward agricultural regions have been the source of some puzzlement to economists. Adding to this puzzle is the fact that these rates can take on an unbelievably wide range of values, often within the same area. In one region of the Philippines – a study[1] shows 15 per cent of the rice farmers paid interest charges over 200 per cent, while 20 per cent of them took loans at a zero interest.[2] These figures for the Philippines are by no means exceptional. The experience is much the same in other LDCs, particularly in south-east Asia (Wharton, 1962; Bailey, 1964; Reserve Bank of India, 1977; Rahman, 1979).

An important question which arises is why arbitrage between sectors does not lead to more homogeneous and lower rural interest rates. Suppose that interest in the rural sector is 120 per cent and it is 10 per cent in the organised urban credit market. The question is, why does our *homo œconomicus* not take this opportunity to earn some easy money by borrowing in the urban market and lending in the rural one? If enough people indulge in such arbitrage between the two sectors, then the rural interest would fall and the urban one would rise till parity is restored.

The fact that this does not happen and the interest rate differentials continue to persist calls for explanation. One of the more traditional

[1] The study is by Jose Gapud and is referred to in Griffin (1974).
[2] In real terms this turns out to be around 16 per cent because of implicit charges (Griffin 1974), but clearly that does not destroy the observation that interest rates can take a wide range of values.

136

explanations is the lender's risk hypothesis (see Tun Wai, 1958; Bottomley, 1975; Raj, 1979). This asserts that moneylenders in backward regions face a positive risk of default and once this is taken into account, the *effective* interest rate turns out to be no higher than its counterpart in the organised sector.

To formalise, suppose that a moneylender finds that, on an average fraction q of his loan is not repaid. Then if the lender gives a loan of Rs. L at interest rate i, his expected earning (assuming that no interest is paid on what is defaulted) is

$$(1 + i)(1 - q)L - L.$$

The effective interest rate, d, is got by dividing this by L:

$$d = i(1 - q) - q.$$

Clearly, if $q > 0$, $d < i$. Arbitrage between the sectors would ensure that at equilibrium d is equal to the interest rate in the urban market. Hence, given a positive risk of default, i.e. $q > 0$, we would find i to be above the urban interest rate. Thus the interest rate differentials would persist at equilibrium.

Consider an example in which $q = 0.5$ and the organised sector interest rate is 10 per cent. Hence at equilibrium $d = 0.1$. Inserting these values in the above equation we get $i = 1.2$, i.e. 120 per cent. Therefore to sustain an effective rate of 10 per cent, the actual rate has to be 120 per cent. This is the crux of the hypothesis: the observed high rural interest rates are illusory.

This hypothesis can be useful in some situations. But as a general proposition it is quite inadequate, because in these transactions, thanks to the personalised nature of rural markets, the borrower typically cannot get away without paying. Quoting an important Indian rural credit survey, Raj (1979) points out that moneylenders considered 'only 10 per cent or less' of the loans they gave to agriculturists as 'doubtful'. Risk cannot therefore explain more than a very small amount of the premium on rural interest. For a fuller explanation it is important – as Bottomley (1964) himself points out – to take account of the monopolistic nature of credit markets.

2   Monopolistic markets

The existence of 'personalised relation' between the borrower and the lender is a reflection of the fact that each lender lends only to those over whom he has some control. As Bottomley (1964) correctly observes, the village moneylender's 'monopoly power' arises from his intimate knowledge of the borrower's circumstances. 'It is, therefore, very difficult for a potential competitor to break into a local money market if he comes from another district...' (p. 433).

To formalise a polar case of this suppose that a borrower (who is a price-taker) can get loans only from one moneylender; and let his loan demand function be

$$L = L(i) \qquad L'(i) < 0, \tag{1}$$

where L is the amount of credit and i the interest rate. Let the inverse function of (1) be as follows

$$i = i(L) \qquad i'(L) < 0. \tag{2}$$

This is just another way of looking at the same relation. This demand function for loans is depicted by AD in figure 11.1.

The personalised relation ensures that there is no defaulting and the moneylender chooses L (with i then being given by (2)) so as to maximise his interest earning. Assuming that he has the option of investing his money elsewhere and earning an interest of r on it, his objective function is as follows:

$$\underset{\{L\}}{\text{Max}} \; Li(L) - Lr.$$

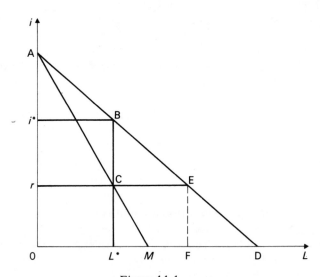

Figure 11.1

The first-order condition of this problem is:

$$r = i(L) + i'(L) L. \tag{3}$$

The left-hand side is the marginal cost of giving loans and the right-hand side (which is equal to $[\partial Li(L)]/\partial L$) represents marginal revenue. Hence (3) is the familiar condition: $MC = MR$, and the equilibrium just described is the standard equilibrium in a monopolistic market. Denoting the chosen values as L^* and i^*, this equilibrium is depicted in a familiar diagram in figure 11.1 where AM represents the marginal revenue curve.

In case the moneylender has access to the urban credit market, r will be the interest rate that can be fetched there and this model would explain why rural interest charges are typically above the urban rate. Also, since we argued that the rural credit economy is fragmented into little monopolistic islands – each one like the one just discussed – the rural economy itself will be characterised by a whole array of interest rates. This is well in keeping with the existing evidence as discussed in the beginning of this chapter.[3]

The above model, however, is open to two important criticisms. First, the analysis presumes that the borrower always has enough money to repay a loan. In reality, given the widespread poverty of rural borrowers, this is unrealistic. Often at the time of repayment the borrower finds himself short of the required cash. He is then forced to repay a part of the debt in terms of whatever he has – land, utensils or even labour. These assets, being odd bits and ends, usually are not marketable. This introduces a new twist to the problem because now the borrower's and the lender's valuation of the asset can be different, and the lender may enter the credit market with the express purpose of acquiring assets kept as security. This is the line pursued in Bhaduri (1977), Basu (1983b) and in other works, like Prasad (1974), Rao (1980) and Borooah (1980). In the next section, I briefly develop some of these ideas.

The second criticism is applicable to monopoly analysis in general, but assumes greater significance in the present context. Return to figure 11.1 and the equilibrium described therein. The lender earns a profit of $BCri^*$. What we do not always realise is that this is not the maximum profit that a monopolist (in this case, the lender) can extract from the buyers (here, the borrower). He could do better if

---

[3] Some have argued effectively (e.g. Bottomley, 1975; Chandarvarkar, 1965) that in reality both lender's risk and the lender's monopoly power act in concert to push up interest rates. Hence the models of sections 1 and 2 of this chapter work in conjunction and are not *alternative* explanations of reality.

he offered the borrower 'all-or-nothing' contracts. It is very important to appreciate this fully.

So far the demand function for loan, i.e. (2), was treated as a 'primitive'. I shall now *derive* it from more basic assumptions. Suppose that the borrower takes loans only in order to invest.[4] Let R denote the total earnings from investment and L be, as before, the total amount of loan. Assume

$$R = R(L) \qquad R'(L) > 0, \ R''(L) < 0.$$

Just like a producer employs workers up to the point where wage equals (the value of) marginal product of labour, similarly here the borrower, given i, chooses L so that i equals 'marginal earnings' from L (i.e. $\partial R/\partial L$). Thus the marginal earnings curve represents the demand curve for loans and the area under this curve is equal to the total earnings of the borrower. Hence the demand curve for loans is given by

$$i = R'(L).$$

This then is the equation of curve AD in figure 11.1.

Now suppose that the moneylender–monopolist considers giving a loan of a certain amount, say $0L^*$, and asks from the borrower for the maximum amount he is willing to pay for this. Clearly he will be willing to pay up to $0ABL^*$.[5] Given that the lender (as assumed earlier) has the option of earning an interest of r elsewhere, his net income will be $ABCr$.

If the lender adopts this strategy of extracting the maximum that the borrower is willing to pay, it is clear that he does best by giving loans equal to $0F$. His net income is then AEr. Since $AEr > BCri^*$, by this strategy the monopolist earns a larger profit than he would by behaving like a textbook monopolist.

This raises some rather fundamental questions about our standard monopoly analysis. These have been written about elsewhere and I briefly comment on them before returning to the problem at hand. What the above discussion makes clear is that the textbook monopolist's equilibrium describes the outcome of a market where, (a)

---

[4] Though I demonstrate the proposition under the assumption that loans are taken for production only, the argument is not difficult to generalise, particularly if one has some familiarity with Hicksian consumer's surplus analysis (e.g. Hicks, 1956).

[5] The offer is the following: here is a loan of $0L^*$. How much will you pay for it if the alternative is getting no loan? Faced with such an 'all-or-nothing' offer the answer will obviously be $0ABL^*$ given that if he gets no loan he earns zero. Remember that this is a monopoly and there is, therefore, no one else the borrower can turn to for credit. It is also assumed that borrowers do not give credit to others.

there is one seller who faces a given demand curve, and (b) he is allowed to use only (what may be called) a 'price strategy', that is, he can fix any price and sell but he cannot impose any other charges. This second assumption is crucial though it is seldom made explicit.

Since by monopoly we mean a market satisfying (a), and since in reality the seller is free to adopt any strategy, it is not clear why in monopolistic markets the outcome should always be as suggested in textbooks. And indeed often it is not. Note that one way in which a monopolist can extract the maximum amount is to impose first a flat charge and, once a person has paid this, to allow him to buy at the *competitive* price. For example, in figure 11.1, if the lender charges the borrower a flat amount equal to AEr and then allows him to take as much loan as he wants at interest rate r, he would be recovering from the borrower the maximum feasible amount. The existence of 'entry charges' or 'membership charges' to certain chain stores or commercial cine clubs could be interpreted as attempts to do precisely this. This same motivation leads to 'tie-in sales' (Burstein, 1960) in which the monopolist sells at the competitive price but tries to tie up these sales with other transactions and to recover the flat charge from these other transactions.

If we believe that in reality monopolists do behave as traditional theory suggests, then some serious open-ended questions remain regarding why they behave in such a manner. It may be argued that monopolists do not offer 'all-or-nothing' contracts or impose flat charges and recover the full surplus because this requires intimate knowledge of the buyers' needs and demand. Though this may be true, it is not clear why they would switch to a 'price strategy', i.e. (b), instead of some other one, unless they are particularly keen to demonstrate the validity of orthodox economic theory.

In the context of agrarian markets the likelihood of 'all-or-nothing' contracts being offered is particularly great because the personalised nature of these markets gives the lender intimate knowledge of the borrower which is not available to monopolists in anonymous industrial economies.

All this discussion makes it clear that there are different approaches that can be adopted in modelling markets depending on how we circumscribe the strategies open to the agents. In a monopolistic credit market, such as the one discussed here, we could assume that the money lender can choose the interest rate at which he will offer loans. I referred to this earlier as a case where the moneylender is restricted to adopting a 'price strategy' (remember that interest is a kind of price) and this may be referred to as the *P-approach* (P for price) to modelling a market.

Alternatively we could assume that the lender faces no restrictions on the type of strategy he uses. This approach makes use of the concept of 'reservation utility' or 'reservation frontier' in an important way and may be referred to as the *R-approach* (R for reservation).[6] The reservation utility, $\tilde{u}$, of an agent in the context of a particular exchange is the utility that he will have if the exchange does not take place. This concept becomes significant because in the R-approach the lender ensures that the borrower gets no more than his reservation utility even after the exchange. This is merely a more general statement of what was shown in the above example where the entire profit accruing to the borrower was siphoned off by the moneylender.

It can easily be shown that Bhaduri (1977) adopts the P-approach. Hence Bhaduri's moneylender is not as extortionate as he could be. That is, implicit in Bhaduri's framework is the assumption that the moneylender's options are restricted to 'price strategies'. The models of Braverman and Stiglitz (1982) and Cheung (1968), on the other hand, are exercises in the R-approach. The analysis in the next chapter demonstrates the use of this approach. For the time being, however, we restrict ourselves to the P-approach as I demonstrate the nature of outcome in credit markets when borrowers have a limited repayment capacity and loans are given against security.

3   Collateral price and interest rate formation[7]

To develop the model of the previous section a step further, assume that while, because of prior ties, the risk of not recovering a loan is zero, it is possible that the borrower is too poor to have enough *cash* for repayment. So some asset of the borrower is treated as security or collateral. If the borrower defaults,[8] an 'equivalent amount' of this asset is relinquished to the lender. In order to decide on what is an equivalent amount, the two agents agree, in advance, on a certain price for the asset. This is called the *collateral price* and,

---

[6] By delimiting the strategies open to the lender in different ways other approaches could be defined.

[7] This section is based on a generalisation and formalisation of Bhaduri (1977), Rao (1980), Borooah (1980) and Prasad (1974), that is, after ironing some flaws.

[8] It should be clear that 'default' in this section has a different implication to what it had in section 1 above. Here 'to default' means 'to default on *cash* payment'. Since all loans are secured there is no question of total default, i.e. getting away without paying in any form.

clearly, the lower this is, the larger the quantity of collateral that the borrower has to forfeit.[9] Hence the underpricing of collateral amounts to the charging of an *implicit interest*.[10]

A complete model of rural credit markets would, therefore, have to explain simultaneously the formation of (at least) the interest rate *and* the collateral price. To construct such a model it is convenient to assume that loans are taken for consumption only. Let p denote the collateral price. The asset used as collateral could be land, jewellery or even odd items, like a standing crop, the promise of labour services or used utensils. Not surprisingly, there are typically no markets for these. Let the lender's valuation of a unit of the collateral in money terms be π and the borrower's valuation of the same be π_B. It is assumed that $\pi < \pi_B$. This is reasonable because, if $\pi > \pi_B$, the two agents would be able to immediately effect a mutually advantageous trade.

Let i be the interest rate, L the amount of loan taken and K the maximum amount of cash the borrower has at the time of repayment. Let $\bar{u}$ be the fraction of the loan that he is forced to default, i.e. the fraction that he is *unable* to pay in cash. Then $\bar{u} = 0$, if $(1+i)L \leqslant K$; and $(1 - \bar{u})(1 + i)L = K$, if $(1 + i)L > K$. This may be written as

$$\bar{u} = \bar{u}(i, L) = \begin{cases} 0 & \text{if } (1 + i)L \leqslant K \\[2ex] 1 - \dfrac{K}{(1 + i)L} & \text{if } (1 + i)L > K. \end{cases} \tag{4}$$

This is the *involuntary* default function. For any i and L, the borrower cannot default less than $\bar{u}(i, L)$, though he can default more, if he so wishes. Of course, he has to compensate for the total default by giving the lender an equivalent amount of the collateral. If $1 + i > \pi_B/p$, a rupee defaulted is less costly than a rupee repaid, from the borrower's viewpoint. Thus in this case he will default the

---

[9] Empirically, secured loans are important in rural usury. According to a Reserve Bank of India (1977) survey, 40 per cent of the loans in 1971 were given against well-defined securities. Atiqur Rahman's (1979) detailed study of credit relations in two regions of Bangladesh reveal that more than 50 per cent of the loans were secured. In the present model the real guarantee to the lender comes from his personal ties with the borrower. The main role of the collateral is as a substitute for cash at the time of repayment.

[10] Implicit charges play an important role in rural credit dealings (Griffin, 1974; Kurup, 1976; Bardhan and Rudra, 1978; Sivakumar, 1978), and take a variety of different forms. As Myint (1964) observes: 'The high rates of interest which peasants have to pay are not only formal interest charges but also in considerable part concealed charges obtained through manipulating the prices of commodities which the peasants buy or sell.'

entire loan. Similarly, if $1 + i \leqslant \pi_B/p$, he tries to default as little as possible given constraint (4). Thus, denoting the proportion of the loan *actually* defaulted by u, we have

$$u = \begin{cases} 1 & \text{if } i > (\pi_B/p) - 1 \\ \bar{u}(i, L) & \text{if } i \leqslant (\pi_B/p) - 1. \end{cases} \tag{5}$$

The total loan demanded by the borrower depends on both the implicit and explicit charges:

$$L = L(i, p) \qquad L_i \leqslant 0, \; L_p \geqslant 0. \tag{6}$$

It is possible to impose some natural restrictions on (6). Notice that if $u = 0$, then the cost of taking a loan does not depend on p and its lowering would thus leave L unchanged. A similar argument holds for $u = 1$ and the raising of i. We may therefore assume that (6) satisfies:

1 If $u = 0$, then L is unchanged for decreases in p. But if $u > 0$, then $L_p > 0$.
2 If $u = 1$, then L is unchanged for increases in i. But if $u < 1$, then $L_i < 0$.

It will also be assumed that there exists a sufficiently small p, say p^0, at which the borrower takes a loan which is small enough not to entail any default and u equals 0. Not only is this assumption realistic, its denial has quite absurd implications.[11]

It is conceptually interesting to examine the factors which lend elasticity to the loan demand function. As i increases or p falls, there would typically be two factors leading to a lowering of L. First the borrower will try and make do with a smaller loan. Secondly, he may turn to other sources like the local shopkeeper or professional moneylender, at terms which were earlier not sufficiently attractive, thereby implying a fall in L (i.e. the loan taken from this money-lender). If the isolation of the credit market is complete, then this second factor is absent and the loan-demand function will be relatively inelastic. (It should, however, be emphasised that because of the existence of the first factor, it is wrong to claim that complete isola-

---

[11] Apart from these no other restrictions are imposed on (6). It may be argued that L should depend on

$$\left[i(1 - u) + \left(\frac{\pi_B}{p} - 1 \right) u \right].$$

But here I use only the more general form implied by (6).

tion implies complete inelasticity.) On the other hand, if the credit market is perfectly competitive – which is grossly unrealistic but unfortunately underlies a considerable amount of traditional thinking – then L will be perfectly elastic with respect to i and p at certain given values. Thus the extent of isolation of the credit market is captured by the extent of elasticity of L.

The lender's income from usury, D, consists of interest earnings and transferred collateral:

$$D = D(i, p) = \left[i(1 - u) + \left(\frac{\pi}{p} - 1 \right) u \right] L. \tag{7}$$

The lender chooses i and p so as to maximise D, subject to (4), (5) and (6). This explains the formation of i and p in isolated or monopolistic credit markets and also sheds interesting light on the *process* of usury.

A complete characterisation of the optimum is cumbersome and does not provide any significant intuition. Consequently, assuming that the optimum exists, and breaking up the problem into two steps, I deduce only a few important properties of the optimum. Note, that there are two possible special cases of this problem. First, p may be treated as exogenous and this could be thought of as a theory of interest determination. Secondly, it may be assumed that i is exogenous and we could have a theory of collateral price. Bhaduri's (1977) model is the former type of special case. In the ensuing paragraphs I consider the second special case and use this as a stepping stone for analysing the general case.

So I begin by treating i as fixed. The lender chooses the collateral price, p, so as to maximise his net income, $D(i, p)$. Assuming that an optimal p exists,[12] let us use $\hat{p}$ to denote it. The principal aspect of $\hat{p}$ which interests us is its relation with π. Is there reason to believe that collateral is generally undervalued, i.e. $\hat{p} < \pi$? The question is of fundamental importance to Bhaduri's work, its subsequent exten-

---

[12] In this case the existence of an optimum p is quite easy to demonstrate. First, it may be checked that the optimum p, if it exists, cannot lie outside the closed interval (p^0, π_B). The main problem arises from the fact that if we define the function $D(i, .)$ on this interval, there will exist a discontinuity at point $\pi_B/(1 + i)$. This follows from (5). Notice that in reality if $p = \pi_B/(1 + i)$, i.e. $i = (\pi_B/p) - 1$, then the borrower is indifferent between defaulting and repaying. This means that at this point we could assume either $u = 1$ or $\bar{u}(i, L)$ (though in (5) I have assumed $u = \bar{u}(i, L)$). This means that we could ensure that $D(i, .)$ is an *upper semi-continuous* function (Berge, 1963, p. 74). Hence, since (p^0, π_B) is compact, $D(i, .)$ must take on a maximum value somewhere within (p^0, π_B) (this is an immediate corollary of theorem 2 in Berge (1963, p. 76)). I am grateful to Jean Waelbrock for pointing this out to me.

sions and discussions, and to the analysis of rural interest rates in general. Fortunately, a clear answer is possible: within the framework of this model *collateral is necessarily undervalued*.

This may be established as follows. From (4) and (5) it is clear that u could be equal to 1 or $\bar{u}$ and $\bar{u}$ could, in turn, be 0 or $1 - K/(1 + i) L$. Hence the optimum situation could be of three types, depending on whether

Case I $\qquad u = 1$

Case II $\qquad u = \bar{u} = 1 - \dfrac{K}{(1 + i) L}$,

or

Case III $\qquad u = \bar{u} = 0$.

In Case I, $D = ((\pi/p) - 1) L$. At the optimum, D must be greater than zero, because otherwise the moneylender would not indulge in usury. Hence $((\pi/\hat{p}) - 1) L > 0$, i.e. $\hat{p} < \pi$.

In Case II, by substituting $u = 1 - K/(1 + i) L$ into (7) we have

$$D = \frac{iK}{1 + i} + \left(\frac{\pi - p}{p}\right) \left(\frac{(1 + i) L - K}{1 + i}\right).$$

The necessary condition for this to be the optimum is $\partial D/\partial p = 0$. Hence,

$$\frac{\partial D}{\partial p} = \frac{[K - (1 + i) L] \pi}{(1 + i) \hat{p}^2} + L_p \frac{\pi - \hat{p}}{\hat{p}} = 0.$$

Since in this case $\bar{u} = 1 - K/(1 + i) L$, we know from (4) that $(1 + i) L > K$. Hence (since $L_p > 0$), for the above equation to be true, $\hat{p} < \pi$.

Finally, given Case III, (4) implies $(1 + i) L \leqslant K$. This means that the entire loan is repaid in cash. Hence the price of collateral has no operational significance.

This establishes that whenever collateral is transferred it is underpriced. Moreover, the earlier literature (Bhaduri, 1977, Borooah, 1980) was only considering cases where default invariably took place, i.e. cases I and II, and in both cases $\hat{p} < \pi$. This result continues to hold in the general case as it is surprisingly easy to demonstrate now.

Consider the simultaneous determination of i and p. The lender chooses these so as to maximise D. Let the chosen values be i^* and p^*. The fundamental question is again whether in this generalised framework there is reason to expect the underpricing of collateral, i.e. $p^* < \pi$.

Since i^* and p^* are optimal, $D(i^*, p^*) \geqslant D(i, p)$, for all i, p. Hence, $D(i^*, p^*) \geqslant D(i^*, p)$, for all p. Hence if the interest rate was exogenously fixed at i^*, then p^* would be the optimal p. But it was precisely in such a framework, i.e. where i was given exogenously, that the underpricing of collateral was proved in the previous section. Hence $p^* < \pi$. This is the generalised framework which earlier writers had in mind though they ended up modelling a special case of it. In Bhaduri's (1977) model p was assumed to be exogenously given and it was *assumed* to be underpriced. The underpricing of collateral has also been noted in many empirical studies (e.g. Bardhan and Rudra, 1978; Kurup, 1976). The model in this section shows *analytically* that collateral will be underpriced. This means that the lender's risk is indeed non-existent. Default is no longer something which the lender fears. He may, in fact, encourage default in order to confiscate the borrower's assets kept as security.

This model was constructed without bringing uncertainty directly into the picture. But many of the features of the model were chosen so as to acknowledge the important role of uncertainty. For example, it is not clear why in this model and the other earlier ones the borrower and the lender go through the exercise of having an interest rate and a *contingent* default agreement? Since they both know what the final outcome will be, why can they not simply agree that 'this is the loan and this will be repaid in terms of this much money and this much land'? Why go through the charade of having a collateral price and an agreement saying that depending on how much is defaulted, collateral will have to be transferred using the collateral price as the conversion rate? The reason, in reality, must be that each believes that he can do better by having a contingent agreement rather than one with the exact form and amounts of repayment prespecified. This could be explained by introducing uncertainty or an assumption of asymmetric information about K. While it is desirable to construct a theory which includes these features in its ambit, the present limited approach is, however, not methodologically flawed. Once we know why complicated contracts exist, we can analyse them in a certainty model in the same way that we analyse the effects of price-taking behaviour in the Edgeworth box because we know that if there were many agents, they would be price-takers, even though in the Edgeworth box there are only two.

Finally an important point about transferring collateral is worth noting. Consider the case where at the time of repayment the borrower finds himself with an inadequate amount of money. In this and in related models it is assumed that the balance is paid by transferring collateral. In reality there is another option which is frequently exercised. This involves taking another loan (often from the same lender, which is equivalent to deferring repayment) to repay the debt. This is, of course, merely postponing the day of reckoning and could well result in the borrower becoming 'bonded'.

Finally, it should be noted that a market may be 'isolated' in two different ways. For example, if landlords in a village trust and give loans only to those with whom he has hereditary connections (e.g. if the tenant's father has been the landlord's or the landlord's father's tenant), then if landlord i gives a better deal to his tenants than does landlord j, there is no way that the tenants of j can shift to i, because hereditary connections, unlike guns and butter, cannot be traded. Thus hereditary connections, caste and community links and a multitude of intricate human relations, the outcome of decades or even generations of history, fragment and isolate markets in a fundamental way. It is to an imperfect market of this kind that the present model pertains.

There is a second way in which markets can get fragmented. If credit transactions are intertwined with some other transactions, for instance, if landlords give credit only to those who work on their land, then again competition in the credit market will break down. In the modern literature such markets are described as 'interlinked' ones. Interlinkage raises a host of very interesting issues which are different from the ones considered in this chapter and which form the subject matter of the chapter that follows.

CHAPTER 12

A Theory of Interlinked Rural Markets

1 Antecedents

An interlinked deal is one in which two or more interdependent exchanges are simultaneously agreed upon. Thus, when a landlord agrees to take on a tenant at a fixed rent and also agrees to provide him with credit at a certain interest rate, he is entering into an interlinked deal. Not only are rural markets frequently characterised by such deals, but it is increasingly being appreciated that interlinkage could be the key to understanding many features of traditional economies. As Bailey (1966, p. 401) writes: 'The watershed between traditional and modern society is exactly this distinction between single-interest and multiplex relationships.'[1] As a result of this appreciation, the subject of interlinkage has received a great amount of empirical attention (see, for example, Bardhan and Rudra, 1978; Platteau, Murickan and Delbar, 1981; Rudra, 1981) and this, in turn, has led to a spurt of theoretical research (among others, Braverman and Srinivasan, 1981; Braverman and Stiglitz, 1982; Mitra, 1983; Basu, 1983). This modern work has antecedents which go back to empirical and impressionistic studies spread over some decades.

Traces of the basic idea occurred in many works in economics and social anthropology (see Bardhan, 1980, for a good survey). Analysing rubber markets, in Malaya, Wharton (1962) emphasized the existence of the 'dealer-lender-merchant' and how this triple role gave him powers which a mere dealer or lender did not possess. Long (1968) stressed the role of interlinkage in his study of Thai and Indian credit markets: 'The merchants who trade with farmers in Asia frequently

---

[1] This is also quoted and discussed in Bardhan (1980, p. 82).

combine the activities of retailer, money-lender and buyer of output'
(p. 277). That such combined activities can lead to very different
market outcomes has been argued by Bharadwaj (1974) in her lucid
monograph on Indian agriculture.

One prominent cause of interlinkage is 'potential risk'. I have
argued in Basu (1983) that a market characterised by potential risk
has an innate tendency to seek another market with which to get
interlocked. This argument is elaborated in what follows. In section 2
below, the concept of potential risk is explained and its role in the
emergence of interlinkage discussed. After that, in sections 3 to 7,
a full theory of interlinked markets is developed and elaborated
upon.

2   Potential risk and the emergence of interlinkage

The role of risk in the emergence of interlinkage is best appreciated
by examining a shortcoming in the lender's risk hypothesis.[2] In this
hypothesis the key variable is q – the proportion of loans defaulted
on an average. What does this really mean?

There can be little dispute that we do not mean that for *every* loan
given, a fraction q is not returned. Neither do we mean that no
matter who the loan is given to, there is a probability of q that he
will default totally. Clearly if the debtor is the lender's tenant or has
some historical ties with him, it is very unlikely that he will be able
to get away; and if, on the other hand, the debtor has no dealings,
nor any prior ties, with the lender, it is likely that he will not repay,
there being hardly any legal machinery in backward regions to
enforce repayment. In fact, it is not very unrealistic and for analytical
purposes it is convenient to assume that for every moneylender (who
is also often a landlord), among all potential borrowers there is a set
of people from whom he can always recover his loans, in cash or
otherwise, and over the rest he has no 'control'. In addition, let us
assume that the control areas of different lender-landlords are distinct.

In this set up, q – the *average* proportion defaulted – must be some
kind of a weighted average of the two probabilities:[3] 0 for those over
whom the lender has 'control'[4] and 1 for the others. Given each land-

---

[2] The lender's risk theory was discussed in chapter 11 section 1 and it may be useful to
reread it before proceeding further.
[3] Even if we had not made the polar assumption that one group can never default and
others always do, q would continue to be a weighted average.
[4] 'Control' can take a variety of forms including the threat of social sanctions.

lord's q, and the fixed urban interest rate, r, we can compute the equilibrium i for each landlord in accordance with the lender's risk theory. Suppose that each landlord is charging his equilibrium i. The credit market is then in equilibrium according to the lender's risk theory. But in such a situation the borrowers can very easily do better. They have to simply rearrange their creditors: each should go to a lender who has no control over him.

Thus if a landlord does not discriminate between potential borrowers, he will end up attracting all 'lemons' and eventually go bankrupt. In reality all landlords realise this. Indeed 'natural selection' ensures that they all do. So they generally give loans to those over whom they have control. Hence, while there is a risk of default if a loan is made to a carelessly chosen borrower, a phenomenon which will be referred to as *potential risk*, there is no risk of default when a lender *actually* gives a loan because he would have ensured that the debtor is one over whom he has control.

So, even if risk cannot directly explain the exorbitant rural interest rates in a manner suggested by the lender's risk hypothesis, it plays a crucial indirect role. It is potential risk which *fragments* the market, thereby encouraging the emergence of monopolistic moneylenders.

At this point it is important (as was noted in chapter 11) to distinguish between two kinds of isolation. If a lender gives credit only to those with whom he has some hereditary connections or to those belonging to the same subcaste as him, then there exists 'barriers to entry' and the kind of model discussed in chapter 11, sections 2 and 3 may be applicable.

If, on the other hand, lenders cover their risk by giving loans to those with whom they conduct other economic exchanges, then a new and very interesting dimension enters the analysis. For instance, assume that landlords have 'control' only over their tenants or employees and so they give loans only to them. This is a case where the labour and credit markets are 'interlinked'. Now, suppose that a labourer finds the interest his landlord charges too high. He cannot turn to another landlord for credit, simply because the landlord would not give it to him, and that in turn because, if he did, the labourer would not repay. The credit market is, therefore, isolated. But there is a difference now. The labourer has one option – to shift lock, stock and barrel – that is, he can go to another landlord and try to persuade him to employ him and also to be his creditor. Whether the shift is worthwhile or not will depend not only on the interest charges of the new landlord but on the *package*, i.e. interest and wages, that the new landlord is willing to offer.

This is the beginning of interlinkage between factor markets and, as just discussed, at the core of it lies the credit market with its potential risk. What is the nature of an interlinked 'market'? What will be the structure of wages and interest rates in such a market? These are questions that I turn to in the section that follows. But before that, a comment on policy.

It is known that backward regions in LDCs suffer from acute credit shortages. Not only does this cause much hardship for the poor but this has been identified as one of the key factors which impede innovation and investment. Governments have responded to this by trying to provide institutional credit through banks and other financial organisations. However, the record of such projects has been quite dismal. Time and again, credit has been given out, recovery has been very poor and finally the project has had to be abandoned.

One way of improving the efficiency of credit markets is to make the legal machinery in the rural sector more effective, so that contracts are not easily violated.[5] This would not only help the government to run its financial institutions more effectively, but, more importantly, it would diminish reliance on personal relations and help the flow of non-institutional credit between regions and from the urban to the rural sector.

Before proceeding to the model, note that the credit market is not the only one embodying potential risk. Interlinkage is here viewed as a consequence of individual rationality, and the urge to find insurance in the face of uncertainty. An obvious example of a market with potential risk is the credit market and hence this is used here as the cornerstone. Similar risk-based explanations have been suggested by Wharton (1962) and Bottomley (1964) (see also Akerlof, 1970, p. 499). Potential risk can, however, be found in other markets as well, for instance, that for consumer durables. That is why we generally prefer to buy shoes from a well-known company with a reputation to maintain and second-hand cars from acquaintances rather than from the anonymous advertisement columns of newspapers. To a lesser extent the same risk is there even in the purchase of perishables for which quality differences are not easily discernible. In a modern society, large departmental stores and the legal machinery are institutions which provide cover against such risks. In backward economies, interlinkage is the obvious response. It should be clear

---

[5] Social norms could also play an important role in this, as discussed in chapter 1. A useful discussion of the principles involved in designing a successful rural credit policy may be found in Lipton (1977, pp. 300–2).

from this that my choice of credit and labour markets, in constructing a theory of interlinkage, is purely for reasons of illustration.

3 Partial equilibrium in an interlinked market

Consider a rural region which has l landlords and N identical peasants. There is no law to ensure that a loan taken by a peasant will be repaid and thus, in keeping with the above analysis, it is supposed that the only way that a peasant can get a loan is to tie himself for a year as an employee to a landlord. It is being assumed for simplicity that this is the only form of employment that landlords provide. It is simple to extend the model to permit share tenancy and this is done in an appendix to this chapter. From his own landlord the worker can get as much loan as he wants but he cannot default. Let w be the wage for a year's work that a peasant gets from his employer-landlord and i be the interest rate at which he can borrow from his landlord. Let u be a function such that a higher value of u implies a more acceptable package from the peasant's point of view. It is convenient to think of u as a utility index. It may be assumed that

$$u = f(w, i) \qquad f_1 > 0, \ f_2 \leqslant 0. \tag{1}$$

We may rewrite (1) as follows

$$w = \phi(i, u) \qquad \phi_1 \geqslant 0, \ \phi_2 > 0. \tag{2}$$

It is assumed that the amount borrowed by the peasant. L, depends on the interest rate:[6]

$$L = L(i) \qquad L'(i) \leqslant 0. \tag{3}$$

It is reasonable to expect that at sufficiently high interest rates peasants cease to take loans. Hence I assume that there exists $\bar{i}$ such that for all $i \geqslant \bar{i}$, $L(i) = 0$ and for all $i < \bar{i}$, $L'(i) < 0$. Clearly interest rates are inconsequential to a peasant if he is anyway not taking loans. Hence, for all $i > \bar{i}$, $f_2 = 0$ and $\phi_1 = 0$. This is the reason why some of the relations in (1) and (2) were specified as *weak* inequalities.

---

[6] Some may find the more general specification, namely $L = L(i, w)$, more acceptable, but there are two ways of justifying the simpler assumption: it is possible to think of the peasant's basic utility function suitably separable (e.g. $\Omega = \Omega^1(L) + \Omega^2((1+i)L) + \Omega^3(w)$) so that L turns out to be a function of i only. Secondly, even if we begin with the more general form, $L = L(i, w)$, since (as we shall see later) landlords ensure that peasants are on their reservation frontier, w depends on i, and *in effect* L depends on i only.

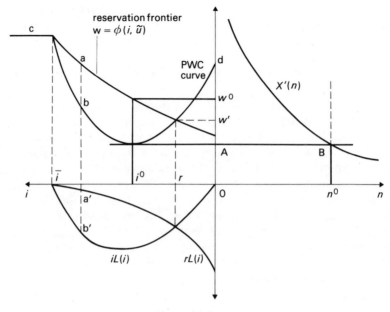

Figure 12.1

To begin with, (1) (or, alternatively, (2)) and (3) are treated as 'primitives', i.e. their specifications are independent of each other and are exogenously given to us. The special case where (1) and (3) are both derived from one basic utility function and utility depends on intertemporal earnings is taken up later.

For the partial equilibrium analysis assume that there is a 'reservation utility', $\tilde{u}$, for all peasants, which means that as long as a landlord offers a package, (w, i), which has an index below $\tilde{u}$, that is $f(w, i) < \tilde{u}$, no labourers come to him. But if he offers $\tilde{u}$ or more, there is an endless supply of labour. Thus, for the time being, I ignore the fact that this region has only N peasants. In the general equilibrium the number becomes important and it is used to determine endogenously the value of the utility index.

In the immediate context the index is exogenously given, which means there is a frontier in the (w, i)-space, given by $\tilde{u} = f(w, i)$, which defines the limits to which a peasant can be pushed. The reservation frontier is illustrated in figure 12.1.

The frontier is an important tool of analysis for interlinked systems. It will be argued that in bringing about an equilibrium, the frontier in an interlinked market plays the same role as does price in a conventional market. In other words, price is replaced by the reservation frontier and it is the movement up and down of the entire frontier which brings about a general equilibrium.[7]

The partial equilibrium approach can be rationalised by assuming that the rural region is a small one and workers are free to migrate to and from an adjacent sector where they can always get a package (w, i) which gives them u.

Let us now look at the decision problem of the landlords. Assume that output, X_j, produced by landlord j is a function of the number of employees, n_j, that he has. Hence

$$X_j = X_j(n_j) \qquad X_j'(n_j) > 0, \ X_j''(n_j) < 0 . \tag{4}$$

A typical marginal product curve is shown in the top right quadrant of figure 12.1. Assuming that each landlord has to pay the same wage to and charge the same interest from all his employees (in the case of landlord j, these being w_j and i_j) and that these are given in real terms, landlord j's yearly earning from cultivation is $X_j(n_j) - w_j n_j$.

The landlord has access to the organised credit market where he keeps his money at an exogenously given interest rate, r_j. We treat r_j as his opportunity cost of lending money to the peasants. While r_j will be referred to as an interest rate in the organised or urban sector, it is possible to give it a wider interpretation. It could be the rate of return landlord j expects on investment or the expected earning from the urban share market. Basically r_j is the opportunity cost of money given as loan to the peasants and what is important is that it is assumed to be parametrically given. Given this wider interpretation and also because credit markets – even in the organised sector – exhibit a variety of interest rates and different landlords have access to different ones, there is no reason to expect that $r_i = r_j$, for all i, j.[8] It is assumed that the landlord has enough money to take care of the entire credit demand of his workers. The landlord's net interest earning is therefore equal to $n_j(i_j - r_j) L(i_j)$.

The landlord's objective is

$$\underset{\{w_j, i_j, n_j\}}{\text{Max}} \ \pi_j = X_j(n_j) - w_j n_j + n_j(i_j - r_j) L(i_j)$$

subject to

$$w_j = \phi(i_j, \tilde{u}).$$

---

[7] This *direct* analogy is not possible if peasants have non-identical indifference curves in the (w, i)-space.

[8] We are of course assuming that there is no inter-landlord borrowing.

Dropping the subscript j wherever there is no possibility of confusion, and substituting the constraint in the objective function, the landlord's objective may be restated as

$$\text{Max}_{\{i,n\}} \pi = X(n) - \phi(i, \tilde{u}) n + n(i - r) L(i). \tag{5}$$

This implies the following first-order conditions:

$$X'(n) = \phi(i, \tilde{u}) - (i - r) L(i) \tag{6}$$

$$L(i) + (i - r) L'(i) = \phi_1(i, \tilde{u}). \tag{7}$$

Solving these two equations we get i_j and n_j in terms of the exogenous variables:

$$i_j = i_j(\tilde{u}, r_j) \tag{8}$$

$$n_j = n_j(\tilde{u}, r_j). \tag{9}$$

Once we get i_j, we can compute w_j from the equation of the reservation frontier, i.e.

$$w_j = \phi(i_j, \tilde{u}). \tag{10}$$

Landlord j is in equilibrium if i_j, w_j and n_j are such that they solve (8), (9) and (10).[9] The rural sector is in equilibrium when each landlord j, has chosen his respective optimal $[i_j, w_j, n_j]$. More formally $[i_j, w_j, n_j]_{j=1...l}$ is an equilibrium configuration if it satisfies (8), (9) and (10) for all j. The total employment in the rural sector in equilibrium is $\Sigma_{j=1}^{l} n_j(\tilde{u}, r_j)$.

Observe that equations (6) and (7) are block recursive: we can first solve (7) and get the equilibrium interest rate, and then using that solve (6) and get the equilibrium n_j. This characteristic makes it easy to represent this model geometrically. Actually the block recursion is obvious directly from the landlord's objective function (5) which may be rewritten as

$$\pi = X(n) - nC(i, \tilde{u}, r) \tag{11}$$

where

$$C(i, \tilde{u}, r) = \phi(i, \tilde{u}) - (i - r) L(i). \tag{12}$$

[9] In order not to get enmeshed in the problems of existence, it is simply assumed that equilibrium, both partial and general, exists throughout this model. As long as the assumptions of a model do not logically imply non-existence, a direct assumption that equilibrium exists is logically as consistent as the more indirect approach of deriving the existence from more basic assumptions. For those who prefer otherwise, continuity of $L(i)$ and $w = \phi(i, u)$ and the assumption that $\lim_{n \to \infty} X'(n) = 0$ ensure the existence of this equilibrium.

Clearly $C(i, \tilde{u}, r)$ is the per worker cost (PWC) to the landlord. Note that for every given n, π is maximised by minimising $C(i, \tilde{u}, r)$. Since $\tilde{u}$ and r are exogenous to the landlord, he has to choose i so as to minimise the per worker cost. Having done this, he could then maximise π with respect to n.

In the bottom left quadrant of figure 12.1, plot two curves, $iL(i)$ and $rL(i)$. Recalling our assumption that for a sufficiently large i demand for loans goes to zero, it is clear that for all $i \geqslant \bar{i}$, $iL(i) = rL(i) = 0$. Since $L'(i) \leqslant 0$, $rL(i)$ falls monotonically as i increases. Note that $iL(i) = rL(i) > 0$ can happen only if $i = r$. Thus the two curves intersect where $i = r$. The vertical gap between the two curves shows $(i - r)L(i)$. This is negative for $i < r$. Subtract this gap from the reservation frontier vertically (i.e. ab = a'b') and we get the line marked cbd which shows $C(i, \tilde{u}, r)$, i.e. the PWC corresponding to different interest rates. This curve will be referred to as the PWC-curve. Since the landlord minimises $C(i, \tilde{u}, r)$, he chooses the lowest point on the PWC-curve. He therefore sets the interest rate at i^0. The wage he pays can be read off the reservation frontier and is shown in figure 12.1 as w^0.

Now, n is chosen to equate $X'(n)$ to the minimum PWC. This is obvious from (6) and may be written as:

$$X'(n) = C(i^0, \tilde{u}, r) \tag{13}$$

where i^0 is the interest at which PWC is minimised. The equilibrium n is denoted by n^0 in figure 12.1.

4   A general equilibrium

The fact that this region has N peasants has so far been ignored. In the partial equilibrium analysis it was shown that given $\tilde{u}$ the aggregate demand for labour was $\Sigma_{j=1}^{l} n_j(\tilde{u}, r_j)$. Now assume that this region is a closed economy. There is no reason why the aggregate demand for labour should be equal to the supply of labour,[10] N, for an arbitrarily chosen $\tilde{u}$. However, we could vary $\tilde{u}$ so that demand

---

[10] It is assumed that labourers are willing to work no matter how much utility they get from work (though of course between two jobs they would prefer the one offering a higher utility). In other words, the supply curve of labour vis-à-vis $\tilde{u}$ is vertical at N. It is easy to relax this assumption.

equals supply. That is precisely the closing equation for a general equilibrium:

$$\sum_{j=1}^{l} n_j(\tilde{u}, r_j) = N. \tag{14}$$

Hence, $[(i_j, w_j, n_j)_{j=1...l}, \tilde{u}]$ is an equilibrium configuration of interest, wage, employment and utility if and only if these values satisfy equations (8), (9) and (10), for all j, and equation (14).

In the next sections we explore the properties of our model, but before that it is worth pausing to examine the process which brings about this equilibrium and in particular the role of $\tilde{u}$.

In the partial equilibrium analysis we pretended that $\tilde{u}$ was given, i.e. the reservation frontier was fixed, and landlords were asked how many workers they would demand. By changing $\tilde{u}$ an aggregate demand curve can be constructed. A possible case is illustrated in figure 12.2. Note that the derivation of this demand curve is analogous to the derivation of a traditional demand curve where agents are asked to treat price as given and state their demands. Fortunately, as with most traditional demand curves, the present one turns out to be downward sloping. This can be demonstrated using figure 12.1. The reader may check this and skip, if he so wishes, the ensuing mathematical proof.

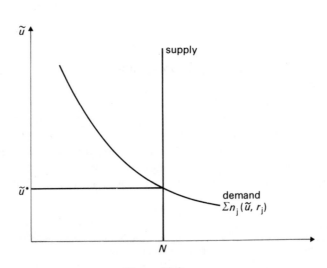

Figure 12.2

A standard mathematical approach would be by differentiating the first-order conditions (6) and (7). An alternative approach which requires little formal mathematics and is also intuitively satisfying is as follows.

Consider landlord j, without using the subscript. Let n^0, i^0 be the landlord's chosen values given $\tilde{u}^0$; and n^*, i^* be his chosen values given $\tilde{u}^*$. Since, as argued above, the landlord chooses i to minimise $C(i, \tilde{u}, r)$,

$$C(i^*, \tilde{u}^*, r) \leqslant C(i^0, \tilde{u}^*, r).$$

Let $\tilde{u}^* < \tilde{u}^0$. Then,

$$C(i^0, \tilde{u}^*, r) < C(i^0, \tilde{u}^0, r),$$

since $\phi_2 > 0$ (see equation (2)). These two inequalities together imply

$$C(i^*, \tilde{u}^*, r) < C(i^0, \tilde{u}^0, r).$$

Since n is chosen so as to satisfy (13), the above inequality implies $X'(n^*) < X'(n^0)$. This in turn implies $n^* > n^0$, since $X''(n) < 0$ (see equation (4)). Thus $\tilde{u}^* < \tilde{u}^0$ implies $n^* > n^0$. Since this is true for all landlords, $\tilde{u}^* < \tilde{u}^0$ implies

$$\sum_{j=1}^{l} n_j^* > \sum_{j=1}^{l} n_j^0.$$

This establishes the downward slope of the demand curve.

That $\tilde{u}$ in this interlinked market plays the role which price plays in conventional market analysis is now obvious. If $\tilde{u}$ is set too high, $\Sigma n_j(\tilde{u}, r_j) < N$, i.e. labour is in excess supply. That means workers would be willing to accept a lower $\tilde{u}$, and competition will drive $\tilde{u}$ down till (14) is satisfied. If $\tilde{u}$ is initially very low, a reverse process establishes (14). Since $\tilde{u}$ represents a frontier in the (w, i)-space, it is clear that it is the movement of this frontier which brings about an equilibrium in an interlinked market.

The fact that $\tilde{u}$ is determined by these economic forces does not preclude the possibility of it persisting around the subsistence level. This is explained by assuming that the labour supply curve has a cut-off point: workers agree to supply labour only if they are assured of getting a subsistence utility or more. This would imply that for a *class* of labour-demand curves, the equilibrium $\tilde{u}$ would be the subsistence one.

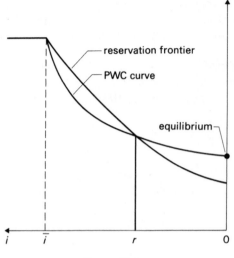

Figure 12.3

5   The structure of wages and interest

A number of characteristics of rural markets which have been observed in various field studies and have been casually theorised about by earlier authors is captured in this simple model.

First, as is obvious from figure 12.1, in general equilibrium, i_j need not be equal to r_j and in particular can be greater than r_j. Thus 'abnormally' high rural interest rates can persist without resulting in any arbitrage. On the other hand i_j can also be less than r_j, a possibility demonstrated in figure 12.3 where $i_j = 0$. It is interesting to note that i_j could never be zero in Bhaduri's (1977) framework. This happened because in his framework loan demand was inelastic and while there was isolation in the credit market there was no explicit interlinkage. This paper shows how isolation naturally gives rise to market interlinkages and that once this happens rural interest can in certain situations be zero. The existing evidence (see for example Bardhan and Rudra, 1978) validates this possibility. One should be warned, however, that a zero interest should not be taken as an indicator of peasants being well off. In interlinked markets peasants who pay no interest typically get lower wages, which could be well below the marginal product of labour. Equations (6) and (10) establish the more general proposition that

$$i_j < r_j \leftrightarrow X_j'(n_j) > w_j, \tag{15}$$

i.e. a landlord, who charges an interest rate below the interest in the organised sector to which he has access, pays a wage less than the marginal product of labour. Note that since the implication in (15) is a two-way one, the widespread prevalence of exorbitant rural interest rates would suggest that marginal product of labour would often be below the wage rate. This could be one explanation of the widely discussed phenomenon of low marginal productivity in the rural sector.

It would, however, be wrong to suppose that $i_j = r_j$ is merely a case of coincidence. An important special case of this model arises if we assume that the peasants' behaviour is the outcome of *intertemporal earnings* maximisation. In that case, as is discussed later, and proved in Appendix 2, $i_j = r_j$ for all j. Of course, (15) continues to be valid but only in a trivial sense.

What is possible here and continues to be possible in the intertemporal earnings approach is that different landlords charge different interest rates and pay different wages. What the theory of interlinkage tells us is that the dispersions in the prices of these two, i.e. credit and labour, are not arbitrary. In particular, it suggests the following hypothesis: for all, i, k,

$$i_j < i_k \leftrightarrow w_j < w_k. \tag{16}$$

This follows from the fact that at equilibrium $f(w_j, i_j) = f(w_k, i_k)$, for all j, k, i.e. (unskilled) workers who get a higher wage pay a higher interest on loans so that the utility index is the same. This is one explanation of the observation that in rural regions there often exists neighbouring villages paying different wages and this persists without causing any migration. Similarly for interest rates: interlinkage makes it impossible for peasants paying a high interest rate to go for credit to the neighbouring landlord who charges his workers a lower interest. To do so in the presence of potential risk, he has to give up his earlier job and work for the neighbouring landlord, i.e. shift totally. And that is not worthwhile because $f(w_j, i_j) = f(w_k, i_k)$.[11]

Note that this utility equivalence result is stronger than (16), and depends critically on the assumption of identical preferences among peasants. On the other hand, (16) would continue to hold even with

[11] This result is discussed by Braverman and Srinivasan (1981). This is not really a surprising result but a certain amount of importance has been attached to it because of its differences with Marshall's (1920) analysis of equilibrium in share tenancy (see chapter 10 above). Observe that in its present form which is identical to that in Braverman and Srinivasan ('All contracts are utility equivalent') this proposition hinges on the assumption of identical preferences. A more general statement of the same idea is as follows: at equilibrium no worker t would prefer to work in place of worker s at the terms (i.e. i and w) that s is receiving.

non-identical preferences. Hence (16) is the hypothesis which we would expect to be valid even though the stronger proposition, $f(w_j, i_j) = f(w_k, i_k)$ for all j, k, may not be.

The above analysis clarifies one feature of interlinkage which is not always clearly understood. Having observed differing wages (or other prices) between villages many have sought to explain this in terms of interlinkage. What is, however, often not appreciated is that interlinkage explains these differences only by showing that in a more fundamental sense there is equality, i.e. all jobs are equally acceptable. In reality it could indeed be the case that peasants in one village are better off than workers in another village. To put it more generally, there exists workers who would prefer to be in the shoes of other workers. A theory of interlinkage cannot, in itself, explain this. Instead we need to resort to an old argument, one making use of the concept of transfer costs or barriers to entry, which in turn could be the consequence of custom. For example, if there are impediments to labour mobility for reasons of caste then utility differences may persist undisturbed. A number of barriers to entry in the labour market have been discussed by Sen (1975, pages 53–5).

Dispersion in the price of a commodity, like wages, is caused by isolation in the market for that commodity, i.e. the labour market. Isolation in turn can be caused by both interlinkage of markets and the existence of transfer costs. If it is caused solely by interlinkage, then we would find that the wage differentials are offset by price differentials in other markets (in the present model, interest). If on the other hand isolation is caused solely or additionally by the existence of transfer costs, then the wage differentials would not cause balancing differentials elsewhere.

A second conceptual issue that is highlighted by our model of interlinked markets is that many expressions which are quite standard in conventional market analysis are extremely misleading, in the present context. Many of the same people, who have been responsible for this new perspective of agrarian relations, have, however, continued to use expressions which are borrowed from another realm and have thus contributed to a not inconsiderable amount of semantic confusion. For example, consider a general equilibrium in an interlinked market with $i < r$. This, as shown earlier, implies $X'(n) > w$. Would we in this case say that the labour market is imperfect because workers are not getting their marginal product? The answer is not very obvious. While workers are not getting their marginal product they are getting credit at an interest below the organised sector rate. Moreover, if instead of wages we look at the per worker cost, we find that in equilibrium it is equal to the marginal product, $X'(n)$. Actually when deals are interlinked, it is no longer correct to think of wages as payment for labour and interest as payment for loans. The (w, i) vector jointly reflects the price of labour and loans. It is futile to try and separate the two and say how much each costs.

Another problem relates to the term monopoly. Consider the general equilibrium situation depicted in figure 12.1. Here the rural interest, i, is above the organised market interest. This sort of a situation is often described by saying that the credit market is *monopolistic*. Now, one standard feature of a monopolistic market is that if the seller raises his price a little bit only he does not face a zero demand. But consider a single landlord raising, *ceteris paribus*, his interest rate by a small amount, beginning from the equilibrium in figure 12.1. This would imply a movement directly to the left, starting from (i^0, w^0). This would mean offering peasants a package (w, i) which is less acceptable than what is available on the market. In other words the landlord loses all demand for credit. Thus he clearly cannot be described as a monopolist or even as monopolistic. On the other hand, he can raise interest without losing customers if he also raises the wage rate, so as not to push (w, i) below the equilibrium reservation frontier. Thus he does have power to affect the interest rate unlike a competitive supplier of loans. The point is, if we consider the joint deals in labour and credit, the model constructed here is a competitive one. But if we examine each 'market' separately, like the credit market or the labour market, then both descriptions, monopoly and competition, raises problems. It may thus be preferable to describe these individual 'markets' by using the more neutral term 'isolated'.

It is for these reasons that one agrees with Bharadwaj's (1974, chapter 1) claim that the problem of underdevelopment is not one which can be understood by tinkering with the standard competitive model by introducing a dose of monopoly here and a shot of monopsony there.

> What does complicate the analysis, however, is the fact that markets become interlocked through price and non-price links, given that market and social power is vested in the dominant rural classes and that the dominant party often combines multiple functions, thus enjoying a superior position simultaneously in a number of markets. (Bharadwaj, 1974, p. 4)

This is not always fully appreciated. For instance, Wharton's (1962) study which begins with an insightful account of interlinkage ends up with a rather staid analysis of monopsony. Similarly Griffin (1974) in his concerned account of Asian agriculture, while never hesitating to point out the severe limitations of the traditional model, does, often make claims which are appropriate only in the traditional framework. The tendency to equate price dispersion with 'imperfection' and a coincidence of marginal product and wage with 'efficiency' are examples of this.

At the same time there is a risk of excess at the other end. While the existing critiques of standard equilibrium models are extremely destructive, when it has come to alternative *constructions* the suggestions have not been equally radical and some of the same criticism continue to apply.[12] For example, Bhaduri's (1977) model has more in common with the traditional approach than what is generally believed. Similarly the idea of interlinkage is not *as* beyond the ambit of market analysis as some seem to suggest. It is true that each separate 'market' is fundamentally different from a competitive one or monopoly (and to ignore that would lead us into errors mentioned in the above paragraph), but multiple deals defined with adequate care can be subjected to market analysis as is transparent in my model and not so transparent in others.

6   The intertemporal earnings approach

Till now (1) and (3) have been treated as primitives. It is arguable and in most traditional analysis it would be presumed that since both these functions pertain to the peasant, they are derived from the peasant's *basic* utility function. This in itself would not give us any interesting special cases. But if in addition we assume that the peasant's basic utility depends on his intertemporal profile of earnings then we get a result which is at first sight rather surprising: at equilibrium, $r_j = i_j$ for all j, i.e. each landlord charges his peasants an interest rate equal to his opportunity cost of lending money. In brief, rural interest rates are not usurious. If they are high, it is only because the cost to the landlords, of lending money to the peasants, is high.[13]

It is easy to misunderstand this result. The fact that interest rates are not 'inexplicably' high does not mean that peasants are not being

---

[12] This is of course quite understandable. Moreover this in itself is no reason to believe that the traditional approach is correct. If we found that modern medicine was failing us we would not treat that as a reason for resurrecting the witchdoctor.

[13] I owe this result entirely to Jacques Drèze.

subjected to extortion. As we shall see in a moment, the implication is precisely the reverse.

It is true that the special case arises under severe restrictions on the characterisation of a peasant's preference. For instance, a peasant must attach no significance to wages other than as a source of earnings. That is, status and 'recognition' aspects of income – to use Sen's (1975) term in a slightly different context – are ruled out; and (what is the other side of the same coin) there is assumed to be no stigma attached to the taking of loans. While I do not make these assumptions in this chapter, they are quite pervasive in the literature and consequently this result is of interest.

While a formal proof is relegated to the end of this section (geometric) and Appendix 2 (algebraic), the main idea is not difficult to grasp. Let r be the interest rate the landlord earns from depositing his money in the organised sector. By lowering the rural interest rate to r, the landlord allows the peasant to make greater use of money. That is always worthwhile for a landlord who is powerful enough to hold the peasant at his reservation utility and extract the excess money for himself: if two individuals are sharing a cake and the amount that one person gets is fixed, it is clearly to the other person's advantage to take any measure that would expand the cake.[14, 15]

Hence $i = r$ is not a sign of the peasant's wellbeing. The landlord sets $i = r$ only because markets are interlinked and he can extract all the advantages that accrue to the peasants by keeping i low. For analogous reasons discussed in the previous chapter, if monopolists were more powerful than what they are and they had a good idea of their customers' demand structures, they would not charge monopoly prices. They would instead lower prices to the level that would prevail in competition and extract the additional consumers' surplus by imposing 'flat' charges or by some 'tie-in' mechanism (Burstein, 1960).

While the above discussion, for aesthetic reasons, suppresses the landlord subscript j, what we have actually shown is that for each landlord j, $i_j = r_j$. This in turn implies that $X_j'(n_j) = w_j$, i.e. each landlord equates wages to the marginal product of labour. However, as long as different landlords have different opportunity costs of money and given the imperfections of capital markets there is no reason to expect otherwise, barring coincidences, $i_j \neq i_k$ and $w_j \neq w_k$ given

---

[14] In the general model i could persist above r because the greater benefit accruing to a peasant by lowering i may not always be extractable by the landlord without loss of value.

[15] It is, however, not necessary that landlords will be better off in the general equilibrium if they all lower i to r, though each landlord is better off by doing so.

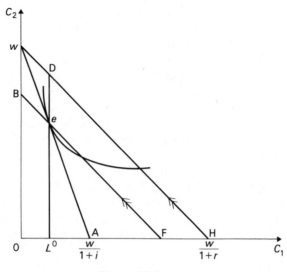

Figure 12.4

$j \neq k$. Even in this special case, interlinkage helps explain price dispersion. Of course, as before, those paying higher interests get higher wages such that utility levels across peasants happen to be the same. In other words, while both the hypotheses embodied in (15) and (16) continue to be valid, only the latter is *relevant* in the context of the special case.

Before proceeding to the next section, a geometric proof of this proposition is presented, making use of some simplifying assumptions. Some readers may prefer to read Appendix 2 instead.

Suppose there are two periods, 1 and 2, and the peasant takes his loan in period 1. In period 2 he receives his wage and repays his loan. Hence his intertemporal earnings profile is $[L, w - (1 + i) L]$. Denoting consumptions in periods 1 and 2 by C_1 and C_2, we have $C_1 = L$ and $C_2 = w - (1 + i) L$, which implies $C_2 = w - (1 + i) C_1$. In figure 12.4, let the line wA represent this budget constraint, given a certain w and i. Assume $i > r$. The proof is completed by showing how the landlord could do better by lowering the interest rate to r.[16] Since preference depends on intertemporal earnings (or consumption), indifference curves can be drawn in the (C_1, C_2)-space representing the peasant's preference. Let the peasant choose point e and let the indifference curve represent his reservation utility. He is there-

---

[16] A similar proof goes through if we assume $i < r$.

fore borrowing L^0 from the landlord. The landlord's PWC, ignoring its intertemporal character, can be represented in figure 12.4. In the same figure draw the line depicting $C_2 = w - (1 + r) C_1$. This is shown by wH. The landlord's net interest earning from the worker, $(i - r) L^0$, is then shown by eD. Hence the PWC is $w0 - eD$. Let the landlord lower the interest rate to r and wages from $w0$ to B0. Then the budget constraint of the peasant becomes BF. The landlord's PWC is now given by B0 (since he has no interest earnings), which is equal to $w0 - Bw = w0 - eD$, i.e. the PWC in the original situation. But note that with the new budget constraint, BF, the peasant is on a higher indifference curve than in the original situation. Hence the landlord can lower wages a bit more without losing his worker. Hence he can have a PWC smaller than in the original situation.

7   Response to exogenous changes

Let us return to the question of technological innovation which, as discussed in chapter 1, has been the source of much controversey. First consider a single landlord who has the option of making an innovation which will shift the marginal product curve of labour upwards. It is.reasonable to assume that a single landlord cannot change the prevailing utility levels of peasants.[17] Thus to a single innovating landlord the reservation frontier is given, which means, and this is obvious from the left-hand side of figure 12.1, that the per worker cost remains unchanged to the landlord. So with an innovation which shifts $X'(n)$ curve to the right, he employs more labour. Therefore he benefits unambiguously from the innovation and the benefit has two sources: his existing labour force becomes more productive and he employs more people.

Though this framework has important differences with Bhaduri's (1973) model, the above argument is, in essence, the same as the one forwarded in chapter 9 as a critique of Bhaduri's stagnation hypothesis. What is happening here is that as a single landlord innovates he ensures that he keeps his peasants pushed against the reservation frontier, the position of which is determined by the behaviour of *all* landlords and peasants taken together and is unaffected – for all practical purposes – by the actions of a single landlord. He therefore reaps the full benefits of his innovation.

[17] In other words, single landlords are reservation frontier takers just like in conventional market analysis individual agents are supposed to be price takers. It is well-known that a rigorous explanation of this in a general equilibrium framework raises problems.

If all landlords innovate together the consequences are very different though. It is clear from figure 12.1 that for a given $\bar{u}$, innovation would result in each landlord demanding a greater amount of labour. This implies a rightward shift of the aggregate demand curve for labour in figure 12.2. Hence equilibrium $\bar{u}$ rises. Thus peasants become better-off if all landlords innovate together. The status of landlords' welfare is, however, ambiguous. It is possible to construct upward shifts of the marginal product curve in different ways and show that the landlords may or may not be better off. From this, one may be tempted to argue that rural stagnation is a consequence of *group* decision on the part of landlords, but such a theorem has other difficulties as discussed in chapter 9, section 3.

Another exogenous change worth examining is a credit squeeze in the organised sector. Since the credit market in this analysis is not rationed, a natural way to define a credit market squeeze in the organised sector is in terms of a rise in its interest rates. Let $(r_1^0, \ldots, r_l^0)$ be the original structure of interest faced by the landlords and let $(r_1^*, \ldots, r_l^*)$ be the new structure. We assume that there is a credit market squeeze, i.e. $r_j^* \geqslant r_j^0$, for all j and $r_k^* > r_k^0$, for some k. The consequence of this in the rural sector is as follows: the peasants are worse off as a consequence of changes in the structure of rural interest and wages. In the generalised model there is no definite *a priori* directional effect on rural interest: it could rise or fall. In the utility-theoretic special case, however, a credit squeeze in the organised sector gets directly transmitted to the rural sector for the obvious reason that $r_j = i_j$ for all j. All this is obvious from figure 12.1. For a particular landlord, if r goes up, with $\bar{u}$ constant, his PWC will rise and thus the demand for labour will fall. Hence the aggregate demand curve for labour shifts left in figure 12.2, implying a fall in $\bar{u}$.

The impact of the credit squeeze on landlords is uncertain. Consider a single landlord. His profit can be represented in the top right quadrant of figure 12.1 as the area under the marginal product curve and above the PWC line. In the situation depicted in the diagram this is equal to the area above AB. Since technology is unchanged, the only way the profits can drop is if the PWC line (i.e. AB) shifts up. Therefore it is obvious from the diagram that a drop in the profit of landlord j is necessarily accompanied by a drop in the number he employs, n_j. Hence, if starting from an equilibrium, as urban interest rates rise, every landlord is worse off, $\Sigma_{j=1}^l n_j$ falls, which means the general equilibrium condition (14) cannot be satisfied. Therefore, (a) all landlords cannot be worse off, and by the same argument, (b) they cannot all be better off.

However, (a) need not necessarily be true in general because it hinges on the assumption of inelastic labour supply. If labour supply was upward sloping, i.e. $N = N(\tilde{u})$, $N'(\tilde{u}) > 0$, then (a) would no longer be true, though (b) remains unaffected. If there is an unlimited labour supply at the subsistence utility, then a credit squeeze would imply an increase in unemployment and also a drop in landlords' welfare. What cannot be captured in this model, but could be the case in reality, is that a credit squeeze would affect investment adversely and have a detrimental long-run impact.

Finally, it is worth examining the consequences of removing potential risk. In order to remove potential risk institutional changes would be required. For example, a sense of values may be inculcated which make people desist from defaulting or the government's legal machinery in the rural sector may be strengthed. However it be achieved, the question which concerns us here is that, once potential risk is ruled out, what happens to wages and interest rates. Assume that landlords j and k were charging interest rates r_j and r_k and $r_j > r_k$. Once potential risk is removed a worker of landlord j can go to landlord k and ask for credit at a rate r which is between r_j and r_k. This he can now do while retaining his job with j. Such trades will continue till the dispersion in interest rates is greatly reduced; and, of course, by the utility equivalence result, wage dispersion will also be reduced. This would imply that landlords who have a high opportunity cost of money will cease to give loans on the rural markets and those with a low opportunity cost will earn super-normal profits.[18] In short, a conventional market equilibrium will emerge and this is not surprising because interlinkage in this model had germinated from the presence of potential risk.

It is difficult to explore formally the welfare effects of an institutional change like the removal of potential risk. This is because in reality working for rural owner-operators and feudal landlords is not the only opportunity open to the peasants. Typically there would exist other more anonymous forms of employment opportunities where, however, credit is not available as from a feudal landlord. A feudal landlord may pay poorly but he provides the peasant with some insurance. To quote from Breman (1974, p. 193):

> The allowance he [the farm servant] receives is not sufficient for him to be able to cope with eventualities such as divorce and remarriage, illness,

---

[18] In order to have a normal solution, it is necessary to assume that landlords have a finite amount of money to give out as loans or that they face an increasing opportunity cost of giving credit.

continuous rain during the monsoon, or collapse of a wall of his hut. On such occasions the master cannot refuse too often to come to his assistance – at least if he wishes to keep his servant. ... [Hence], the farm servant has at least a possible source of credit, even though laboriously obtained. Aside from the security of a minimal income this is for the farm servant the compensatory side of servitude.

In the original situation, with potential risk in the credit market, it was the need for insurance – money on a rainy day – which ensured that the peasants would come to the rural landlords and consequently in our main analysis these alternative opportunities could be ignored. Once the government removes potential risk, the two functions of finding a job and having an insurance are no longer intertwined. The peasant can then work in the more anonymous capitalist farms and turn elsewhere for his loans. Clearly a broader and more complex framework is needed for a realistic assessment of the implications of removing potential risk or other institutional changes.

While institutions and customs play a significant role in moulding our economic lives, and much has been written about them, economists are not yet in a position to provide a satisfactory 'integrated' analysis. Some rudimentary remarks on the nature and role of extra-economic forces are retained for the concluding chapter.

Appendix 1   Share tenancy and interlinkage

The 'tenure' relation in this model was a 1-year contractual system with wage payment. Extending this to an interlinkage model involving *share tenancy*, instead, is a straightforward exercise. I illustrate this here by using a very simple characterisation of share tenancy: the landlord's production function is the same as above; so that we may write it, suppressing the subscript, as

$$X = X(n).$$

But now the landlord does not pay a wage to his tenants. Instead he pays them a fraction, t, of the output. Using w to denote a peasant's income (so that (1) and (2) remain unchanged) we have

$$w = \frac{tX(n)}{n}. \tag{A1}$$

The landlord's control variables in this share tenancy model are i, n and t (as opposed to i, n and w in the main model). Hence the landlord's objective is

$$\text{Max}_{\{i,n,t\}} \pi = (1-t)\, X(n) + n(i-r)\, L(i),$$

subject to

$$\frac{tX(n)}{n} = \phi(i, \tilde{u}). \tag{A2}$$

(A2) follows from (2) and (A1) and it simply asserts that tenants must get their reservation utility, $\tilde{u}$.

The landlord's objective can be restated as

$$\text{Max}_{\{i,n\}} \pi = X(n) - \phi(i, \tilde{u})\, n + n(i-r)\, L(i)$$

Since t does not occur in this expression, the maximisation is done with respect to $\{i, n\}$, which is exactly what was done in the main model (see (5)). Once the optimal i and n have been found, (A2) gives the value of t. Hence the model gives us a theory of the formation of interest rate, employment and the rental proportion. Since t can be converted to w using (A1), the general equilibrium solution and analysis can be conducted in the same way as in the basic model.

Appendix 2   The algebra of the intertemporal earnings approach

While the exact temporal structure of the transactions is unimportant for proving that $r_j = i_j$, for all j, assume that the peasant takes the loan in period one and repays it in period two which is also the period in which he receives his wage. Hence, since his utility depends on his earnings profile, $\Omega = \Omega(L, w - (1 + i)\, L)$, where Ω denotes his utility. The analysis is simpler if we assume the function is additively separable in which case we could represent it as

$$\Omega(w, i, L) = \alpha(L) + \beta(w - (1 + i)\, L)$$

$$\alpha' > 0, \ \beta' > 0, \ \alpha'' < 0, \ \beta'' < 0. \tag{A3}$$

The peasant chooses L to maximise Ω. Hence[19]

$$\alpha'(L) - (1 + i)\, \beta'(w - (1 + i)\, L) = 0. \tag{A4}$$

---

[19] The second-order condition is satisfied since $\alpha'' < 0, \ \beta'' < 0$.

Let

$$V(w, i) \equiv \underset{\{L\}}{\text{Max}} \ \Omega$$

and let $\tilde{V}$ be the reservation utility. Then the landlord chooses w and i so as to

$$\underset{\{w,i\}}{\text{Min}} \ K = w - (i - r) L, \tag{A5}$$

subject to

$$V(w, i) \geqslant \tilde{V}.$$

In this case it is never worthwhile for the landlord to charge usurious interest rates. This may be shown by contradiction. Let i^*, w^* and L^* be the equilibrium values and let $i^* > r$. Now consider what happens if the landlord lowers i to $i^0 = r$ and w to $w^0 = w^* - (i^* - r) L^*$. Then $w^* - (i^* - r) L^* = w^0 - (i^0 - r) L^0$, where L^0 is the peasant's loan demand when interest and wage are i^0 and w^0. Thus (A5) implies that with i^0 and w^0 the landlord is as well off as before.

Note that

$$w^* - (1 + i^*) L^* = w^0 - (1 + i^0) L^*.$$

Therefore,

$$\Omega(w^0, i^0, L^*) = \Omega(w^*, i^*, L^*) \equiv V(w^*, i^*).$$

Note that w^0, i^0, L^* does not satisfy (A4) since w^*, i^*, L^* does satisfy (A4). Thus, given w^0 and i^0, L^* is not the optimum loan demand. Thus

$$V(w^0, i^0) \equiv \Omega(w^0, i^0, L^0) > \Omega(w^0, i^0, L^*) = V(w^*, i^*) = \tilde{V}.$$

Hence the peasant is better off than before. Therefore by lowering the interest rate and wage, as above, the landlord remains equally well-off and the peasant is above the reservation utility. It is easy to see that the landlord can do better by lowering wages even further so as to push the tenant to the reservation frontier. Thus i^*, w^* is not the landlord's optimum. This contradiction establishes that i cannot be greater than r in equilibrium. It is obvious that for similar reasons i cannot be less than r. Thus $i = r$ and clearly the result carries over to the general equilibrium.

PART IV

Concluding Remarks

CHAPTER 13

The Limits of Economic Analysis

1 Introduction

In the preceding pages non-economic issues and methodological questions have received only cursory attention. The aim of this chapter is to comment on some of these matters which cropped up earlier but had to be hushed up in order not to lose the thread of the main argument. No single topic therefore dominates the ensuing pages which may, in a sense, be thought of as a series of appendices.

A concept which lies at the periphery of conventional economics is 'power'. Most economists would agree that it plays an important role in society but hardly anybody knows in exactly what way. Much has been written on the subject but nothing that can be described as definitive. The next section begins with some comments on 'power'. These are no more than stray observations in the context of issues dealt with in this book, and their purpose is to provoke research which may lead to new ideas.

Section 3 below defends some of the methods used in this work and the last section sums up.

2 On power, custom and social institutions

It is often argued that our elegant theoretical models are useless in the context of the less developed economy with its many imperfections and lopsided distribution of power. This contains two arguments at once. The first one asserts that if a theory is elegant and the reality messy, then the theory cannot be apt for the occasion. This is quite obviously a fallacy. It stems from confusing the properties of a model with those of its object of study.

The second and the more serious argument is that since power is seldom discussed in our theories but it is of consequence in reality, our theories must be irrelevant. This argument misses the point that not to speak about power does not necessarily imply a denial of its role. Consider the standard Arrow–Debreu model of general equilibrium, which is reticent on questions of power. However, to the extent that this model takes the initial endowments of individuals to be exogenously given, it leaves room for power. Suppose, for the sake of argument, that power affects only the endowments of individuals and an individual's power does not depend on the endogenous variables of the model. In that case power would play a role in determining the outcome of markets, and this role would not negate the validity and relevance of the Arrow–Debreu model. Thus the presence of power in reality does not *automatically* imply that our theories are inadequate. But, of course, they nevertheless may be. After all it is not clear that power does work exclusively through the structure of individual endowments. Also, an agent's power may well depend on the outcome of the market place.

Power has many facets. It affects the workings of markets in ways, some of which are, as yet, too complex for us to replicate in our models. There are, nevertheless, some areas of development economics[1] where one aspect of power asymmetry between agents has been built into the framework – at times, I suspect, unwittingly.

I illustrate this with the model of interlinkage developed in the previous chapter. The peasant, it may be recalled, chooses whether to work or not and the amount of loan to take. The landlord chooses the wage and the interest rate, i.e. (w, i). So each agent has his *control area* and no one uses force on the other. It may therefore appear that there are no asymmetries in the model. But actually the model is not yet fully specified. Its outcome will depend crucially on which agent is assumed to know the other's 'reaction function'.[2] For intance, in the model in chapter 12, as in other models of this genre, it is supposed that (a) the landlord knows the peasant's reaction function (i.e. the peasant's choice in response to alternative offers of packages, (w, i)), and (b) the landlord makes his choice first and then the peasant chooses.

---

[1] Mainly the models of landlord–tenant relationship and also the recent models of interlinkage: Bhaduri, 1977; Braverman and Srinivasan, 1981.

[2] An example of a 'reaction function' can be found in the appendix to chapter 7.

		serf's house			
		red		blue	
landlord's house	red	4	10	0	0
	blue	0	0	10	4

Figure 13.1

As far as theory goes, there is no reason why we could not have made the opposite assumption that, (c) the peasant knows the landlord's reaction function, and (d) the peasant chooses his variables first.[3] This could result in a different equilibrium with the peasant much better off than in the other approach.[4] Hence, in our model of interlinkage at least one kind of asymmetry, in favour of the landlord, is built in. And in some sense this could be thought of as *one* manifestation of power asymmetry.

Those familiar with oligopoly theory will recognise that landlord–tenant interactions of the above kind are similar to the Stackelberg model of duopoly with the landlord playing the role of the 'leader'. How the choice of a 'leader' affects the outcome is easy to illustrate game-theoretically.

I shall consider a variant of the game known as the 'Battle of the Sexes'. A small feudal village is deciding on its choice of colours for the landlord's mansion and the serf's hut. The utilities that the landlord and the serf get from alternative colour schemes is shown in the *pay-off matrix* in figure 13.1. In each box the left-hand figure shows the utility that the landlord gets and the right-hand one shows the serf's utility. Thus if both houses are painted red, the serf gets 10 utils and the landlord gets 4 utils. The pay-off matrix makes it clear that both agents agree that a mono-coloured village is preferable to a bi-coloured one. The conflict is about what this single colour should

[3] A direct switch, with the landlord still controlling (w, i) and the peasant controlling the volume of credit and the decision to work is not possible. But such an exercise becomes possible once we suitably redefine the control variables.

[4] One case where the outcomes of the two approaches would definitely be different is in a partial equilibrium type situation where both landlords and peasants have their respective reservation utilities, u_l and u_p, arising, for instance, from the existence of another sector to which they are free to migrate. In this case depending on which set of assumptions, (a) and (b), or (c) and (d), is adopted the peasant or the landlord would be pushed against his reservation utility. For a result in between these two extremes we would need a bargaining model: see Bell and Zusman (1976).

be. The landlord prefers blue; this gives him 10 utils. But the serf prefers, for reasons not toally incomprehensible, red.[5]

The game is symmetric and each agent has a similar area of control, namely, each can choose the colour of his own house. Despite this symmetry the outcome will be skewed depending on who is assumed to have the right of first choice. If the landlord chooses first he will opt for blue. *Given this*, the serf will also choose blue and the landlord will get 10 utils. If, on the other hand, the serf chooses first, it is easy to check, the landlord gets 4 utils. This illustrates the significance of whether we assume (a) and (b), or (c) and (d). The first approach leads the landlord to be vastly better-off. What is interesting is that this outcome coincides with what would happen if the landlord was a tyrant who chose not only for himself but also for his serfs. In that case he would order that both houses be painted blue. This would entail an open exercise of power. The landlord can, however, reach the same outcome more subtly, by giving the serf the freedom to choose the colour of his hut, but by retaining the innocuous looking right to choose first.[6, 7]

As argued earlier, many economists writing on agrarian relations have used the kind of asymmetry assumption just described. The deeper question as to what gives rise to this asymmetric power structure remains open. Finally, it ought to be stressed that power works in many ways and the above discussion pertains to only one kind of power and there is no attempt to argue that this is the most important kind.[8]

[5] This game is known as the 'Battle of the Sexes' because its origin is in analysing a typical conflict between husband and wife planning an evening out. He prefers to go to the bull fight, whereas her preference is for the ballet. Both of them would, however, prefer to go to the same place rather than different ones. Hence the pay-off matrix could be thought as being identical to that in the landlord–serf conflict. If the wife has made up her mind about going to the ballet the husband is better off going to the ballet as well. If, on the other hand, he manages to make it clear first that he is definitely going to the bullfight, then his wife will follow suit. Hence, in this game stubbornness, and more importantly, one's reputation for it, clearly pays (see, Luce and Raiffa, 1957).

[6] For simplicity, I have been discussing this problem in terms of who chooses first. Even if we assume that the agents choose simultaneously, the same asymmetry can be shown to arise. It is important to note that, we are not allowing 'mixed strategies'. If these are permitted then the outcome of this game may be symmetric (see Aumann, 1976, chapter 2).

[7] This is related to the interesting cake-sharing problem. You and another person wish to share a cake. One will cut and the other choose. Consider first a homogeneous cake. Clearly you should be indifferent between cutting and choosing because the final outcome will be the same. Next consider a cake which has on it a cherry, which your friend, unlike you, loves. A little bit of thought will make it obvious that now you would be better off if you cut.

[8] A discussion of a different kind of power in the same economic context is contained in Desai (1981).

In some ways, the impact of custom, caste and social institutions on market outcomes is more obvious than that of power. One popular attitude among economists towards social institutions is to treat them as mere decorations. According to this view, the situation which we would expect to emerge in the absence of such institutions is the situation that emerges. A less popular but probably more realistic approach is contained in Akerlof's engaging paper (Akerlof, 1976) which treats the caste system as exogenously given, and shows how it may persist because it is in the interest of each agent to abide by its rules. This is because, like money, everyone believes that everyone else believes in the caste system and it becomes a 'self-fulfilling prophecy'. Caste, in Akerlof's theory, is not inconsequential. It may indeed lead the economy into a low-level equilibrium trap.

Social institutions and custom can also affect the functioning of an economy by setting up barriers to mobility. Thus in certain situations, it may not be possible for a peasant to become a landlord, not only for economic reasons but because of social restrictions. Similarly, if there are different types of labour, e.g. skilled and unskilled, institutions like caste could hamper movement between these categories. This would imply that the wage differentials between these groups of labour would not be equal to the cost of acquiring skill. While caste is an obvious example, in reality there exist many subtle and less visible institutions which have the same effect. For example, there are instances of understanding among landlords not to employ a peasant who has deserted his master and of the administration aiding such a system.[9]

Another example in a similar vein is the discussion in chapter 9 of how custom may impede innovation. All these cases, however, ignore the possibility of a two-way relation between social institutions and economics. To attempt here an analysis of such interactions in any depth would be foolhardy. It is preferable, instead, to illustrate this with a specific problem.

In his book, Breman (1974) has studied[10] an interesting question: How can we explain the disappearance of the system of bonded

---

[9] 'They are slaves of the soil and as such are not at liberty to leave the estate to which they belong. The owner of the estate, a Brahmin, is quite unable to cultivate the land without their help.' This is from a letter from the Collector of Trichinopoly to the Collector of Salem seeking help to round-up absconding peasants, and is quoted in Kumar (1965, p. 42) from the proceedings of the Board of Revenue, Madras, 30 June 1919. Younès (1979) has attempted a theoretical model of serfdom with complete barriers to labour mobility, based on the 'demesne-tenures system'

[10] See page 70ff.

labour from so many regions?[11] He begins by considering a theory of Nieboer (1910) which suggests that an increased abundance in labour supply obviates the necessity for bonded labour, and in, particular, the *hali* system disappeared 'owing to a process of pauperisation under colonial rule', which resulted in an increase in 'the percentage of agricultural labourers'.[12] This is a kind of conspiracy theory of servitude. When labour is plentiful, wages are anyway low; so landlords have nothing to gain from the institution of bondage and so it does not exist. As labour becomes scarce, the system emerges to keep wages low. That the effect of the institution of bondage is to depress workers' welfare is obvious enough. What is interesting about this hypothesis is that the *institution* of bondage is, in turn, supposed to be a consequence of economic factors.

It may be interesting to note in passing that the hypothesis is incomplete in one obvious sense. If labour continues to become less abundant, then again it is reasonable to expect that bondage would come under strain because now each landlord would benefit immensely by breaking the implicit agreement and wooing the workers of other landlords. As this strain increases, we would expect the institution to wither away. Hence the relation between the institution of bondage and labour abundance may well be a U-shaped one, with the institution withering away either because there is too much labour or there is too little. The causation is different at the two ends. In the case of labour abundance the landlords have no need for the system. In the extreme shortage case, the landlords feel the need but there is too much competition among themselves for them to abide by the rules of a tacit agreement.

> The lords [of Ile de Ré] ... resorted to agreements between themselves in the twelfth and thirteenth century for mutual assitance in the capture of fugitive serfs; agreement which provided for an exchange of captives or gave the right of pursuit in another's territory. But so considerable did the problem of fugitives become, and so great the hunger for labour that, despite treaties and mutual promises, an acute competition developed to entice and steal the serfs of a neighbouring domain. (Dobb, 1945, p. 46)

---

[11] He raises this question in the specific context of the *hali* system in Gujarat but this analysis has wider appeal and I treat it as such.

[12] Breman goes on to show why this theory is inadequate, but that need not concern us here. In fact, no attempt is made here to suggest that bondage is, in reality, sustained in this manner. This theory is presented only as an illustration of how institutions and the marketplace could have a two-way relation.

3   Some comments on method

While economists have a sense of methodology, i.e. they can usually write economics without making methodological blunders, they are dismal whenever they try to articulate their methodological position or to write a paper while consciously following some method. If I had to pick out a work of Milton Friedman which I think is the least defensible, I would unhesitatingly choose his paper on methodology: Friedman, 1953. His writings on economics are so good because he has generally been shrewd enough not to follow the principles outlined in this paper. Some of his followers have been less fortunate.

In what follows, I want very briefly to defend two methodological *aspects* of this book, without making any attempt to spell out and defend any overall methodology.

First, note that this monograph uses both 'partial' and 'general' equilibrium techniques. This may be construed as a weakness because there is a popular belief that the only correct approach is a general equilibrium one and that a 'partial' approach ought to be eschewed. The frailness of this argument becomes clear once we appreciate that models are typically of different *degrees* of generality though we use a 0-1 language.[13] A model is not completely general as long as what is treated in it as exogenous is, *in reality*, affected by some endogenous variable of the model.[14] Hence, thanks to the great complexity of reality, it is unlikely that we will be able to construct a completely general model, and more importantly, even if we do, there will be no way of being sure that we have.[15] Viewed in this way, what I have done in this book is to develop and discuss models of different degrees of generality and it is not clear that this is a particularly reprehensible thing to do.

Secondly, a word about the use of different levels of precision in this book. It is true that vague generalisations and verbosity ought to be criticised in science. We should try and be precise, but that does not mean that we have to deny that imprecision too has a role. Our every-day speech is extremely imprecise but nevertheless we manage

[13] Many logical problems and paradoxes can arise from this use of a 0-1 language where the underlying concept is 'fuzzy' (Basu, 1983a). This can lead not only to wrong answers but, with graver implications, to wrong questions.

[14] It should be clear that in any model much more than just the exogenous *variables* are exogenously given. For instance, in a standard general equilibrium model what is exogenously given includes the form of the utility and production functions. This is unlikely to be true in reality, thereby indicating the possibility of an even more general model.

[15] The problem is akin to the one faced in expressing a 'basic' value judgment (Sen, 1970, chapter 5).

to convey a great amount to one another – and perhaps more than what we would if we always tried to be precise. One reason for this must be that the presuppositions of different minds are similar.[16]

In economics many concepts are used without them ever having been properly defined. This is not *always* undesirable. In fact, in introducing a difficult concept, like power or rationality, an economist faces two options. He could first define it carefully and then use it; alternatively he could proceed directly to use it hoping that people have a reasonably uniform notion of the concept or at least will learn its meaning as they read on. This is exactly how a child learns. No one tries to teach a child what a circle is by defining it. Instead we keep using the word and pointing out circles to him. And gradually the child learns its meaning and understands exactly what his father means when he refers to a *circular* garden, even though neither the child nor the father can define it.

4   Concluding remarks

Development economics is a vast and verbose subject. To write a short monograph on it therefore entails a formidable choice problem. In this book this is partly taken care of by confining attention to works which have a definite theoretical content and by the decision to dwell at length on recent advances – critically examining them and suggesting new directions. But a subject does not emerge from no-where. So I have had to go back to earlier works, presenting and formalising some of the main ones.

[16] In the essay, 'A plea for clear thinking' (in B. Russell, *Portraits from Memory and Other Essays*, Simon and Schuster, 1951), Bertrand Russell wrote: 'In 1917, Wilson pro-claimed the great principle of self-determination, according to which every nation had a right to direct its own affairs' (pp. 187–8). Having observed this, Russell quite rightly pointed out that since the word 'nation' was not well defined, Wilson's principle was imprecise: 'Was Ireland a nation? Yes, certainly. Was northeast Ulster a nation? Protestants said yes, and Catholics said no.... In Petrograd, as it then was, during the time of Kerensky a certain single house proclaimed itself a nation ... and appealed to President Wilson.... This, however, was felt to be going too far.' With this example Russell was emphasizing the confusion that can arise from a loose statement, and he added that if 'President Wilson had been trained in logical accuracy', he should have specified the conditions under which his principle was to be used. This is, however, too tall a demand because it is unlikely that the conditions, *even if* well defined in Wilson's mind, would be simple enough to be expressible in words. What is more important here is that even without these conditions being stated, Wilson's principle does convey something to us which is probably not totally at variance with what Wilson had in mind. This happens because there is a certain amount of homogeneity in the presumptions in different human minds. Language abounds in terms which we cannot define but which convey broadly the same information to different minds.

The traditional development economist's perspective has been a very broad one – not only aggregating over goods and people but spanning vast stretches of time. This has its use but also its limitations; as much of this book tries to show, it is important to analyse the smaller segments of this canvas. The book was organised in three main parts plus this concluding one. The first part took a fairly aggregated view of the economy and its concerns were primarily with macroeconomic problems: stagnation, unemployment, inflation and growth. The first disaggregation occurred in Part II where the economy was conceived of as comprising two sectors: the urban and the rural. Migration, unemployment and wage rigidities were then studied in the context of a dual economy. Considerable emphasis was laid on the neglected and yet important question of the emergence of dualism. The third part consisted of a properly disaggregated analysis of several aspects of backward rural economies, in particular, the causes of technological stagnation, the consequences of different forms of land tenure and the nature of rural credit markets. In chapter 12, some of these issues, discussed earlier in isolation, were put together in a model of interlinked factor markets.

This is not a normative book in that it contains very little direct discussion of economic policy. It is, instead, an attempt to explain and understand some of the more salient characteristics and problems of the less developed economy. It is, of course, hoped that this may contribute to the design of more meaningful policies. Consider the problem of urban unemployment in dual economies. The standard response to this has been to create more urban jobs. Not surprisingly, this has not led to any remarkable success. To treat this problem effectively, we have to first understand how labour markets work in dual economies and to recognise the *existing structure of incentives*. Simplistic plans which disregard the latter may help win votes but are unlikely to mitigate unemployment.

An important purpose of this book was to try and lend clarity and rigour to the major ideas and debates in the subject. There are situations where imprecision has a role. This was argued a moment ago. But in development economics, jargon and a deliberate prolixity have been used as a facade where ideas are scarce. The lack of lucidity has been the basis of numerous pseudo-debates and has also aided the popular tendency to confuse positive and normative issues. Thus many reject monetarism not because they believe it is empirically invalid but because they feel that to accept monetarism is to advocate unfettered capitalism.

References

Adams, D. W. and Rask, N. (1968), Economics of cost-share leases in less developed countries, *American Journal of Agricultural Economics*, **50**.

Agarwala, N. (1979), On Leibenstein's theory of disguised unemployment, *Indian Economic Review*, **14**.

Akerlof, G. (1970), The market for 'lemons': Quality uncertainty and the market mechanism, *Quarterly Journal of Economics*, **84**.

Akerlof, G. (1976), The economics of caste and of the rat race and other woeful tales, *Quarterly Journal of Economics*, **90**.

Allen, F. (1982), On share contracts and screening, *Bell Journal of Economics*, **13**.

Ames, D. W. (1962), The rural Wolof of the Gambia, in P. Bohannan and G. Dalton (eds) *Markets in Africa*, Northwestern University Press.

Anand, S. and Joshi, V. (1979), Domestic distortions, income distribution and the theory of optimum subsidy, *Economic Journal*, **89**.

Arrow, K. J. (1982), A cautious case for socialism, in I. Howe (ed.) *Beyond the Welfare State*, Schoeken Books.

Aujac, H. (1950), Une hypothèse de travail: L'inflation, conséquence monétaire du comportement des groupes sociaux, *Economie Appliquée*. English translation (1954), Inflation as the monetary consequence of the behaviour of social groups: A working hypothesis, *International Economic Papers*, **4**.

Aumann, R. J. (1976), *Lectures on Game Theory*, Stanford University, mimeo.

Bacha, E. L. (1978), An interpretation of unequal exchange from Prebisch-Singer to Emmanuel, *Journal of Development Economics*, **5**.

Bagchi, A. K. (1973), Some implications of unemployment in rural areas, *Economic and Political Weekly*, **8**, Special number, August.

Bailey, F. G. (1964), Capital, saving and credit in Highland Orissa (India), in R. Firth and B. S. Yamey (eds) *Capital, Saving and Credit in Peasant Societies*, Allen and Unwin.

Bailey, F. G. (1966), The peasant view of bad life, *Advancement of Science*, December.

Bardhan, P. K. (1980), Interlocking factor markets and agrarian development: A review of issues, *Oxford Economic Papers*, **32**.

Bardhan, P. K. (1983), *Land, Labor and Rural Poverty*, Columbia University Press and Oxford University Press.

Bardhan, P. K. and Rudra, A. (1978), Interlinkage of land, labour and credit relations: An analysis of village survey data in East India, *Economic and Political Weekly*, **13**, Annual Number, February.

Bardhan, P. K. and Srinivasan, T. N. (1971), Crop sharing tenancy in agriculture: A theoretical and empirical analysis, *American Economic Review*, **61**.

Basu, K. (1980), *Revealed Preference of Government*, Cambridge University Press.

Basu, K. (1980a), Optimal policies in dual economies, *Quarterly Journal of Economics*, **95**.

Basu, K. (1981), Causality and economic theory, *Indian Economic Review*, **16**.

Basu, K. (1983), The emergence of isolation and interlinkage in rural markets, *Oxford Economic Papers*, **35**.

Basu, K. (1983a), Fuzzy revealed preference theory, *Journal of Economic Theory* (forthcoming).

Basu, K. (1983b), Implicit interest rates, usury and isolation in backward agriculture, *Cambridge Journal of Economics* (forthcoming).

Basu, K. and Roy, P. L. (1982), Share, size and subsistence: Revisiting some old controversies on tenancy, *Economic and Political Weekly*, **17**, 24 July.

Bauer, P. T. (1946), The economics of planting density in rubber growing, *Economica*, **13**.

Bauer, P. T. (1971), *Dissent on Development*, Weidenfeld and Nicolson.

Behrman, J. R. (1973), Price determination in an inflationary economy: The dynamics of Chilean inflation revisited, in R. S. Eckaus and P. N. Rosenstein-Rodan (eds) *Analysis of Development Problems*, North-Holland.

Bell, C. and Zusman, P. (1976), A bargaining theoretic approach to cropsharing contracts, *American Economic Review*, **66**.

Berge, C. (1963), *Topological Spaces*, Oliver and Boyd.

Béteille, A. (1974), *Studies in Agrarian Social Structure*, Oxford University Press.

Bhaduri, A. (1973), A study in agricultural backwardness under semi-feudalism, *Economic Journal*, **83**.

Bhaduri, A. (1977), On the formation of usurious interest rates in backward agriculture, *Cambridge Journal of Economics*, **1**.

Bhaduri, A. (1983). *The Economic Structure of Backward Agriculture*, Academic Press.

Bhagwati, J. N. (1958), Immiserizing growth: A geometrical note, *Review of Economic Studies*, **25**.

Bhagwati, J. N. and Srinivasan, T. N. (1974), On reanalyzing the Harris–Todaro model: Policy rankings in the case of sector-specific sticky wages, *American Economic Review*, **64**.

Bharadwaj, K. (1974), *Production Conditions in Indian Agriculture*, Cambridge University Press.

Bliss, C. J. and Stern, N. H. (1978), Productivity, wages and nutrition: Part I The theory; Part II Some observations, *Journal of Development Economics*, **5**.

Bliss, C. J. and Stern, N. H. (1982), *Palanpur – Studies in the Economy of a North-Indian Village*, Oxford University Press.

Blomqvist, A. G. (1979), Urban unemployment and optimal tax policy in a small, open dual economy, *The Journal of Development Studies*, **15**.

Boeke, J. H. (1942), *The Structure of Netherlands India*, Institute of Pacific Relations.

Boeke, J. H. (1953), *Economics and Economic Policy in Dual Societies*, Institute of Pacific Relations.

Borooah, V. (1980), High interest rates in backward agricultural communities: An examination of the default hypothesis, *Cambridge Journal of Economics*, **4**.

Bose, P. S. (1982), Determination of rent under share tenancy: An analytical exercise, *Indian Economic Review*, **17**.

Bottomley, A. (1964), Monopoly profit as a determinant of interest rates in underdeveloped rural areas, *Oxford Economic Papers*, **16**.

Bottomley, A. (1975), Interest rate determination in underdeveloped rural areas, *American Journal of Agricultural Economics*, **57**.

Braverman, A. and Srinivasan, T. N. (1981), Credit and sharecropping in agrarian societies, *Journal of Development Economics*, **9**.

Braverman, A. and Stiglitz, J. (1981), Landlords, tenants and technological innovations, World Bank, Development Research Centre, Working Paper.

Braverman, A. and Stiglitz, J. (1982), Sharecropping and the interlinking of agrarian markets, *American Economic Review*, **72**.

Breman, J. (1974), *Patronage and Exploitation*, University of California Press, Berkeley.

Brown, D. J. and Atkinson, J. H. (1981), Cash and share renting: an empirical test of the link between entrepreneurial ability and contractual choice, *Bell Journal of Economics*, **12**.

Burstein, M. L. (1960), The economics of tie-in sales, *Review of Economics and Statistics*, **42**.

Byres, T. J. (1972), The dialectic of India's green revolution, *South Asian Review*, **2**.

Cagan, P. (1956), The monetary dynamics of hyperinflation, in M. Friedman (ed.) *Studies in the Quantity Theory of Money*, University of Chicago Press.

Campos, R. (1964), Economic development and inflation with special reference to Latin America, in OECD *Development Plans and Programmes*, OECD, Development Center.

Canavese, A. J. (1982), The structural explanation in the theory of inflation, *World Development*, **10**.

Cardoso, E. A. (1981), Food supply and inflation, *Journal of Development Economics*, **8**.

Chakrabarty, S. K. (1977), *Price Behaviour in India, 1952-70*, Macmillan.

Chakravarty, S. (1977), Reflections on the growth process in the Indian economy, in C. Wadhva (ed.) *Some Problems of Indian Economic Policy*, Tata McGraw-Hill.

Chandarvarkar, A. G. (1965), The premium for risk as a determinant of interest rates in underdeveloped rural areas: Comment, *Quarterly Journal of Economics*, **79**.

Chayanov, A. V. (1966), *The Theory of Peasant Economy*, Irwin.

Chenery, H. B. and Bruno, M. (1962), Development alternatives in an open economy: The case of Israel, *Economic Journal*, **72**.

Chenery, H. B. and Strout, A. M. (1966), Foreign assistance and economic development, *American Economic Review*, **56**.

Cheung, S. N. S. (1968), Private property rights and sharecropping, *Journal of Political Economy*, **76**.

Chichilnisky, G. (1980), Basic goods, the effects of commodity transfers and the international economic order, *Journal of Development Economics*, **7**.

Corden, W. M. (1974), *Trade Policy and Economic Welfare*, Clarendon Press.

Corden, W. M. (1980), Trade policies, in J. Cody, H. Hughes and D. Wall (eds) *Policies for Industrial Progress in Developing Countries*, Oxford University Press.

Corden, W. M. and Findlay, R. (1975), Urban unemployment, intersectoral capital mobility and development policy, *Economica*, **42**.

Currie, J. M. (1981), *The Economic Theory of Agricultural Land Tenure*, Cambridge University Press.

Dagnino-Pastore, J. M. (1963), Balanced growth: An interpretation, *Oxford Economic Papers*, **15**.

Dasgupta, P., Marglin, S. A. and Sen, A. K. (1972), *Guidelines for Project Evaluation*, United Nations Industrial Development Organisation, United Nations.

Datta Chaudhuri, M. K. (1981), Industrialisation and foreign trade: The development experiences of South Korea and the Philippines, in Lee (1981).

Debreu, G. (1959), *Theory of Value*, Yale University Press.

Desai, M. (1981). Power and agrarian relations: Some concepts and measurements, London School of Economics, mimeo.

Dixit, A. (1983), The multi-country transfer problem, *Economics Letters*, **13**.

Dobb, M. (1945), *Studies in the Development of Capitalism*, Routledge.

Drèze, J. (1975), Existence of an exchange equilibrium under price rigidities, *International Economic Review*, **16**.

Drèze, J. (1979), Demand estimation, risk-aversion and sticky prices, *Economics Letters*, **4**.

Elkan, W. (1973), *An Introduction to Development Economics*, Penguin.

Enke, S. (1962), Economic development with unlimited or limited supplies of labour, *Oxford Economic Papers*, **14**.

Epstein, T. S. (1967), Productive efficiency and customary system of rewards in rural South India, in R. Firth (ed.) *Themes in Economic Anthropology*, Tavistock Publications.

Ezekiel, H. (1960), An application of Leibenstein's theory of underemployment, *Journal of Political Economy*, **68**.

Fields, G. (1975), Rural–urban migration, urban unemployment and underemployment, and job-search activity in LDCs, *Journal of Development Economics*, **2**.

Findlay, R. V. (1959), International specialisation and the concept of balanced growth comment, *Quarterly Journal of Economics*, **73**.

Flemming, J. M. (1955), External economies and the doctrine of balanced growth, *Economic Journal*, **65**.

Friedman, M. (1953), The methodology of positive economics, in M. Friedman (ed.) *Essays in Positive Economics*, Chicago University Press.

Friedman, M. and Friedman, R. (1980), *Free to Choose*, Pelican.

Furnivall, J. S. (1939), *Netherlands India, A Study of Plural Economy*, Cambridge University Press.

Furtado, C. (1964), *Development and Underdevelopment*, University of California Press, Berkeley.

Gamble, D. P. G. (1955), *Economic Conditions of Two Mandinka Villages: Kerewan and Keneba*, London: Colonial Office.

Geanakoplos, J. and Heal, G. (1983). A geometric explanation of the transfer paradox in a stable economy, *Journal of Development Economics*, **13**.

Ghose, A. K. and Saith, A. (1976), Indebtedness, tenancy and the adoption of new technology in semi-feudal agriculture, *World Development*, **4**.

Griffin, K. (1974), *The Political Economy of Agrarian Change*, Macmillan.

Gunning, J. (1983), Basic goods, the effects of commodity transfers and the international economic order: Comment, *Journal of Development Economics*, **13**.

Gunning, J. (1983a), Rationing in an open economy: Fix-price equilibrium and two-gap models, *European Economic Review*, **23**.

Haberler, G. (1961), Terms of trade and economic development, in H. S. Ellis (ed.) *Economic Development for Latin America*, St Martin's Press.

Hahn, F. (1977), Exercises in conjectural equilibria, *Scandinavian Journal of Economics*, **79**.

Hallagan, W. (1978), Self-selection by contractual choice and the theory of sharecropping, *Bell Journal of Economics*, **9**.

Harris, J. R. and Todaro, M. P. (1970), Migration, unemployment and development: A two-sector analysis, *American Economic Review*, **60**.

Haswell, M. (1975), *The Nature of Poverty*, Macmillan.

Hendry, D. F. (1980), Econometrics – alchemy or science?, *Economica*, **47**.

Hicks, J. R. (1956), *The Revision of Demand Theory*, Oxford University Press.

Hicks, J. R. (1974), *The Crisis in Keynesian Economics*, Basil Blackwell.

Higgs, H. (1894), 'Metayage' in western France, *Economic Journal*, **4**.

Hirschman, A. O. (1958), *The Strategy of Economic Development*, Yale University Press.

Islam, N. (1957), External economies and balanced growth, *Indian Economic Journal*, **5**.

Jevons, S. (1871), *The Theory of Political Economy*, Macmillan, Penguin edition.

Johnson, D. G. (1950), Resource allocation under share contracts, *Journal of Political Economy*, **58**.

Jorgenson, D. W. (1967), Surplus agricultural labour and the development of a dual economy, *Oxford Economic Papers*, **19**.

Joshi, H. and Joshi, V. (1976), *Surplus Labour and the City*, Oxford University Press.

Kaldor, N. (1934), Mrs. Robinson's 'Economics of imperfect competition', *Economica*, **1**.

Kalecki, M. (1954), El problema, del financiamiento del desarrollo economico,

El Trimestre Económico. English translation (1955), The problem of financing economic development, *Indian Economic Review*, **2**. Reprinted in Kalecki (1976).

Kalecki, M. (1960), Unemployment in underdeveloped countries, *Indian Journal of Labour Economics*, **3**. Reprinted in Kalecki (1976).

Kalecki, M. (1968), The difference between crucial economic problems of developed and underdeveloped non-socialist economies, in M. Kalecki (1968) *Essays on Planning and Economic Development*, PWN Warsaw. Reprinted in Kalecki (1976).

Kalecki, M. (1976), *Essays on Developing Economies*, Harvester Press, Humanities Press.

Kesselman, J. R. (1979), Formulating fiscal policies to expand employment in Indian industry, *Economic and Political Weekly*, **14**.

Kumar, D. (1965), *Land and Caste in South India*, Cambridge University Press.

Kurup, T. V. N. (1976), Price of rural credit: An empirical analysis of Kerala, *Economic and Political Weekly*, **11**, 3 July.

Lee, E. (ed.) (1981), *Export-led Industrialisation and Development*, ILO.

Lee, E. S. (1966), A theory of migration, *Demography*, **3**.

Leibenstein, H. (1957), *Economic Backwardness and Economic Growth*, Wiley.

Leibenstein, H. (1957a), Underemployment in backward economies, *Journal of Political Economy*, **65**.

Leibenstein, H. (1958), Underemployment in backward economies: Some additional notes, *Journal of Political Economy*, **66**.

Lewis, W. A. (1954), Economic development with unlimited supplies of labour, *The Manchester School*, **28**.

Lewis, W. A. (1958), Unlimited labour: Further notes, *Manchester School*, **32**.

Lipton, M. (1977), *Why Poor People Stay Poor: A Study of Urban Bias in World Development*, Temple Smith.

List, F. (1841), *Nationale System der Politischen Œkonomie*. English translation (1885), *National System of Political Economy*, Longman.

Little, I. M. D. (1981), The experience and causes of rapid labour-intensive development in Korea, Taiwan Province, Hong Kong and Singapore and the possibilities of emulation, in Lee (1981).

Little, I. M. D. and Mirrlees, J. A. (1974), *Project Appraisal and Planning for Developing Countries*, Heinemann.

Little, I. M. D., Scitovsky, T. and Scott, M. (1970), *Industry and Trade in Some Developing Countries*, Oxford University Press.

Long, M. (1968), Interest rates and the structure of agricultural credit markets, *Oxford Economic Papers*, **20**.

Luce, R. D. and Raiffa, H. (1957), *Games and Decisions*, Wiley.

Malinvaud, E. (1977), *The Theory of Unemployment Reconsidered*, Basil Blackwell.

Marshall, M. (1920), *Principles of Economics*, 8th edition, Macmillan (first edition, 1890).

Mathur, A. (1966), Balanced *v.* unbalanced growth – A reconciliatory view, *Oxford Economic Papers*, **18**.

Mazumdar, D. (1976), The rural–urban wage gap, migration and the shadow wage, *Oxford Economic Papers*, **28**.

Mckinnon, R. I. (1964), Foreign exchange constraints in economic development and efficient allocation, *Economic Journal*, **74**.

Meier, G. M. (1963), *International Trade and Development*, Harper and Row.

Mendras, H. (1970), *The Vanishing Peasant*, MIT Press.

Mill, John S. (1848), *Principles of Political Economy*, J. W. Parker.

Mirrlees, J. A. (1975). Pure theory of underdeveloped economies, in Reynolds (1975).

Mitra, P. (1983), A theory of interlinked rural transactions, *Journal of Public Economics*, **20**.

Mukherji, B. (1975), Peasants in semi-feudal agriculture – A note on A. Bhaduri's model', *Indian Economic Review*, **10**.

Mundell, R. A. (1968), *International Economics*, Macmillan.

Myint, H. (1964), *The Economics of Developing Countries*, Hutchinson.

Myrdal, G. (1968), *Asian Drama*, Pantheon.

Nakajima, C. (1970), Subsistence and commercial family farms: Some theoretical models of subjective equilibrium, in C. R. Wharton (ed.) *Subsistence Agriculture and Economic Development*, Aldine.

Navarrete, A. and Navarrete, I. M. (1951), La subocupacion en las economias poco desarrolladas, *El Trimestre Económico*. English translation (1953), Underemployment in underdeveloped economies, *International Economic Papers*, **3**.

Neary, P. (1981), On the Harris–Todaro model with inter-sectoral capital mobility, *Economica*, **48**.

Negishi, T. (1961), Monopolistic competition and general equilibrium, *Review of Economic Studies*, **28**.

Nelson, R. R. (1956), A theory of the low level equilibrium trap in underdeveloped economies, *American Economic Review*, **46**.

Newbery, D. M. G. (1975), Tenurial obstacles to innovation, *Journal of Development Studies*, **11**.

Newbery, D. M. G. (1975a), The choice of rental contract in peasant agriculture, in Reynolds (1975).

Newbery, D. M. G. (1977), Risk-sharing, sharecropping and uncertain labour markets, *Review of Economic Studies*, **44**.

Nieboer, H. J. (1910), *Slavery as an Industrial System*, Burt Franklin.

Nurkse, R. (1953), *Problems of Capital Formation in Underdeveloped Countries*, Basil Blackwell.

Okhawa, K. (1972), *Differential Structure and Agriculture – Essays on Dualistic Growth*, Kinokuniya Bookstore Co. Ltd.

Olivera, J. (1964), On structural inflation and Latin American structuralism, *Oxford Economic Papers*, **16**.

Pandit, V. N. (1978), An analysis of inflation in India, 1950-75, *Indian Economic Review*, **13**.

Park, Y. C. (1981), Export-led development: The Korean experience 1960-78, in Lee (1981).

Platteau, J. Ph., Murickan, J. and Delbar, E. (1981), Interlinkage of credit, labour and marketing relations in traditional marine fishing, *Social Action*, **31**.

Prasad, P. H. (1974), Reactionary role of usurer's capital in rural India, *Economic and Political Weekly*, **9**, Special Number, August.

Prebisch, R. (1959), Commercial policies in underdeveloped countries, *American Economic Review*, **49**.

Rae, J. (1834), *Some New Principles on the Subject of Political Economy*, Hilliard, Gray and Co.

Rahman, A. (1979), Usury capital and credit relations in Bangladesh agriculture: Some implications for capital formation and capitalist growth, *Bangladesh Development Studies*, **7**.

Raj, K. N. (1979), Keynesian economics and agrarian economies, in C. H. H. Rao and P. C. Joshi (eds) *Reflections on Economic Development and Social Change*, Allied Publishers.

Rakshit, M. (1982), *The Labour Surplus Economy*, Macmillan.

Ranis, G. and Fei, J. C. H. (1961), A theory of economic development, *American Economic Review*, **51**.

Rao, C. H. H. (1971), Uncertainty, entrepreneurship and sharecropping in India, *Journal of Political Economy*, **79**.

Rao, J. M. (1980), Interest rates in backward agriculture, *Cambridge Journal of Economics*, **4**.

Rao, V. K. R. V. (1952), Investment, income and the multiplier in an underdeveloped economy, *Indian Economic Review*, **1**.

Ravenstein, E. G. (1885), The laws of migration, *Journal of the Royal Statistical Society*, **48**.

Ravenstein, E. G. (1889), The laws of migration, *Journal of the Royal Statistical Society*, **52**.

Reserve Bank of India (1977), *Indebtedness of Rural Households and the Availability of Institutional Finance (All-India Debt and Investment Survey 1971-2)*, RBI, Bombay.

Reynolds, L. G. (1975) (ed.), *Agriculture in Development Theory*, Yale University Press.

Ricardo, D. (1817), *The Principles of Political Economy and Taxation*, John Murray.

Robbins, L. (1968), *Theory of Development Economics in the History of Economic Thought*, Macmillan.

Robinson, J. (1937), *Essays in the Theory of Employment*, Macmillan.

Rodgers, G. B. (1975), Nutritionally based wage determination in the low-income market, *Oxford Economic Papers*, **27**.

Rosenstein-Rodan, P. N. (1943), Problems of industrialisation in eastern and south-eastern Europe, *Economic Journal*, **53**.

Rudra, A. (1981), *Indian Agricultural Economics, Myths and Realities*, Allied Publishers.

Salop, J. and Salop, S. (1976), Self-selection and turnovers in the labour market, *Quarterly Journal of Economics*, **40**.

Scitovsky, T. (1954), Two concepts of external economies, *Journal of Political Economy*, **17**.

Scitovsky, T. (1978), Market power and inflation, *Economica*, **45**.

Seers, D. (1962), A theory of inflation and growth in underdeveloped economies based on the experience of Latin America, *Oxford Economic Papers*, **14**.

Sen, A. K. (1962), An aspect of Indian agriculture, *Economic Weekly*, **14**, Annual Number, February.

Sen, A. K. (1966). Peasants and dualism with or without surplus labour, *Journal of Political Economy*, **74**.

Sen, A. K. (1968), *Choice of Techniques*, 3rd edition, Basil Blackwell (first edition, 1960).

Sen, A. K. (1970), *Collective Choice and Social Welfare*, Oliver and Boyd.

Sen, A. K. (1973), Behaviour and the concept of preference, *Economica*, **40**.

Sen, A. K. (1975), *Employment, Technology and Development*, Clarendon Press.

Sen, A. K. (1981), *Poverty and Famines: An Essay on Entitlement and Deprivation*, Clarendon Press.

Sheehey, E. J. (1980), Money, income and prices in Latin America: An empirical note, *Journal of Development Economics*, **7**.

Singer, H. (1949), Economic progress in underdeveloped countries, *Social Research*, **16**.

Singer, H. (1950), The distribution of gains between investing and borrowing countries, *American Economic Review*, **40**.

Sivakumar, S. S. (1978), Aspects of agrarian economy in Tamil Nadu: A study of two villages. III. Structure of assets and indebtedness, *Economic and Political Weekly*, **13**, 20 May.

Smith, A. (1776), *The Wealth of Nations*, Strahan and Cadell.

Spillman, W. J. (1919), The agricultural ladder, *American Economic Review, Proceedings*, **9**.

Srinivasan, T. N. (1979), Agricultural backwardness under semi-feudalism – Comment, *Economic Journal*, **89**.

Srinivasan, T. N. and Bhagwati, J. N. (1983), On transfer paradoxes and immiserizing growth, Part I: Comment, *Journal of Development Economics*, **13**.

Stiglitz, J. E. (1974), Alternative theories of wage determination and unemployment in LDCs: The labour turnover model, *Quarterly Journal of Economics*, **88**.

Stiglitz, J. E. (1974a), Incentives and risk sharing in sharecropping, *Review of Economic Studies*, **61**.

Stiglitz, J. E. (1976), The efficiency wage hypothesis, surplus labour and the distribution of labour in LDCs, *Oxford Economic Papers*, **28**.

Sunkel, O. (1958), La inflation chilena: un efoque heterodoxo, *El Trimestre Económico*, **25**. English translation (1960), Inflation in Chile: An unorthodox approach, *International Economic Papers*, **10**.

Sweezy, P. M. (1939), Demand under conditions of oligopoly, *Journal of Political Economy*, **47**.

Taylor, L. (1979), *Macromodels for Developing Countries*, McGraw-Hill.

Thirlwall, A. P. (1972), *Growth and Development*, Macmillan.

Todaro, M. P. (1969), A model of labor migration and urban unemployment in less developed countries, *American Economic Review*, **59**.

Todaro, M. P. (1976), *Internal Migration in Developing Countries*, ILO.

Tun Wai, U. (1958), Interest rates outside the organised money markets of underdeveloped countries, *I.M.F. Staff Papers*, **6**.

UNECLA (1950), *The Economic Development of Latin America and Its Principal Problems*, by Raúl Prebisch, United National Economic Commission for Latin America.

Wharton, C. (1962), Marketing, merchandising and moneylending: A note on middlemen monopsony in Malaya, *Malayan Economic Review*, **7**.

Wonnacott, P. (1962), Disguised and overt unemployment in underdeveloped economies, *Quarterly Journal of Economics*, **76**.

Younès, Y. (1979), On the relation between organisation of production and forces of production in a given socio-economic structure, CEPREMAP, mimeo.

Young, A. (1928), Increasing returns and economic progress, *Economic Journal*, **38**.

Subject Index

195

Name Index

Adams, D. W. 124
Agarwal, N. 96, 104
Akerlof, G. 152, 179
Allen, F. 4
Ames, D. W. 113
Anand, S. 72
Arrow, K. J. 6, 15, 176
Atkinson, J. H. 134
Aujac, H. 35
Aumann, R. J. 178

Bacha, E. L. 54
Bagchi, A. K. 134-5
Bailey, F. G. 136, 149
Bardhan, P. K. 130-1, 134, 143, 147, 149, 160
Basu, K. 39, 65, 73, 79 121, 135, 139, 142, 149-50, 181
Bauer, P. T. 12, 134
Behrman, J. R. 34
Bell, C. 130, 177
Berge, C. 145
Béteille, A. 4
Bhaduri, A. 39, 110-11, 111, 113, 117, 120, 139, 142, 145, 146-7, 160, 164, 167, 176
Bhagwati, J. N. 49, 78-9, 81
Bharadwaj, K. 150, 163
Bliss, C. J. 96, 102, 104-5, 125
Blomqvist, A. G. 80-1
Boeke, J. H. 60
Borooah, V. 139, 142, 146
Bose, P. S. 135
Bottomley, A. 137, 139, 152
Braverman, A. 110, 142, 149, 161, 176
Breman, J. 8, 118, 169, 179
Brown, D. J. 134
Bruno, M. 45
Burstein, M. L. 141, 165
Byres, T. J. 120

Cagan, P. 33
Campos, R. 38
Canavese, A. J. 35
Cardoso, E. A. 36-8
Chakrabarty, S. K. 34
Chakravarty, S. 65
Chandarvarkar, A. G. 139
Chayanov, A. V. 124
Chenery, H. B. 45
Cheung, S. N. S. 109, 124-7, 130, 134, 142
Chichilnisky, G. 49-51, 53

Corden, W. M. 44, 73, 75
Currie, J. M. 125

Dagnino-Pastore, J. M. 13
Dasgupta, P. 27
Datta Chaudhuri, M. K. 55
Debreu, G. 14-15, 176
Delbar, E. 149
Desai, M. 110, 178
Dixit, A. 49
Dobb, M. 180
Drèze, J., 14-15, 17, 45

Elkan, W. 54
Enke, S. 64
Epstein, T. S. 121
Ezekiel, H. 96

Fei, J. C. H. 64
Fields, G. 75, 82
Findlay, R. V. 14, 73, 75
Fleming, J. M, 10, 22
Friedman, M. 44, 181
Friedman, R. 44
Furnivall, J. S. 60
Furtado, C. 35

Gamble, D. P. G. 113
Gapud, J. 136
Geanakoplos, J. 49
Ghose, A. K. 110
Griffin, K. 110-11, 120, 136, 143, 164
Gunning, J. 45, 50, 52-3

Harberler, G. 54
Hahn, F. 16
Hallagan, W. 131-3
Harris, J. R. 61, 67, 69-78, 80-2, 86
Haswell, M. 105
Heal, G. 49
Hendry, D. F. 34
Hicks, J. R. 35, 140
Higgs, H. 125
Hirschman, A. O. 13, 23

Islam, N. 22

Jevons, S. 3
Johnson, D. G. 109, 111, 123, 125, 127, 135
Jorgenson, D. W. 64
Joshi, H. 76
Joshi, V. 72, 76

197